The MARK of

ATLANTIC CROSSINGS

Rafe Blaufarb, Series Editor

The MARK *of* REBELS

Indios Fronterizos *and* Mexican Independence

BARRY M. ROBINSON

THE UNIVERSITY OF ALABAMA PRESS
Tuscaloosa

The University of Alabama Press
Tuscaloosa, Alabama 35487-0380
uapress.ua.edu

Hardcover edition published 2016.
Paperback edition published 2021.
eBook edition published 2016.

Typeface: Minion

Cover image: Spanish and indigenous conquest of Colotlán
Cover design: Michele Myatt Quinn

Paperback ISBN: 978-0-8173-6046-7

A previous edition of this book has been cataloged by the Library of Congress.
ISBN: 978-0-8173-1920-5 (cloth)
E-ISBN: 978-0-8173-8995-6

For Linnea

And lastly, keep in mind, as I do, the *Mark of Rebels* with which the people of Colotlán are viewed and even treated by their neighbors, as they are drawing attention to their actions against the whole society and public tranquility. . . . I am ready with my life, and all my fortune, to secure for Your Majesty by whatever means possible the peace and quiet of these lands, which up until now have been threatened with ruin because of the little subordination in which the indios fronterizos have lived.

Antonio de Vivanco to Viceroy Martín de Mayorga, 1781

Contents

Illustrations

Figures

Tables

Acknowledgments

I would not have encountered the Colotlán Frontier or told the story of its indios fronterizos without the support of many colleagues, friends, and family over the years.

The advice and guidance of my academic mentors as I developed this project is greatly appreciated, and I am particularly thankful for Jane Landers, whose gracious and genuine support has shaped my professional life as constructively as her suggestions and critique helped to shape this project. Right from the beginning of my career Lyman Johnson provided an example of the model Latin Americanist to which I continue to aspire. Under his advice I made the decision to set out upon this academic path. Little did I know that it would lead me, literally and figuratively, around the Atlantic World.

Years of archival research could not have been possible without institutional support, and I am grateful for the assistance provided by Vanderbilt University, Samford University, and Queens University of Charlotte. Local research grants from the Robert Penn Warren Center for the Humanities and the Vanderbilt Department of History first led me into the Mexican archives from 2001 to 2004. Other individuals at Vanderbilt deserve thanks for their contribution to the early stages of this project, and I would like to mention Marshall Eakin, Daniel Usner, J. Leon Helguera, and Simon Collier in particular.

Vital research assistance was provided through faculty development grants from Samford University that allowed me to return to Mexico, and to extend my research to the Archivo General de Indias and the Archivo General de Simancas in Spain, and I'd also like to thank my Samford colleagues for their advice and support along the way.

Each research trip to Mexico was made more fruitful by the wonderful people I met in the archives, and I would like to recognize Alicia Susana Palacios Alvarado, Juan Delgado Haro, the two Cristínas, and the entire staff of the Archivo Histórico del Estado de Zacatecas for their patience and kindness. Likewise, the staff of the Archivo General de la Nación, and Adrian Ortíz Martínez and José Luis Godínez Raya in particular, worked above and beyond the call of duty to photocopy an enormous amount of material for me before I left the AGN. In Guadalajara, Dra. Águeda Jiménez Pelayo and the staff of the Centro de Investigaciones Histórica Matías de la Mota Padilla also provided invaluable assistance, as did Director Carlos Fregoso Gennis, Encargada Juana Irma, and the rest of the staff of the Biblioteca Pública del Estado de Jalisco and the Universidad de Guadalajara. Numerous others in Guadalajara, Aguascalientes, Zacatecas, Jérez, and Colotlán helped make living and working in Mexico a fruitful and memorable experience, among them Joe Green and Rosa, Jorge Gómez Naredo, and Paulina Ultreras Villagrán.

New colleagues at Queens University of Charlotte have been supportive of my research, for which I am very grateful, and I would especially like to thank our department chair, Suzanne Cooper Guasco, and my former dean (and now provost) Lynn Morton for providing some crucial research time in my schedule as I completed the final revisions to the manuscript.

Each editor and staff member at the University of Alabama Press has displayed professionalism and courtesy in their interactions with me, and I'd like to thank Dan Waterman, Joseph Powell, Wendi Schnaufer, S. Scott Rohrer, and Jonathan Berry for their encouragement and editorial support as the book moved toward publication.

A great many friends have been a source of encouragement, critique, and inspiration over the course of this project. Among them I highly value the friendships formed through Vanderbilt's Graduate Christian Fellowship, who gave us a sense of community in Nashville and beyond.

None of my adventures would have been possible without my beloved family, which has been a source of strength for many years. Dad, thank you for being a loving, generous point of reference; a father who inspired the best in me. I wish you could be here to celebrate with us, but am grateful for the time that we shared, and for the encouragement that you and Mom gave me over the years. Son, I look forward to sharing these stories with you some day, and I hope that you discover a passion for your own journeys, wherever they may lead you.

A faithful confidante accompanied me on my quest to follow the story of Padre Calvillo's indios fronterizos, and Linnea, you have been my editor, reviewer, travel companion, and muse. All I can do is thank you as we celebrate what is truly a shared accomplishment. Cerulean dreams of you still crash around vacant episodes of my heart, and I remember that time we walked in Puebla.

The MARK *of* REBELS

Introduction

Local Loyalties in an Imperial Context

The Colotlán region lies in the heart of Mexico's Western Sierra Madre, a place of canyons and indigenous pueblos, of cacti and centuries-old ghosts. To the east, situated just off the Guadalajara-Zacatecas highway, the ruins of La Quemada serve as one of the few remaining markers of the region's pre-Hispanic past. Back up in the canyons, towns that sprang from the convergence of Spanish colonial settlements and indigenous communities now lie dormant, diminished by centuries of conflict and emigration. More recently, state officials initiated efforts to bring socioeconomic renewal to the Colotlán area. In 2000, the University of Guadalajara opened a new campus for northern Jalisco in the municipality of Colotlán, charged with fostering educational and economic development in what was considered a marginalized region.[1]

The effort to uncover the historical roots of the "marginality" of places like Colotlán has underpinned the academic studies of generations of Latin Americanists. Their quest to explain large-scale socioeconomic inequality has served as the central problem of Latin American history, whether framed in terms of economic dependency and underdevelopment; political discussions of imperialism, *caudillismo*, and other barriers to the formation of democratic institutions; or in efforts to uncover the cultural foundations of social disparities. Decades of scholarship have been dedicated to the pursuit of the enigmatic answers to this question.

The period of Spanish-American independence is a pivotal moment in this history of disparity. While few independence movements promised radical social transformation, even fewer delivered. Late colonial social patterns persisted beyond independence from Spain, well into the nineteenth century and, in some ways, to the present day. Understanding how social relationships and ethnic identities shaped independence goes a long way toward explaining this persistence. In postindependence Latin America, landowning creole elites asserted control over the new national political institutions. This control ensured that the twin colonial legacies of hierarchical social structures and racialized power relations would persist well into the twentieth century. Nowhere was this more evident than in the Mexican struggle for independence, where popular rebellions exploded in 1810 but then lost momentum and receded as the decade wore on. Independence was achieved through an 1821 compromise that guaranteed the maintenance of the Catholic religion, (official) racial equality, and political independence. Even so, independence erased many of the privileges accumulated by indigenous communities during the colonial era.

This book takes a new look at Mexican independence, from the perspective of an indigenous population caught in the heart of the struggle. Their story suggests that Mexico's transition from colony to nation can only be understood by revisiting the origins of the colonial system and by recognizing the role of Spain's indigenous allies in both its construction and demolition. By reconstructing late colonial social relationships, this book relates events in the region to broader patterns of identity, loyalty, and subversion throughout the Americas.[2] This approach shifts the discussion of Mexican independence from systemic, impersonal approaches to an examination of local social relationships.[3] Analysis of indigenous identity, the intertwined notions of conquest and frontier, and the pardon process are all central to this inquiry.

Throughout New Spain, the colonial social order underwent tremendous strain in the decade or so of the independence wars, with the eruption of widespread popular violence in the initial stages of insurrection threatening to rip the viceroyalty apart. Ethnic identities developed over the colonial period came under assault from late colonial imperial reforms and the hardening racial attitudes of Spanish neighbors. With the onset of the 1810 insurrection, the indigenous pueblos of Colotlán mobilized local legacies of resistance, and social upheaval convulsed the entire region and overflowed outward in a brief confluence with the "Hidalgo Revolt." A double-edged suppression of the rebellion recovered the loyalties of important regional creole leaders and a substantial section of Colotlán's indigenous population. The Spanish Crown utilized the *indulto*, or royal pardon, to restitch the political and social fabric of New Spain. This strategy limited social polarization and prevented a critical rupture between creole elites and the popular classes. Those indigenous rebels who had sought to regain local autonomy through insurrection were left without access to external sources of political legitimacy in the new Mexican nation.

Unraveling the Conquest

Recent scholarship on early colonial Mesoamerica has begun to revise our interpretation of the "Spanish" Conquest. Historians are paying more attention to the role of non-Europeans in defining the emergent colonial order, including those indigenous communities that took on the role of conquistador for themselves.[4] Given the new imperative to redefine the role of indigenous allies in the events we collectively label "the conquest," how can we best identify these communities? Why did they participate in actions that seem to have expanded the Spanish colonial regime? How did these communities and their descendants remember such events in subsequent decades (and even centuries)? How well does the victor/vanquished dichotomy hold up to ethnohistorical scrutiny? As new studies have started to address these questions, the conventional narrative of a Spanish Conquest as something practiced *by* Europeans *upon* others has begun to unravel. Scholars are beginning to recognize how indigenous values and practices shaped the new colonial system. An underlying concern of this scholarship is the degree to which indigenous inhabitants of Mesoamerica appropriated the powerful role of conquistador for their own purposes.[5] This attenuation or inversion of the conventional conquest dynamic was extensive, and it is clear that the native inhabitants of the Americas took on the role of conquistador for different reasons.[6]

Just as our reinterpretation of "conquest" is transforming our understanding of colonialism's establishment, it should also inform our interpretation of colonialism's closing stages. The social ramifications of indigenous communities' adoption of conquistador identities extended far beyond the early colonial period.[7] These customs of conquest remained active in northern Nueva Galicia (western Mexico) through the late eighteenth century. The primarily indigenous inhabitants of this region (known officially as the Colotlán Frontier) claimed privileges and authority based on their ancestors' service to the Crown during the region's initial colonization and on their own service as militiamen in more recent episodes of subjugation.[8] By the 1780s, the status and identity of these self-identified *indios fronterizos* (Frontier Indians) were called into question by changing colonial notions of ethnicity, the incorporation of mixed-race newcomers into the indigenous communities, and divergent cultural strategies among and within the pueblos.[9]

The ensuing narrative describes an era when different indigenous conceptions of authority and loyalty—both wrapped in the rhetoric of conquest—came into conflict. This period of social unrest occurred at a portentous moment in the history of the Americas. Colonial conceptions of race, social status, and political relations were shifting across the hemisphere. In Spanish America, the imperial reforms instituted by the Bourbon monarchy throughout the eighteenth century sought a more efficient mechanism for bureaucratic control and the collection of revenues. The reforms fostered resentment among local creole elites and sparked economically motivated and ethnically tinged rebellion throughout the empire. The great Andean rebellions of 1780–81 come to mind most prominently, but other examples abound.[10]

Up through the 1980s, historians of Latin America often interpreted these events as direct reactions to the Bourbon reforms and as precursors of the independence struggle.[11] Both of these assessments are persuasive generalizations, but other scholarship on social unrest shows how similar rebellions with a variety of aims and outcomes had occurred throughout the colonial period.[12] The unraveling of the colonial system cannot be understood without examining the preexisting social networks and cultural tensions within which it occurred.[13] Among indigenous communities, cultural imagery harkening back to remembered indigenous pasts frequently underpinned more immediate sources of rebellion.[14] Dynamic notions of ethnic identity often lay at the heart of social conflict. Such was the case in late colonial Colotlán.

Encountering Colotlán

I first encountered the Colotlán Frontier after reading a biographical sketch of an independence-era priest named Pablo José Calvillo in José María Miquel i Vergés's *Diccionario de Insurgentes*.[15] While flipping through the book's many snapshots of prominent and not-so-prominent rebels, a line in the entry for Calvillo drew my attention: "Calvillo brought 7000 Indians to Guadalajara, a group that was versed in the use of the bow and arrow, and that, in the end, gave a very poor result in the famous battle of Puente de Calderón."[16] The fact that the Indians supposedly gave a poor performance in the battle was of little note; the same critique could be leveled against the entirety of the insurgent "army" led by Padre Hidalgo, whose potency and momentum was crushed and splintered by a much smaller royalist force on January 17, 1811. What struck me was the mystery of where the Indians had come from, and why they had followed this Spanish priest from their homes to fight for Mexican independence, assuming that was their objective. I was familiar with Hidalgo, whose heroic role in the independence struggle has been taught to generations of students of Latin American history.[17] But while I knew that a large portion of New Spain's population at the time was indigenous, Hidalgo's rebel army had usually been portrayed as a racially mixed throng of peasants, the product of centuries of subjugation and *mestizaje*.

Further investigation of Padre Calvillo's story continued to intrigue me, as I learned that, instead of dying a martyr's death like Padre Hidalgo and fellow insurgent leader Ignacio Allende, Calvillo applied for a pardon from Spanish military and religious authorities. He confessed that he had been "the head leader of those Bandits," having "convinced all of those [indigenous] inhabitants to join the insurgency," and "persuaded them to [participate in] the defense of the unjust cause." I learned that Calvillo's pardon and abandonment of the insurgency proved to be more of a rule than an exception, forming part of an intense battle for loyalties waged during this period. But important questions still remained. Who were these Indians who fought with Calvillo? Had he really been the driving force behind their participation in the rebellion? Where had they come from, and what was their relationship to the Spanish Empire whose foundations were shaken by Hidalgo's revolt, and to the Mexican nation eventually fashioned out of the independence struggle?

These questions led me to Colotlán. When I first began to research the Colotlán Frontier, it seemed not to exist, other than as a relatively small, remote town in northern Jalisco with a declining population.[18] It turned out that this town had once been the *cabecera* (district capital) of a much larger region known as the Frontera de Colotlán, originally designated a "Frontier" because of its strategic location as a buffer between sizable "unpacified" indigenous populations of the central Western Sierra Madre and the route between the silver mining centers of Zacatecas and the provincial capital of Guadalajara. Late colonial New Spain included a diverse assortment of regional societies ranging from the heavily populated and productive Bajío and Oaxaca, where densely settled indigenous populations were highly integrated within Spanish-controlled society, to the Provincias Internas of the far north, where Spanish imperial control was tenuous at best and racially diverse inhabitants negotiated loosely connected relationships amid cycles of trade and conflict. Colotlán, where Spanish authority swept over the indigenous population early in the colonial period but never quite managed to exert control over their labor or tribute, represents a mix of these extremes.[19] The Valley of Mexico, Oaxaca, Michoacán, and the Bajío are arguably the most studied regions of the colonial period, and our knowledge of the northern Provincias Internas has benefited recently from a burgeoning Borderlands scholarship, but the central Western Sierra Madre in general, and the Colotlán Frontier in particular, have been largely overlooked.[20] Much of the oversight stems from the fact that the Colotlán region was divided between different states after independence and is no longer a coherent region politically. The historiographical inattention is also a result of Colotlán's proximity to the mining centers of Zacatecas, the most productive silver area in the colonial world outside of Potosí in Upper Peru. Most scholarship on the center-west of New Spain focuses on the Zacatecan mining centers rather than the nearby ranchos and indigenous pueblos, usually mentioning them only in passing.[21]

In fact, royal authorities carved one of these mining centers right out of the middle of the Colotlán region after a particularly fruitful silver discovery in the early eighteenth century, converting that section into a separate *gobierno* (political district) and renaming it Bolaños. The Spanish then removed all Indians from the newly created district except for those working in the mines. The perceived importance of the Colotlán region increased, and a series of jurisdictional disputes between the viceregal authorities in Mexico City and the *audiencia* of Nueva Galicia frequently shifted the political borders of the region in the late colonial period. At times, the opposing authorities used the genuine threat of indigenous violence as a rationale for changing the command structure of the area. The social and ethnic tension stemming from the displacement of Colotlán's indigenous communities by mining settlement and production has been all but forgotten in the principal historiography of late colonial New Spain and early Mexico. This is a serious oversight considering the important role of these strained relations in the devastation of the Zacatecan mining industry during the independence struggle.

As in the case of many empires, the Spanish imposed jurisdictional boundaries upon the people and territory under their control in colonial New Spain without much regard for indigenous conceptions of space and region. Colonial administrators attempted to resettle indigenous populations in the interest of the civilization and "pacification" of lands ostensibly under imperial control.[22] Such actions on the part of the Spanish regime present an obstacle for historians interested in describing the lives and environments of the primarily indigenous underclass who fought in the rebellions leading up to Mexican independence. The leaders of the newly independent Mexico essentially followed the borders of Spanish administrative districts in partitioning their new nation, and most historians have drawn from the jurisdictional boundaries set by the Spanish or the Mexican state in ordering their discussions of independence-era history. As a result, the history of this region and its people at the end of the colonial period must be pieced together from a range of sources.

This project incorporates an extensive array of source material, including documentary collections and travel accounts, but the principal body of evidence comes from archival records from eleven different repositories in Mexico and from the Archive of the Indies and Archive of Simancas in Spain. These documents include collections of civil litigation and criminal cases, pardon documents and statements of loyalty, census data (*padrones*), royal edicts, official correspondence, petitions from indigenous pueblos, and ecclesiastical and military records. The individuals in these documents cover a wide range of the social spectrum, including all racial, gender, and class categories. I have also compiled a database of individuals who lived in the region during the independence period—including several hundred documented participants in the pardon process—along with various descriptors, including names, dates, kinship, social or ethnic status, location, and other relevant information.[23] In addition to more commonly used methods of textual analysis, this database serves as a basis for analysis of pueblo-level loyalties and identities.

Colonial Periphery, Indigenous Center

The terms used in this book to identify the geographic and social contours of the Colotlán region merit some consideration. "Frontier," in particular, is a loaded term and can convey widely different meanings within Latin American scholarship, let alone the historiography of British America and the United States. Generally, scholarly usage of the term has moved from characterizations of a frontier as the geographical area along the edge of the inexorable advance of "civilization" to conceptions of frontiers as zones of cultural interaction that can be viewed from multiple angles of interpretation.[24]

The term Colotlán Frontier is a direct translation of *La Frontera de Colotlán*, the official designation used by Spanish colonial authorities to describe the large political district constituting most of the communities in the mountainous region of the Western Sierra Madre in what is now northern Jalisco, southwestern Zacatecas, and parts of Nayarit and Aguascalientes (see figure I.1).[25] It is also the term most frequently used by the inhabitants of the region themselves during the late colonial period, although the topographical descriptor "the canyons" was also used, and is the only term still applied to the region as a whole in the present day. In this study the term "Colotlán region" will encompass the slightly broader area including the neighboring canyons of Juchipila and Tlaltenango, Valle de Huejúcar, and the closest Spanish towns and settlements on the edges of the official gobierno. In many respects the Colotlán Frontier also served as a "frontier" in the more recent ethnohistorical use of the term; a site of intensive cultural interaction that can be explored from the inside out as much as from the outside looking inward. In her discussion of ethnic spaces in Sonora, Cynthia Radding

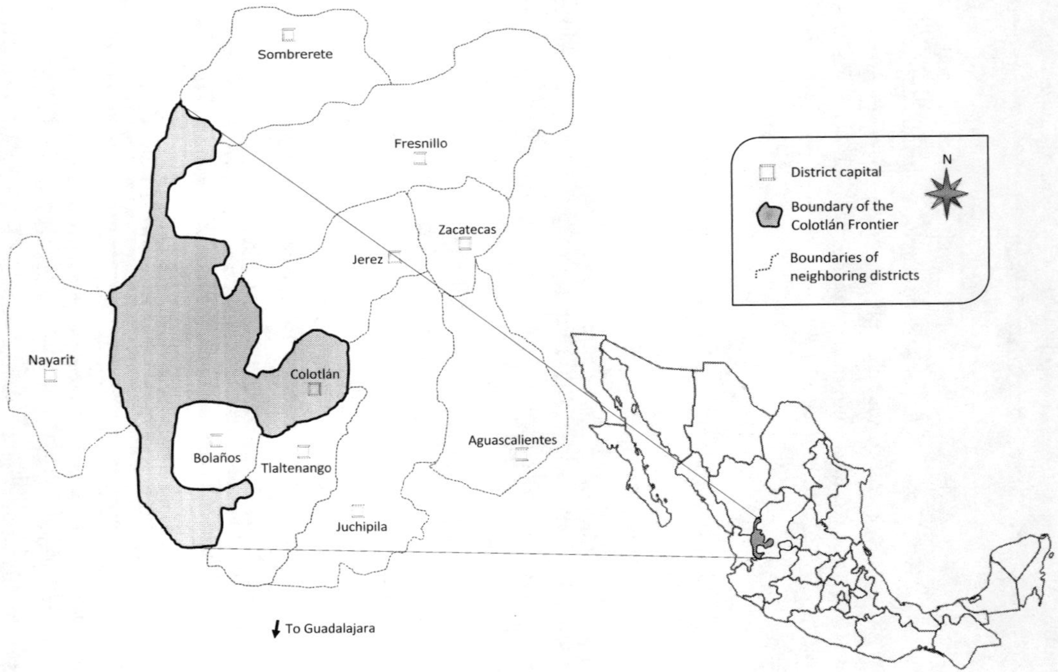

Figure I.1. Districts of the Colotlán region in relation to modern Mexico. The Colotlán Frontier spanned portions of the modern-day states of Jalisco, Zacatecas, Nayarit, and Aguascalientes. Map by author.

argues for the importance of a "view from the periphery"—in her case an examination of the "social ecology" of Sonoran *serrano* communities—for understanding other historical developments such as modernization and class formation.[26] This study of Colotlán goes one step further by inverting conventional conceptions of center and periphery in Spanish America. It views the Colotlán region as a cultural center, with more recognized and better-studied areas of nearby Spanish colonial society coming into the narrative from the periphery, just as they would have appeared to the inhabitants of the Colotlán Frontier.

The cultural "center" in this conceptualization was essentially an indigenous one for most of the colonial period. Most inhabitants lived in the indigenous pueblos of the Colotlán Frontier and the neighboring canyons of Tlaltenango and Juchipila. They formed the principal military force in the area, and their presence defined outside observers' characterizations of the region until after Mexican independence. Still, by the late eighteenth century the region's pueblos had absorbed Tlaxcalan colonists, some members of Spanish military or ranching families, and free blacks, *mulatos*, and other *castas* from the mining centers of Zacatecas and Bolaños.[27] Considering the cultural diversity among the different indigenous groups of this portion of Nueva Galicia—a kingdom encompassing much of western and northern New Spain with its capital in Guadalajara—a more detailed account of the ethnic composition of this "indigenous center" requires an overview of the colonial history of the region.

This is the purpose of Chapter 1, which sets up the context of cultural interaction in the Colotlán region from the Conquest to the late eighteenth century, with a particular focus on the relationship between the indigenous communities and representatives of Spanish authority. This account shows how the Tlaxcalan allies of the Spanish superimposed a Conquest model for understanding identity and social relations onto earlier traditions of indigenous resistance. Their descendants employed both of these cultural forms in their interactions with Spanish officials and residents of neighboring districts. These indios fronterizos, as they came to be known, participated in the relatively late conquest of neighboring Nayarit. They then used this service to the Spanish regime to preserve their status in the social conflicts of the eighteenth century. At the same time, they upheld their own memories and traditions of resistance as a caution to possible Spanish threats to their status and privileges. Such threats were increasingly present as Spanish concern for securing mineral wealth from nearby Zacatecas—and later from within the Colotlán region itself—drew the attention and energies of Spanish elites and settlers. By the late colonial period casta newcomers had integrated themselves into some of the region's pueblos, causing conflict *within* some, while forming alliances in others and increasing the ongoing formation of a new fronterizo—but still substantially and overtly indigenous—identity.[28]

Chapter 2 uncovers the social underpinnings of local and regional authority and important late colonial ethnic transformations by narrating the events of a significant moment of conflict and relational shifting in 1780 and 1785. A group of indios fronterizos calling themselves the Señores Colotecos attempted to wrest control of the region away from official representatives of the Spanish regime. Their authority carried no official weight beyond their ability to convince their fellow indios fronterizos of their legitimacy, yet for a significant amount of time, they managed to do just that. While it lasted, the effectiveness of the Señores Colotecos' control over the region's pueblos stemmed from their ability to serve as an outlet for fronterizo concerns, and as an ostensible mechanism for taking action against Spanish officials, neighbors, clergy or even fellow indios who obstructed fronterizo goals. This chapter shows that authority in the Colotlán region was continuously contested, almost always took on ethnic undertones, and needed both external and internal underpinning to be sustained. In the face of late colonial reform and hardening conceptions of race, competing factions drew upon different conceptions of fronterizo identity to bolster their claims to authority and status.

A second episode of social conflict forms the basis of Chapter 3's narrative, focusing on a dispute over land. Agrarian pressures have figured prominently in analyses of late colonial and independence-era New Spain, and this chapter explores the local dynamics underpinning such tensions. The resulting narrative shows how local interpersonal—and intercommunal—relationships served as the most significant venues and the most direct reasons for social conflict; these relationships fed on and subsumed disputes over land and labor caused by demographic pressures. Throughout the conflict over the use of a particular valley, the communities involved recognized specific bonds of allegiance, whether on their part or that of their adversaries. Social divisions aligned vertically rather than horizontally, and the concept of indio fronterizo was malleable enough to include allied newcomers from outside the pueblo. In the end, the complicated social interplay between the various factions of New Spanish society discussed in the chapter—*hacendados* and *vaqueros*, miners, merchants, Spanish officials, priests, parishioners, castas and indios—functioned as a tangled web of disputes and loyalties.

Chapter 4 explores the moment of connection between the people and history of the Colotlán region and the larger events of the independence period. Beginning with a comparative look at the revolutionary period throughout the Americas, the chapter shifts to an exploration of the social and ethnic composition of the insurgency in Colotlán, showing how the insurrection grew out of strong roots in the region's indigenous past, mobilized in 1810 by pueblo leaders and local personalities. This indigenous quality of the insurrection then grafted into the larger Hidalgo Revolt through alignment with creole commanders with viceroyalty-wide connections. But a considerable gulf—largely ethnic in its origins and its consequences—existed between the aims of the vast majority of the rebels and the higher-level creole elite leadership. During this period, the status and privileges the indios fronterizos had sought to recover and protect continued to fade into the past, unable to survive either the late colonial reforms of the Spanish regime or creole conceptions of race and property in the formation of a new nation-state.

Chapter 5 takes a step back by explaining the workings and historical context of the pardon process across New Spain, and by identifying broad patterns of involvement. I then return to the Colotlán region to reconsider the story of Padre Calvillo and the events of the later insurgency in the region. The story of the shifting loyalties that dramatically altered the course of the insurrection conveys many of the principal themes developed in the previous chapters, including the importance of family connections, the reciprocal honoring of obligations as a means of garnering and maintaining respect and status, and the tension between the concerns of indigenous communities and those of creole *vecinos* (property-owning neighbors).[29] The chapter shows how the pardon process served as a re-integrative force, holding together or reforming many of the traditional relationships of the New Spanish social order during the tumultuous independence period, and thus providing a basis for the eventual consensus and compromise that resulted in an independent Mexico. The book concludes with an epilogue that considers the connection between creole political ascendance and social banditry in the Western Sierra Madre.

1

Conquest Identities and the Indios Fronterizos of Colotlán

> [The Indians of Colotlán] hardly have an appropriate kind of Government, maintaining the false idea of being important Fronterizos, when they have nothing to make them such, since the indios of Nayarit [have long since been conquered and] are more domesticated and more peaceful and without comparison less rebellious than the Colotecos; and I would rather choose to live with the Indians of Nayarit than among the Colotecos, as I have not heard that the Indians of Nayarit have killed any of the officials who have been placed over them. What, then, can remedy this situation? I judge that the answer lies in making them Tributaries.
>
> —Report of Pedro Antonio Trelles Villa de Moros, *corregidor* of the mining center of Bolaños, 1783

The European colonization of the Americas followed a pattern of conquest and settlement that began with the earliest encounters in the Caribbean and continued on through at least the late nineteenth century. But this was not simply a European project. Indigenous communities frequently allied themselves with European conquerors, often participating as conquistadors in their own right.[1] The implications of this indigenous participation have the potential to reshape our understanding of the colonial era, and of the independence period. Native communities played a fundamental role in shaping and maintaining the colonial system, and they also had a greater stake in its dissolution than has yet been recognized.

Frontier areas, on the edges of these colonial systems, opened up opportunities for social fluidity and cultural adaptation that did not exist elsewhere.[2] In the Colotlán Frontier, native allies of the Spanish parlayed their service as conquistadors into the establishment of a "Frontier Indian" status that granted them special privileges and a measure of autonomy from the surrounding Spanish settlements. As the epigraph above suggests, these fronterizo communities valued and defended their special status up through the late colonial period, when it came under attack from their Spanish neighbors.

The Initial Conquest of Colotlán

A number of different indigenous groups inhabited the Colotlán region before the arrival of the Spanish and their native allies in the 1530s. Groups speaking a variety of southern Uto-Aztecan languages included Cazcanes, Coras, Guachichiles, Huicholes, Tepehuanes, and Zacatecos. These groups occupied a region dominated by the Sierra Madre Occidental, with deep canyons funneling rivers through the highlands. Cultures were diverse, with certain groups like the Cazcanes living in more sedentary agricultural settlements while others like the Huicholes inhabited smaller family-based rancherias spread throughout the mountains.[3] Evidence also remains of earlier and more sophisticated civilizations, which built great fortresses such as Chicomostoc, also known as La Quemada.

The Spanish and their indigenous allies initially referred to the region's native population as Chichimec, a generic term of Nahuatl derivation referring to many "uncivilized" indigenous groups outside of Spanish control. Although subsequent events would lead to their partial incorporation into colonial society, at this point most of the indigenous groups of the Colotlán region were still included in the Chichimec designation. The Spanish and their Indian allies encountered fierce indigenous resistance from the time of their earliest expeditions.[4] Soon after the first missionaries entered the region, the Mixtón war of 1541, named for the range of mountains near Colotlán that separates the valleys of Tlaltenango and Juchipila, erupted.[5] Spanish settlers had "pacified" the area just to the south, and Franciscan friars had begun to evangelize the outlying areas.[6] According to an anonymous friar cited in Renato Haro Ortega's Historia de Colotlán, at a gathering of Indian leaders in Tlaltenango, individuals claiming to be "messengers of Tecoroli" proclaimed that this messianic figure would resurrect their ancestors, and that "those who believed in [Tecoroli] and renounced the teachings of the friars to follow him would not suffer, would never die, would be rejuvenated, and could have as many women as they wanted and not just one, as the friars commanded. He that was content with just one woman would die immediately. Then Tecoroli would go to Guadalajara, to Jalisco, to Michoacán, to México, to Guatemala, and to all the places where there are Christians from Spain, and would kill them all."[7] This tradition of messianism among the indios of the Colotlán region, manifested in the person of Tecoroli during the Mixtón war, would persist into the early nineteenth century, when indigenous resistance would take similar form in the messianic figure of "El Indio Mariano."[8]

In 1541, indigenous inhabitants from Colotlán, Tlaltenango, and Tepe-

Figure 1.1. Conquest of Juchipila by the Spanish and their indigenous allies. From Alfredo Chavero, *Lienzo de Tlaxcalla* (Mexico: Litográfica del Timbre, 1892), Figure 58.

Figure 1.2. Conquest of Tlaltenango by the Spanish and their indigenous allies. From Alfredo Chavero, *Lienzo de Tlaxcalla* (Mexico: Litográfica del Timbre, 1892), Figure 61.

Figure 1.3. Conquest of Colotlán by the Spanish and their indigenous allies. From Alfredo Chavero, *Lienzo de Tlaxcalla* (Mexico: Litográfica del Timbre, 1892), Figure 70.

chitlán soon joined with groups from Juchipila, Jalpa, and Nochistlán in open conflict against the Spanish and their native allies. The Indians pillaged Spanish settlements near the region and continued farther south. After a fierce battle on the outskirts of Guadalajara in late September, Viceroy Antonio de Mendoza managed to subdue the uprising with the aid of additional indigenous allies, and in December he eliminated remaining opposition in Colotlán.[9] This early resistance was recorded in the *Lienzo de Tlaxcala*, a cotton canvas painted by Tlaxcalan allies of the Spanish between 1550 and 1564, and provided an indigenous perspective of the conquest. The artists depicted charging Spanish horsemen and their Tlaxcalan allies attacking indigenous archers in Xochipilla (Juchipila), Tlaltenãpã (Tlaltenango), and Colotlán, respectively (see figures 1.1, 1.2, and 1.3). In the Colotlán figure the warriors fight with the image of a scorpion above their heads.[10]

Tlaxcalan Indios Hidalgos and the Settlement Period

In 1584 the viceregal government attempted to apportion the indios of Colotlán into *encomiendas*, but the ongoing Chichimec war of 1561–89 doomed the effort.[11] Beginning in 1591, the viceregal government introduced several

Tlaxcalan settlements as a part of Spanish pacification efforts. Velasco's rationale revealed the Spanish dependence on native participation in the colonization of Mexico: "In as much as the Chichimec Indians from diverse nations in New Spain and New Galicia are in outright warfare and rebellion against my Royal Service, causing grave injuries, death, and thefts, destroying the peaceful pueblos and the cattle-ranching estates, and robbing and raiding Spaniards and travelers along the roads, and given that when it was attempted to remedy this situation with great loss of soldiers and warriors, it couldn't be totally accomplished and resolved [we request] the Indian Principales of the City of Tlaxcala to assist us with four hundred married Indian couples who will settle with the said Chichimecs in order to instruct them so that through their presence the Chichimecs will live in peace, . . . forming established Republics . . . and Pueblos of Christian People."[12] The Christianized Tlaxcalans, allies of the Spanish since the earliest period of the Conquest, played a key role in the expansion of Spanish imperial authority by functioning as conquistadors and settlers throughout Mesoamerica, and by resettling in colonies in frontier areas.[13]

The Tlaxcalan colony in the Colotlán district included 690 married people, 187 children, and 55 single or widowed people, spread into five settlements, including San Andrés. The viceroy instructed the Tlaxcalans to introduce agricultural practices to the indigenous inhabitants of Colotlán, and to teach them how to build houses, and whatever else was necessary to attain the desired goal of acculturation. He also instructed them to form repúblicas de indios of "Christian People, so that the priests can take charge of them, instruct them, and administer the sacraments for the salvation of their souls."[14] In return, the viceroy exempted the Tlaxcalans from tribute, calling them, their descendants, and their dependents "Hidalgos," or nobles. He also permitted them to live separately from the Spaniards and Indian groups indigenous to the region, exempted their markets from the alcabala (sales tax), and permitted them to bear arms and ride horseback using saddles.[15] Throughout the rest of the colonial period the tribute exemption was extended to native indigenous communities, as they intermarried with the Tlaxcalan colonists and performed militia service for the Spanish regime.[16]

It is important to clarify that relations between the Tlaxcalans and indigenous communities native to the region did not begin with peaceful cooperation and ethnic integration. The Tlaxcalans valued the special status and *fueros* (privileges granting special exemptions to a specific group) that had accompanied their role as indios conquistadores during much of the sixteenth century, and they extended a Conquest model onto the social relations in the Colotlán region.[17] Their settlement in the region resulted in immediate resistance. In 1592 Huicholes and Tepecanos (Tepehuanes), who were reduced to the new, joint Chichimec-Tlaxcalan settlement at San Andrés del Teúl, rose up against the newcomers, with the surviving Tlaxcalans taking refuge at an outpost of the Chalchihuites mining camp to the north in the district of Sombrerete. This would later become the pueblo of Nueva Tlaxcala.[18] Sporadic uprisings would continue throughout the colonial period, usually originating in the less assimilated pueblos in the west and northwest, near neighboring Nayarit and Durango. San Andrés del Teúl was refounded some years later, a part of the *doctrina* of the Franciscan monastery at Chalchihuites, along with several other indigenous villages under the jurisdiction of the gobierno of Colotlán.[19]

In addition to the Tlaxcalan settlement, 1591 also marked the establishment of the first permanent mission at San Luis de Colotlán by Franciscans from Zacatecas. With the exception of a portion of the province of Nayarit, controlled by Jesuits until their expulsion in 1767, Franciscans controlled the missionary effort in all of Nueva Galicia throughout most of the colonial period.[20] As later events will make clear, although the evangelization of the Frontera pueblos was never complete, the church's presence supported Spanish colonial conceptions of corporate society, and also facilitated the formation of important relationships between particular communities and priests.[21] Additionally, evangelization allowed for the establishment of lay brotherhoods, or *cofradias*, that could serve as communal support networks and secure repositories of local resources.

Throughout the colonial period the pueblo of San Luís de Colotlán was divided into three barrios: Tlaxcala, Soyatitán, and Tochopa. The division was originally along ethnic lines, with the first corresponding to the descendants of the Tlaxcalan colonists and the other two to indigenous groups native to the region.[22] Over the course of the seventeenth and eighteenth centuries, most of the principal ethnic groups present at the time of conquest disappeared as distinct language and cultural communities, and aside from a smaller number of speakers of the Tepehuan, Huichol, and Cora languages, most people came to speak either Spanish or a variant of Nahuatl.[23] Those families with the strongest claims to Tlaxcalan ancestry held positions of leadership in the Frontier pueblos, but anyone with a family connection to the indios conquistadores could claim the status of an *indio flechero* militiaman and enjoy the corresponding rights.[24] These privileges gave the indigenous communities of the frontier a degree of relief from the commercial and tax abuses that prevailed in other parts of the viceroyalty of New Spain during much of the colonial period.[25]

A late colonial report on the Colotlán Frontier noted that *mulatos advenedizos* joined indigenous communities "in order to enjoy [their] freedom and [tax] exemptions." By 1780, the Huichol, Cora, and Tepehuan ethnic

Table 1.1. Estimated Population of the Colotlán Region in the Late Colonial Period

Location	Indigenous Population	Spanish/ Mestizo Population	Casta Population	Total Population
Colotlán Frontier	15970	4946	2100	23016
Juchipila	8086	10137	4245	22468
Tlaltenango	8190	3200	1100	12490
Bolaños	849	2430	722	4001
Aguascalientes	8617	8648	3357	20622
Nueva Galicia	117705	108437	65045	291187

Source: Data derived from "Informes sobre las fronteras de San Luis Colotlán, 1783," AGN, Indiferente de Guerra, vol. 83, exp. 2; and Peter Gerhard, María del Carmen Velazquez Chávez, Bernardo Carlos Casas, and Dorothy Tanck de Estrada.

groups would be the only discernibly non-acculturated indigenous groups remaining in the Colotlán region, and they were mostly located in smaller villages and *rancheria* settlements to the west.[26] The "demographic *mestizaje*" identified by some scholars of the late colonial period—in which indigenous and Spanish communities became less geographically segregated during the eighteenth century–occurred to a degree in Colotlán, but to a lesser extent than elsewhere.[27] Around 1790, the population of the Colotlán Frontier was about 69 percent indigenous, compared with roughly 40 percent for Nueva Galicia (see table 1.1). It is important to recognize that the Colotlán region remained heavily indigenous, with the heritage and identity of previous generations maintained and utilized by indigenous pueblos.[28] Those castas who eventually married into local pueblos took on an ostensibly indigenous identity, and by the end of the eighteenth century the social lines between indigenous and nonindigenous communities in the region were still evident, even if cultural markers like language and dress were becoming increasingly blurred.[29]

Developing a New Fronterizo Identity

In fact, the cultural context of the Colotlán Frontier reflected a gradual, subtle ethnic transformation toward an indio fronterizo identity.[30] The preservation of their fueros offered an attractive cultural option for individuals from outside the region willing to serve in the militias in exchange for certain social freedoms that were available only to Spaniards in other parts of the viceroyalty.[31] Significantly, there was little intermarriage between Indians and Spaniards in the Colotlán region, resulting in a relatively small *mestizo* population, especially outside of the larger towns.[32] Thus, while the special status of *indios hidalgos* broadened to include non-Indian individuals like the aforementioned mulatos advenedizos, it reinforced the indigenous character of the Colotlán Frontier. It did not, however, signify an increasing mestizaje in the strict indio-plus-Spaniard sense of the term. The Conquest model still formed an important part of the collective identity of the pueblos of the Colotlán Frontier throughout the colonial period, but it would be the indios fronterizos—as the cultural descendants of the Tlaxcaltecan indios conquistadores—and not the Spanish who composed the greater part of the region's social and military force.[33]

So, the seventeenth and eighteenth centuries brought a degree of restricted assimilation to the complex and diverse Spanish Empire, as well as cultural attrition and transformation, albeit in a limited linguistic and mostly intraindigenous manner. Meanwhile, haciendas and smaller ranches from surrounding districts expanded and moved closer and closer to pueblo lands, although Spanish settlement in the Colotlán Frontier itself remained sparse. The recruitment of the Tlaxcalan colonists had furthered a number of Viceroy Velasco's political and religious objectives from the 1591 colonization. Ostensibly available to Spanish military authorities for actions against indigenous communities to the north and west that were still outside the scope of imperial authority, the indios fronterizos did occasionally help pacify unruly groups and suppress revolts in neighboring regions.[34] However, large-scale military operations had, for the most part, ceased in the central-western Sierra Madre by the mid-seventeenth century, with remaining unassimilated groups either reduced, shifted farther to the north, or shielded from Spanish settlements by the indios of the Colotlán Frontier.[35] In this regard, the Frontier Indians served as a cultural buffer, protecting the Zacatecan mining zones and the more established agricultural areas closer to Guadalajara throughout the duration of the seventeenth century.

Significantly, though, this cultural buffer worked both ways. First, the communities of indios fronterizos shielded Cora, Huichol, and some Tepehuan communities in the western portion of the Frontier and in neighboring Nayarit from Spanish intrusion. A number of pueblos, particularly among the Huicholes, remained free from Franciscan and Jesuit evangelization efforts up until just before the turn of the eighteenth century, along with almost the entire neighboring district of Nayarit.[36] Second, the intermingling that occurred between formerly Tlaxcalan and Chichimec (mostly Caxcan and Tepehuan, but also some Cora and Huichol) communities transformed the Tlaxcalan communities themselves, particularly with respect to their relationship with the outside Spanish regime. In fact, the Tlaxcalans' descendants periodically joined indigenous communities native to the region in rising up against the Spanish during the seventeenth century. During one of these incidents, the rebels killed a *capitán protector* (governor) of the Colotlán Frontier.[37] Just after the turn of the eighteenth century, another uprising originated in the pueblo of Nostic, originally a Huichol community that gradually interconnected with the indios flecheros. The rebellion ostensibly began over mistreatment at the hands of a capitán protector by the name of Silva, but was probably also related to encroaching lumbering activities based out of nearby Monte Escobedo in the Jerez district. This 1704 uprising spread from Nostic to nearby Mezquitic, and then to San Luis de Colotlán itself, eventually resulting in the death of Governor Silva after the rebels stormed his residence.[38] Considering later occurrences, it seems likely that Silva took harsh action against the indios of Nostic that the indios of Colotlán interpreted as threatening the indios fronterizos as a whole.

After receiving viceregal authorization and funds, outside forces joined by a loyal *indio cacique*, known only as Calderilla, suppressed the 1704 uprising.[39] Nevertheless, another uprising occurred in 1709, and over the course of the eighteenth century the indios flecheros of San Luis de Colotlán would publicly memorialize the death of Silva as a warning to subsequent governors who threatened their status.[40] Each year they would "place a cross in the place where they had Assaulted [Silva] as an Example, with the entire pueblo gathered in front of the Casas Reales, in sight of the Captain Protectors that have succeeded [him]."[41] This ritual brings to mind the traditional Spanish "ceremony of possession," the significance of which was memorably revitalized by historian Patricia Seed.[42] Although not accompanied by the reading of a *Requerimiento*, the planting of a cross by these descendants of the Tlaxcalan indios conquistadores represents an unmistakable conquest claim.[43] It served as a warning of the tenuous nature of the Captain Protectors' political legitimacy—dependent as it was on the loyalty of the indios fronterizos —and reinforced the lasting potency of the Conquest model for understanding social relations within the Colotlán region.

Indios Conquistadores Once More: The Subjugation of Nayarit

In the 1720s the Conquest social paradigm materialized into a genuine military enterprise, as indios flecheros from the Colotlán Frontier joined Spanish military commanders in the conquest of the Coras of Nayarit. The aftermath of the 1704 uprising had coincided with the rediscovery of silver in

Tepeque, to the south of Colotlán. In early 1705 an indio mason from Analco (near Guadalajara) started a major silver bonanza, when he showed some ore-rich rocks to the priest of a church he was building in Pochotitán, just to the south of Tepeque.[44] Although silver production would remain low in the area around Bolaños during the next few decades, Spanish settlement was still higher there than in other parts of the Colotlán Frontier. During this period, some indios from the Tepeque-Bolaños area had "fled to the west to take refuge among the still unconquered indios of Nayarit."[45] In addition to having fended off previous evangelization efforts, Nayarit had always remained outside of Spanish military and political control, governed by a traditional Cora ruler known as Tonati. Faced with increasing evangelization efforts in the early eighteenth century, Tonati traveled to Mexico City in early 1721 to negotiate the terms of Spanish entrance into Nayarit and Cora acknowledgment of King Felipe V as sovereign. However, after returning to Nayarit, Tonati changed his mind, and preparations for the conquest began.[46]

In June 1721 some two hundred soldiers from Mexico City, Zacatecas, and Jerez traveled to San Luis de Colotlán to mobilize the Frontier's indio militias. Indios flecheros from San Luis de Colotlán, Huejúcar, and several other Frontier pueblos joined the troops, and the force marched westward through Huejuquilla. After initial, indecisive skirmishes, the Spanish and indios flecheros assaulted the Coras' stronghold and temple atop the Mesa del Tonati on January 16, 1722. After the capture of the Mesa some sporadic resistance continued, but from that point forward the Spanish presence in the region remained constant. The Spaniards and their indigenous allies constructed forts throughout the district and sent various objects of Cora power and veneration to Mexico City, including a former Tonati's skeleton, a stone calendar, and "sacred cups from the temple of the sun."[47]

For the indios fronterizos of Colotlán, participation in the conquest of Nayarit—and later in the subjugation of other unruly pueblos to the west—served more to create ties with individual Spanish military families and justify the special privileges the fronterizos' ancestors had received during the Tlaxcalan colonization of the region in 1591 than it did to strengthen their sense of inclusion in the Spanish Empire. Chapters 2 and 3 describe two of these fronterizo-Spaniard relationships, first centering on the mestizo son of a Spanish military family and later on the relationship between a Spanish commander and an indigenous pueblo who had served with him in the conquest of Nayarit. The militaristic nature of their status vis-à-vis the Spanish regime formed an important part of the self-perception and cultural status of the indios flecheros, and related notions of honor and respect served as central components of fronterizo social networks within the region.

Supplanting the Indio Fronterizo Identity

With Nayarit finally conquered, and Colotlán ostensibly aligned with Spanish interests after it contributed to the conquest, the region experienced a relative lull in social unrest and rebellion until midcentury, when new veins discovered in the Bolaños mines led to a massive silver bonanza. The Spanish government subsequently converted the central section of Colotlán into a separate gobierno, renaming it "Bolaños" in honor of a prominent Spaniard from Tlaltenango who had been driven out of the Tepeque region during the Mixtón war (see figure 1.1). The new district was first moved from the jurisdiction of the Colotlán Frontier and placed under the authority of the *alcalde mayor* of Jerez. In 1754, however, the viceroy appointed a corregidor for Bolaños, answerable directly to Mexico City.[48] The perceived importance of Bolaños—and by association the maintenance of social stability in the Colotlán Frontier—increased significantly after the lucrative silver strikes, and the creation of the new gobierno led to a series of jurisdictional disputes between viceregal authorities in Mexico City and the audiencia of Nueva Galicia in Guadalajara that would last until 1800, when Bolaños, Nayarit, and Colotlán would all be grouped together into one large gobierno under a single military and political governor (with the official title of captain general), directly subject to the viceroy.[49]

Reflecting the more Spanish nature of the mining center's ethnic composition, secular clergy began taking over its spiritual oversight during this same period, but they encountered resistance from resident Franciscans. Definitive secularization of Bolaños's parishes was not accomplished until 1785. This process spread to communities in the surrounding canyons, and San Luís de Colotlán was secularized in 1754–55, Juchipila in 1769, and Tlaltenango after 1772.[50] A 1783 report by Miguel Antonio Gómez, cura of the vecino town of Jerez, decries the lack of outward piety among some of the fronterizo communities. He stated that in the pueblos of San Luis de Colotlán, Santiago, Santa María, Huejúcar, and Tlacosahua, "there are four thousand and five hundred Indios, although many are not pure, but only have the nomenclature. . . . With the misinterpreted Fuero of Soldiers, they are Proud, unmannerly, bad Residents, partisan, protectors of Thieves, killers, and other wicked men, who pervert the natural Simplicity of the Indios. . . . It is believed that the Fronterizos must be made to see that it is not dishonorable to Be Tributaries, that it is conducive to their spiritual and temporal welfare and their greater tranquility and augmentation of their goods, assuring them that they will remain in possession of their Lands and that His Majesty will ensure this accolade [. . . so that] they will easily comply and without much pain, fling down to the Ground the Idol of being Militiamen."[51] The report goes on to list a number of pueblos where the Indians "marry as they please, do not attend mass, and it is suspected that they still practice pagan ceremonies." According to Gómez, those indios who lived in Jérez—a larger villa in the northern part of the region with a greater population of Spaniards and mestizos—were "obedient Christians," though some were "regularly corrupted by the bad example and suggestions of bad men that live on the frontier."[52]

From the late 1770s to 1781, a number of Frontier pueblos led by a core group of several ladino indio leaders and the mestizo son of a former captain general of the Frontier sought to wrest effective political control of the Colotlán region from Spanish officials aligned with the Spanish settlements on the region's periphery. Antonio de Vivanco—the leader of the Spanish *Junta de Guerra* (council of war) who suppressed the uprising—also served as the corregidor of Bolaños. The following year he requested that all of the indios from Colotlán be put under his authority as laborers in the mines, and that a special militia battallion be created in Bolaños to facilitate the process.[53] Although the request was denied, he did manage to acquire the labor of indios from the pueblos closest to Bolaños. Accumulating a vast estate from the silver profits, he was eventually granted the title of Marqués de Vivanco.[54]

Conflicts over the relationship between Spanish interests and the indigenous inhabitants of the Frontier continued into the 1790s. In 1791, the governor of Colotlán petitioned the viceregal government to give him permission to force the "idle" indios to work in the mines.[55] An investigation from 1792–93 referred to "the extortions that are suffered by the indios that work in the royal mines of Bolaños and Zacatecas," and of "the multitude of vagrants and degenerates that there are there."[56] In 1795 Captain Don Simon de Herrera professed the inconvenience of the current method of governing the region, due to the "insubordinations of the *indios*."[57] In many ways these insubordinations reflected a growing Spanish effort to "civilize" the Colotlán Frontier. As the excerpts from the 1783 reports opening this section show, neighboring Spanish vecinos tended to view the indios fronterizos of the Colotlán region as an unruly and "unpure" indigenous society, in which "wicked men" had somehow perverted "the natural Simplicity of the Indios." These attitudes took little notice of the complex ethnic origins of the indios fronterizos as descendants of Tlaxcalan "Hidalgos" and indio conquistadors whose status had been anything but "simple" even in the eyes of the Spanish regime.[58]

The viceregal government in Mexico City continued to view much of the Colotlán region as a frontier in the early nineteenth century, and it maintained militia units in the area to protect the haciendas and settlements in the neighboring districts, which included active silver mines in Bolaños.[59]

The customary tribute exemptions and other fueros accompanying the indio flechero militia status—in effect since the introduction of the Tlaxcalan colonies in the late sixteenth-century—came under increasing attack in the last decade of the eighteenth century, as reform-oriented viceroys attempted to restructure New Spain's military forces to counter both foreign and domestic threats. The utilization of indios flecheros as a relatively inexpensive means of defending the Colotlán Frontier differed from the normal policy of excluding Indians from the ranks of the militia in most other regions of the viceroyalty.[60] The practice of employing these indios flecheros worried many of the Spanish residents of the region, who claimed that the Indians "should only be tributaries" and that "it was not appropriate to put the arms of the King in their hands."[61]

In 1792 Viceroy Juan Vicente Pacheco de Padilla, Conde de Revilla Gigedo, ordered the creation of 19 new companies, including 1,320 mounted militiamen in Colotlán and other northern frontier regions. The regulations for Colotlán stated that nine companies based in eight different locations (with two in Tlaltenango), and totaling 630 men, would be formed "for the interior and exterior defense of the Frontier of Colotlán and the Province of Nayarit."[62] The prevailing vecino perspective toward the indios fronterizos is reflected in the viceroy's rationale for these changes: The disbanding of the fronterizo militia companies "will be the wisest and safest means of disarming the Natives [as we are] now no longer in need of their weak forces. Once the pillages and robberies of the indios fronterizos, not to mention the castas and [other] Nations that distinguish them, have been limited, the only thing left to do will be to make sure that the Naturales of both fronteras [Colotlán and Nayarit] dedicate themselves to the cultivation of their lands and other labors . . . in order to temper their customs, so that they forget about the use of Arms."[63]

Royal officials evidently encountered some difficulty in implementing the policies, as two years later the new companies had not been established. In 1794 Viceroy Miguel de la Grua Talamanca, Marqués de Branciforte, again ordered "the extinction of the old companies of indios flecheros," and the establishment of nine companies of provincial dragoons in the border regions of Colotlán, Bolaños, and Nayarit.[64] Branciforte also ordered the distribution of tracts of land to Spanish families, further proof of the government's continued efforts to "civilize" the area, even as late as the turn of the nineteenth century.[65] The viceregal government would persist in this effort to "Hispanicize" the region's cultural composition up until the onset of the independence struggle. In 1807 Huicholes from "la república de indios de Huajuqiaua [Huejuquilla in Colotlán]" submitted a formal complaint against a requirement to contribute 1.5 reales to create a collection of community funds, and against the forced introduction of twelve *gente de razón* in each pueblo.[66]

In spite of attempts to restrict indigenous movement between the official boundaries of imperial districts, the region's indigenous inhabitants continued to maintain a degree of common identity across pueblos with diverse ethnic backgrounds. In 1800–1802, inhabitants of Colotlán participated in the well-documented rebellion of "El Indio Mariano," in which an indigenous leader of Nayarit gathered a large number of supporters for a plan to overthrow Spanish dominion in favor of a messianic, and probably fictional, descendant of the Tlaxcalan kings who derived his authority from a mysterious golden mask. In a message to Don Tomás Ballesteros, military governor of Colotlán, on April 5, 1801, José Abascal, president of the intendancy of Guadalajara, warned Ballesteros of the probability that the Mariano conspiracy would spread into his jurisdiction. Little more than a week later, Abascal wrote again informing Ballesteros that Indians captured in Tepic had stated that they came from Colotlán to "make an attempt to crown their king." Ballesteros replied that he would take any necessary measures to ensure that the rebellion wouldn't spread to his jurisdiction.[67] Although Spanish authorities soon subdued the "Indio Mariano" uprising, in autumn 1810 the entire Colotlán region erupted in violent rebellion. Local indigenous, mestizo, and creole leaders led several thousand fronterizo rebels in open rebellion against the royal government, sacking haciendas and even some towns. This insurrection in Colotlán would disrupt imperial authority throughout much of the Western Sierra and claim the lives of thousands of the region's inhabitants, including the royal governor. However, before considering those events, chapters 2 and 3 will take a closer look at some key features of late colonial social relations in the region.

The Tlaxcalan allies of the Spanish and communities native to the Colotlán region together superimposed a Conquest model for understanding identity and social relations onto earlier traditions of indigenous resistance. Their descendants employed both of these cultural forms in their subsequent interaction with Spanish officials and vecinos from neighboring districts. These indios fronterizos, as they came to be known, participated in the relatively late conquest of Nayarit, subsequently using this service to the Spanish regime to preserve their own status in the social conflicts of the eighteenth century. At the same time, they upheld their own memories and traditions of resistance as a caution to possible Spanish threats to their status and privileges. Such threats were increasingly present as Spanish interest in securing mineral wealth in nearby Zacatecas and—within the Colotlán region itself—Bolaños drew the attention and energies of Spanish elites and settlers. By the late colonial period casta newcomers had integrated themselves into some of the Frontera pueblos, causing conflict within some, while forming alliances in others and increasing the ongoing formation of a new fronterizo—but still substantially and overtly indigenous—identity. The next two chapters continue this story, demonstrating the powerful connection between ethnic and social status, the essential elements of Frontier authority, and the significance of personal relationships on the local level in establishing rights and claiming control over resources.

2

Indigenous Autonomy in Late Colonial Mexico

In the end Señor we are now prisoners, and the Frontiers have been lost, our authority has flown away, and all hell has broken loose with the most unjust foundation.

—Letter from fronterizo leader Juan Vicencio Fernández de Córdova, written in the Aguascalientes jail, January 1781

On January 23, 1781, a prisoner in the royal jail in the villa of Aguascalientes wrote a letter to Don Antonio Fernández de Córdova, administrator of tobacco rents and the *alcabala* (sales tax) in the pueblo of San Luis de Colotlán. Juan Vicencio Fernández de Córdova, known locally as "Juanico," was the mestizo son of Don Antonio's brother and a local Colotlán "Yndia Tlaxcalteca."[1] He wrote during a stop en route to judgment at the hands of the viceroy in Mexico City, in the company of a strong guard and four fellow prisoners, all Spanish-speaking *indios ladinos* from Colotlán. Nearly two hundred pages of testimony and affidavits also accompanied the prisoners, documenting an enormous list of their crimes and excesses against the representatives of royal authority and against the inhabitants of the Colotlán Frontier.[2] Juanico's letter to his uncle conveys a sense of his justification for his actions and, perhaps more importantly, his conception of his own identity in relation to his fellow fronterizos.

Don Antonio Fernández de Córdova,

Our most esteemed uncle and *Señor*, I have not had the chance to write to you since the day they captured us until this day on which, by the Providence of God, we have happily managed to write from the Royal Jail of Aguascalientes, from which we will leave tomorrow for the Royal Court in Mexico, to where we will assuredly arrive as they have put a pair of irons on each of us . . . since [we left] Zacatecas but this does not matter at all because God is the one who hears the case of every person, and if I have caused such a great offence in defending these Ungrateful Frontiers then may his Will be done.

> I believe *Señor* that, upon receipt of this there are already some *Fronterizos* in Mexico presented before Don Mariano Marin declaring the Infamy and treason with which they arrested us. They have us vexed as to how to attain the appropriate jurisdiction without agreeing with them. In the end Señor we are now prisoners, and the Frontiers have been lost, our authority has flown away, and all hell has broken loose with the most unjust foundation. But I think that is how it has to be. In the end *Señor* we are at the utmost extreme and if at present you do not hurt for us and for me because of what has happened, then for the Glory of my Father by whatever means possible try to encourage these slumbering *Señores de Republicas*[3] when I and everyone here with me have sacrificed for them [such that] here we are after everything, and at present they seem to be the biggest ingrates, since if I would see them in some difficulty like mine I would sacrifice, look at what I have done to guard their rights and Privileges and everything. And I would never stop, as a result of which they are imprisoning us so that these Frontiers can be harassed. In the end the [illegible] are what helps us: We are badly treated in shackles and more. I cannot write more as it is now 10:00 and visiting hour in this Jail. God guard you many years in all holy Grace. Aguascalientes Royal Jail January 23, 1781
> Your most attentive servants and Nephew,
> Córdova Pacheco Lozano Belez[4]

The events leading up to the capture of Juanico and his fellow prisoners occurred at a portentous moment in the history of Spanish America. The imperial reforms instituted by the Bourbon monarchy had created a more efficient mechanism for bureaucratic control and the collection of revenues. The reforms had also fostered resentment among local creole elites and sparked both ethnically tinged and economically motivated rebellion all over the empire, including the *comuneros* in New Granada, a tax revolt in Quito, and Tupac Amaru II's race war in the Andes.[5] Historians have tended to categorize these events as direct reactions to the Bourbon reforms and as precursors of the independence struggle. Both of these assessments are accurate in a general sense, but the events depicted in Chapter 1, as well as other scholarship on ethnically tinged social unrest, show how similar rebellions had occurred throughout the colonial period.[6] New work has begun to demonstrate how myth and millennialism harkening back to remembered indigenous pasts often overlay more tangibly identifiable sources of rebellion.[7] None of the rebellions of this period can be understood without examining the preexisting social tensions and networks within which they occurred.

This approach allows for a more informed view of both the general context of the making and breaking of empire, and the rich local sociocultural settings in which the long-term trajectory of Spanish America was determined.

A Power Vacuum

The story of Juanico and the individuals who accompanied him (known collectively as the "Señores Colotecos") was buried in the archives for nearly 225 years.[8] It encompasses events affecting a substantial region containing thousands of people (see table 1.1). The efforts of the Señores Colotecos to preserve the tradition of indigenous authority in the Colotlán region reveal a shifting ethnic landscape in the 1780s. They attempted to represent themselves as defenders of the indios fronterizos and the heirs of the indigenous conquistadors who settled in the region in the late sixteenth century and participated in the conquest of Nayarit in the early eighteenth. In demanding the loyalty of the fronterizo pueblos, they demonstrated many of the qualities scholars associate with caudillo and cacique figures in the nineteenth century.[9] As the pueblos of the Colotlán Frontier chose to support or oppose the Señores Colotecos, the conflict took on ethnic undertones. The Señores Colotecos advocated a fronterizo identity that incorporated some newcomers of mixed ancestry but denied the authority of powerful Spanish landowners and mining interests.

Virtually all parties involved in the turbulent period of conflict from 1780 to 1785, which resulted in the imprisonment of Juanico and his companions, agreed on one point: the trouble began during the government of Felipe del Villar, Captain Protector (governor) of the Colotlán Frontier from 1774 to 1779. Villar's mishandling of the government provoked a strong reaction in the cabecera (district capital) of Colotlán and the four pueblos immediately to the southwest: Totatiche, Acaspulco, Temastian, and Asqueltan (see figure 2.1).[10] The *principales* (indigenous leaders) of these pueblos accused him of dispossessing them of their land and defrauding the Real Hacienda.[11] In 1777 the viceroy responded to the principales' complaints by ordering "the closest Justicia to the Frontera and the Pueblo of San Luis de Colotlán"—or in the absence of such a person "the nearest subject in charge of administering the royal rents"—to serve Capitán Villar with a 1,000 peso fine. The viceroy also ordered him to explain the reason for his actions against the indios.[12] Villar responded weakly by submitting evidence of his efforts to combat idolatry and the uprisings of the nearby indios Tepehuanes. According to the the indios of Colotlán, however, Villar's arbitrary actions, including the imprisonment of various indios and seizure of their goods, had provoked the indigenous rebellions.[13] Finally, in 1779, authorities in Guadalajara ordered

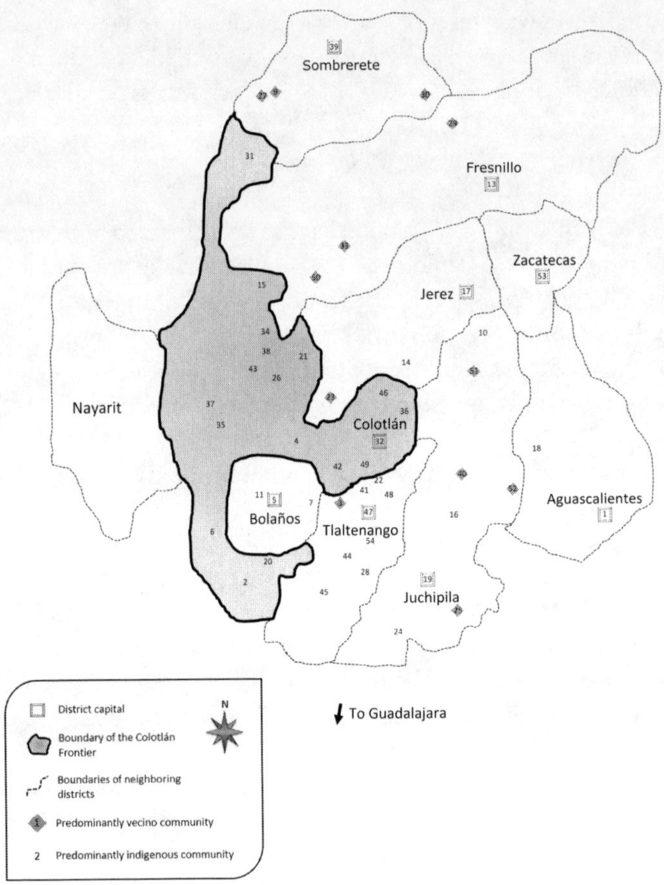

Figure 2.1. Pueblos and towns of the Colotlán region. Predominantly *vecino* communities are marked with a diamond. All others were predominantly indigenous. 1, Aguascalientes. 2, Apozolco. 3, Atolinga. 4, Azqueltán. 5, Bolaños. 6, Camotlán. 7, Coguasco. 8, Coculiten. 9, Chalchihuites. 10, Chicomosoc (La Quemada). 11, Chimaltitán. 12, Durasno. 13, Fresnillo. 14, Huejucar. 15, Huejuquilla. 16, Jalpa (Xalpa). 17, Jerez (Xerez). 18, Jesús María. 19, Juchipila. 20, Mamatla. 21, Mezquitic. 22, Momax. 23, Monte Escobedo. 24, Moyahua. 25, Nochistlán. 26, Nostic. 27, Nueva Tlaxcala. 28, Ocotlán (San Pedro de). 29, Rancho Grande. 30, Saín. 31, San Andrés del Teúl. 32, San Luís de Colotlán. 33, San Mateo Valparaíso. 34, San Nicolás. 35, San Sebastián. 36, Santa María. 37, Santa Catarina. 38, Soledad. 39, Sombrerete. 40, Tabasco. 41, Teocaltiche. 42, Temastián. 43, Tensompa. 44, Tepechitlán. 45, Teúl. 46, Tlalcosagua. 47, Tlaltenango. 48, Tocatic (Tocatique). 49, Totatiche. 50, Valparaíso. 51, Villanueva. 52, Valle de Huejucar. 53, Zacatecas. 54, Zicacalco. Map by author.

Villar to appear before the audiencia as a prisoner within one month, citing as the final straw "the fraud that he is accused of committing against the Tobacco rents."[14] By removing Captain Protector Villar from his position as the highest-ranking royal official in the Colotlán region, this order created a battle for political legitimacy and control over the indio flechero militiamen and the pueblos of the Colotlán Frontier. Significantly, all of the actors in these events recognized that this legitimacy could—and, in fact, must—be established in the eyes of the Frontera communities, not just in the view of Spanish authorities in Guadalajara or Mexico City.

A Cast of Characters: The Colotecos, the *Pocos*, and the "True *Común*"

An overview of the principal individuals and parties involved helps to convey a clear sense of the social dynamics underlying these events. Capitan Felipe del Villar, whose actions and eventual arrest initiated the turbulence, played a role in the power struggle of the 1780s only to the extent that the ongoing lawsuit against him remained a concern for the Fernández de Córdova family and their allies. Consequently, resentment toward Villar formed part of the backdrop of accusations among the pueblos of Colotlán.[15] The key actors in the events following his involuntary departure fall into at least three categories: (1) the *Señores Colotecos*—as supporters of Juan Vicencio Fernández de Córdova and his companions came to call them—and their allies, including a racially diverse group known as the *Pocos*; (2) the pueblos of Huejúcar and Santa María, also known as the Villareños or the loyal pueblos; and (3) the Junta de Guerra—an assembly of powerful Spanish elites from neighboring districts—and its supporters.

As the administrator of tabaccos and alcabalas in Colotlán, Don Antonio Fernández de Córdova would have been a key figure in the suit against Villar, and it is clear that he came down on the side of the indios of Colotlán. At this point Don Antonio had lived among the indios for nearly forty years and, according to the members of the Junta de Guerra, despite his "illustrious birth," "he felt more comfortable following their customs than observing those appropriate to his own blood."[16] Even so, he seems to have served as a relatively inactive patron for his nephew and close allies. Don Antonio's official position and status may have played a role in the removal of Captain Protector Villar, but it was his nephew Don Juan Vicencio Fernández de Córdova (Juanico) who led the effort to maintain the ongoing lawsuit against Villar, and who would eventually be imprisoned for the zealousness of his actions.

Four of Juanico's companions assisted him, and they later joined him in prison: Calixto Pacheco, José de Santiago Velez, Juan de Rivera (principal from the Colotlán barrio of Soyatitán), and Juan Lozano, each one listed as "Light-skinned and ladino Indio."[17] Spanish officials found it necessary to specify the skin color of these men because of the integration of free blacks and mulatos into the region's indigenous population.[18] Both the Spanish and some indios in the Frontera de Colotlán associated African ancestry—and by extension, darker skin color—with lower status. It is not surprising that these men were described as ladino (Hispanicized/acculturated) by the scribe recording the military authorities' report of the events. Although not the case with all of the Frontera pueblos, most indigenous inhabitants of San Luis de Colotlán spoke Spanish and had exercised various customs usually reserved for Spaniards and mestizos ever since the granting of special status to their Tlaxcalan colonist ancestors. Although they would eventually become known as the *Cabecillas* ("ringleaders"), Juanico and his four friends called themselves the "Señores Colotecos," effectively claiming the status of indigenous nobility with strong connotations of connection to place. This claim was not especially difficult to make in the eyes of many of the pueblos of the Frontera de Colotlán, who preserved traditions of descent from the Tlaxcalan *indios hidalgos*. Juanico's Spanish paternal ancestry did not diminish his claim in this regard. Juanico and each of his companions came from the leading families of the three barrios of San Luis de Colotlán and thus already exercised a measure of either formal or informal control over the cabecera of the Colotlán Frontier. Although, with the exception of Juan de Rivera, none of them held the actual title of a pueblo principal (*regidor*, *alguacil*, or *gobernador*, for instance), they represented themselves as such, and they would exercise social and political authority at the pueblo level and beyond in the months after Villar's departure.

Allied with Juanico and his fellow Colotecos—in both their attempts to remove and prosecute Governor Villar and their later efforts to exert social and political authority over the Colotlán Frontier —were the principales and indio militiamen of the pueblos of San Luis de Colotlán, Mezquitic, Nostic, Totatiche, Asqueltán, Temastián, and Apozolco.[19] These pueblos supplied money and material to the suit against Villar and later provided military support for Juanico and his fellow Colotecos. The Colotecos also aligned themselves with an interesting group referred to as *los Pocos* (the lesser ones). A local indio flechero from the pueblo of Huejúcar described some of the Pocos as group of families who had a *gremio* in the barrio of San Pedro in his pueblo.[20] Others were reportedly living in the village of Santiago. The fact that the racially mixed Pocos had formed a gremio in at least one pueblo attests to their rising status in these communities; it also reveals some of the roots of the eventual divisions among the pueblos.[21] Both of these pueblos were north of San Luis de Colotlán, and their principales had been aligned with Villar before his ouster. In Huejúcar, at least, the Pocos seemed to have paid a price for supporting the suit against ex-Governor Villar against the wishes of the village principales.[22] The social divisions among the Pocos and the rest of the village population appeared to have some correlation with race and ancestry. In fact, two of Huejúcar's principales identified their own faction—the non-Pocos—as "the true *Común*," *indios puros* who controlled the "empleos de la Republica." The term común could refer to any given community with certain inherent rights; in indigenous pueblos membership in the común could often convey an entitlement to the use of pueblo land.[23] In Huejúcar, the "true Común" understood their own identity and legitimacy in reference to the cultural heritage of the Tlaxcalan colonists. The pueblo had safeguarded documents confirming their Tlaxcalan ancestors' conquistador status and subsequent participation in frontier military efforts since the sixteenth century.[24] One of the principales, for instance, referred to himself as "Governador Tlaxcalteco."[25] He and his fellow principales described the Pocos—led by the militia Captain Don Joseph Xavier Saturno and his associate Alexo Nuñez—as a minority of some sixty or seventy people "who are in reality a bunch of lobos, Coyotes, and other bad races; thieves, Rustlers, and horse thieving rascals gathered from other places, among which there is just a scattering of native indios from Huejúcar."[26] This characterization represented an overt attempt on the part of the dominant faction to exclude the Pocos from any control of the república de indios and contributed to the Pocos' alignment with the Señores Colotecos, who willingly served as patrons for the rejected minority in return for allegiance.

Along with outside observers, Huejúcar's "true Común" would come to form the center of the opposition to the Colotecos and their aims. Not all of the Frontera pueblos supported the Colotecos in their attempt to exert political control over the region, as will be shown below. Huejúcar represented the most prominent of these "loyal pueblos," as non-fronterizo Spaniards would later term them, but the nearby village of Santa María—along with a number of like-minded smaller communities—would also come to serve as sites of resistance to the Colotecos' plans. The principales and key figures in Huejúcar and San Luis de Colotlán held quite different attitudes toward former Governor Villar and thus reacted differently to his removal from office. For instance, two of the principales of Huejúcar—Ygnacio Alvarado and Laurio Morillo—were reported to have "gone around with Villar" before his fall from grace.[27] It is important to remember, though—as demonstrated in the distinction between the *verdadero Comun* and the Pocos in Huejúcar—that the social rifts among the communities of Colotlán could cut through both intrapueblo and interpueblo lines.

Despite coming down on opposite sides of the Villar dispute, the pueblos of San Luis de Colotlán and Huejúcar shared a number of characteristics. Along with the other Tlaxcalan colony at San Andres del Teúl, both were founded as joint settlements of Tlaxcalan colonists and locally indigenous "Chichimecs"—principally Tepehuanes in San Andres, and Caxcanes or "tochos" in San Luis and Huejúcar—but were generally identified as ladino by the late colonial period.[28] During the 1720s indio flechero militiamen from Huejúcar and San Luis de Colotlán had participated in the conquest of neighboring Nayarit, the last area in this portion of the viceroyalty to be brought under Spanish dominion. As late as 1777, men from both pueblos had joined in the suppression of an indigenous uprising in San Andres, Huejuquilla, and Tensompa.[29] Significant numbers of castas were joining the communities of Huejúcar and San Luis de Colotlán in the late colonial period, and both had undergone the general cultural shift from cultural heterogeneity toward a corporate indio fronterizo identity.

Thus it is clear that both San Luis de Colotlán and Huejúcar—along with their respective allied pueblos—drew from a shared past and had common characteristics. Nevertheless, particular sections of the pueblos' societies formed distinctive relationships with prominent Spanish authorities and members of the local elite, as is evidenced in their respective relationships with former Governor Villar, Spanish authorities in nearby Jerez, and the influential Fernández de Córdova family. As the power struggle after Villar's removal escalated, the divisions within Frontera society would become even more apparent, particularly among the indios fronterizos. And soon another powerful faction would appear on the scene: a Junta de Guerra composed of prominent Spaniards from neighboring districts and led by Antonio de Vivanco, a self-made mining magnate from Bolaños.

"We are the Ones in Power Now"

Before reaching the point where Vivanco's Junta de Guerra enters into the narrative in Colotlán, it is necessary to return to the events following Governor Villar's 1779 departure. Juanico Córdova had served as the unofficial, de facto governor of the barrio of Tlaxcala (one of three in the pueblo of San Luis de Colotlán) at some point preceding Governor Villar's arrest. Drawing upon his status as the son of a respected Spanish creole from a local military family and an India Tlaxcalteca (most likely the daughter of one of the pueblo principales) Juanico exercised significant authority in the fronterizo community. Upon the arrival of the capitán protector's replacement, Don Luis Mendez de Lievana, Córdova and Mendez de Lievana reached an informal agreement whereby Juanico ran public games in which the indios flecheros, tenant farmers (*arrendatarios*), and poorer Spanish laborers competed and gambled with one another, passing a percentage of the take to Lievana as a *coima* (kickback).[30] This deal evidently pleased Mendez de Lievana enough to name Juanico Córdova and his four friends "Visitadores Generales and Apoderados de toda la Frontera." When Mendez de Lievana died within a year after taking office, control of the gambling and resultant revenues passed to Juanico Córdova, who soon moved to exert political control over the entire Colotlán Frontier.[31] After the governor's death, Juanico wasted little time in employing his new status and title in an effort to raise more money from the other Frontera pueblos to sustain the ongoing lawsuit against the deposed Felipe del Villar. His companion, the indio ladino Calixto Pacheco, encouraged him in this endeavor, writing from Tlaltenango in the interim after Mendez de Lievana's death. In the letter he asked Córdova to have the principales of San Luis de Colotlán's three barrios bring twenty pesos each to offer the *comisionado* in Tlaltenango, explaining that "we are the ones in power now."[32] Pacheco recognized that Coloteco control over the Frontera de Colotlán needed to be smoothed over with neighboring Spanish officials, and although he, Juanico, and their associates never fully achieved this aim, they demonstrated a familiarity with Spanish norms of deference and patron-client relationships in this instance and, more substantially, in the exercise of their own authority within the Frontera.

At this point, the only rival to such a claim was Don José Manuel de Aguallo, a resident of San Luis de Colotlán, recently commissioned as Teniente General de la Frontera—subordinate only to the now vacant position of governor—by Antonio de Jauregui, the alcalde of Jerez. Jauregui had no authority to make such an appointment but, as mayor of a predominantly Spanish and mestizo town on the edge of the Colotlán Frontier, he evidently thought that the prospect of a power vacuum in Colotlán merited emergency measures. Córdova and his allies acted to remove Aguallo by forcing him to surrender the key to the pueblo archive and strongbox where the protocolos and instrumentos públicos were kept. They then gave him three days to vacate his house in Colotlán and to leave the pueblo. According to Aguallo, they "arrogantly" stated that "they did not need anyone to govern them, that they were Competent in that regard." Aguallo, who appears to have been rather fainthearted, complied and moved to the nearby pueblo of Santa María, whose inhabitants, in his words, "received him with the utmost obedience, love, and caring." Throughout the course of the dramatic events to come, Aguallo stayed in Santa María, refraining from any challenge of the Colotecos' authority until the eventual arrival of the Junta de Guerra.[33] The Junta would later note the loyalty of the indios flecheros from Santa María "who are of the most faithful, and who have always shown themselves to be good vassals."[34]

Soon Juanico Córdova began riding throughout the region flashing important-looking papers and proclaiming his title as "Apoderado de todas las Fronteras." He proclaimed publicly that he was the only person in charge of the Frontera pueblos and demanded that the indios flecheros and principales of each pueblo contribute money and goods to pass on to Don Mariano Marin, the agent of the pueblos of the Colotlán Frontier in Mexico City. According to the testimony of the leaders of several pueblos, Córdova refused to give receipts for the contributions and confiscated whatever goods he thought sufficient from anyone who did not give him hard currency.[35] According to the principales of Asqueltan, their pueblo gave Córdova 670 pesos, and when they asked him for a receipt he told them that "neither the King, nor His Excellency the Viceroy, who have the most ample faculties to extract money and to punish disobedient people, ordered [me] to give [you] receipts." Despite Juanico's hauteur, in the end they gave him the money, explaining that they had faith in his loyalty to the fronterizos. The principales of Asqueltan also testified that Córdova had "taken eighty cattle from the cofradía of the pueblo, saying that he was going to sell them to submit money to their agent Mariano Marin in Mexico, and that they needed to [do so] because it was necessary to give gifts to the Señores who might favor the Frontera, so that they would give [us] many Privileges."[36]

A number of testimonies from other repúblicas de indios of the Colotlán Frontier are similar, and their words illustrate how members of late colonial New Spanish society viewed the exploitation of local resources for the ostensible well-being of the community as a legitimate function of authority. Other scholars have examined litigation cases between indigenous communities and other entities—government officials, clergy, hacendados, or even other pueblos—demonstrating the frequent use of law as a valued recourse to address (or redress) the concerns of indigenous and African communities.[37] Consequently, the case of the Señores Colotecos is particularly important, as it reveals the personal mechanisms used to coordinate and maintain such efforts. In particular, the responses of the indio fronterizo communities to Juanico's fundraising efforts reveal the social pressures and burdens inherent in pursuing litigation. Their testimonies also demonstrate the potential for exploitation of instances of interaction with extra-regional authorities by individuals like Juanico who could present themselves as cultural intermediaries. Córdova championed the interests of the fronterizo communities—as *he* interepreted them—through his agent in the capital, but he also appropriated resources from local communities to support his efforts to establish himself as the preeminent political authority in the Frontera de Colotlán. Several pueblos and numerous individuals reported burdensome contributions demanded by Juanico and his Colotecos.[38] Significantly, though, they blame him more for his eventual lack of success than for forcing them to contribute. Although many of the actual pueblo principales would later put all of the blame for the eventual turmoil squarely on the shoulders of Juanico and Calixto Pacheco, a number of the pueblos genuinely supported the Colotecos in what was essentially an effort to exert control over local politics. The principales of San Luis de Colotlán, in particular, treated the authority of Juanico and Calixto as implicit in their eventual testimony, and admitted to following Juanico's lead even before the death of Governor Mendez de Lievana.[39] In the end, as the principales of Asqueltan pointed out, personal loyalties served as the decisive factor in this process; in many pueblos Juanico Córdova successfully portrayed himself as the defender of fronterizo society, a recognized member of the community and an advocate for its interests.[40]

Idolatries, Fugitive Indios, and the Colotecos' Effect on Society

The case of Juan Antonio Ramírez, an indio flechero originally from the pueblo of Totatiche, illustrates another element of Juanico's appeal to some members of Frontera society and the pueblo of Asqueltan in particular. A number of years before, Ramírez married an indigenous woman from Asqueltan and went to live in her pueblo. He later claimed that—as an adherent only to the law of the Doctrina– he lived in fear of the "Idolatries of those Bárbaros," until the arrival of Governor Villar. Villar, whom Ramírez described as "a Christian Judge of zeal and charity [with a] good knowledge of our Holy Faith," commissioned Ramírez to make a list "of the Idolatries of the pueblo of Asqueltan." Both Ramírez's self-identification as a God-fearing indio in sharp contrast to the idolatrous "indios bárbaros" and his subsequent commission by Villar show how some indios flecheros had accepted Spanish conceptions of status, while others—who aligned themselves with the Señores Colotecos—adopted a more amalgamated version that privileged defense of fronterizo interests over adherence to Spanish political forms or cultural proscriptions. Ramírez's testimony gives an invaluable sense of both the cultural and religious situation in Asqueltan. He noted that "there are many Rational beings among them in terms of Prose and middling clarity in the Castillan tongue." He went on to acknowledge that Governor Villar "saw fit" to grant him [Ramírez] the title of alguacil mayor in the pueblo. This provides another clue into the reason for the unpopularity of Villar, who appears to have overlooked the practice of pueblos electing their own candidates to pueblo-level office, including Alguaciles Mayores, in favor of pursuing his effort to uncover Asqueltan's idolatries. Following Villar's mandate, Ramírez scrupulously continued noting the pueblo's transgressions, while refusing to participate in their public and ritual dances. Unfortunately for Ramírez, this fostered "such hate, malice, and Passion" against him that, upon the removal of Governor Villar members of the pueblo "raised numerous falsehoods and diabolic fantasies" against him to Don Luis Mendez de Lievana, Villar's replacement. After Mendez de Lievana's death, they complained to Calixto Pacheco who had Ramírez imprisoned in the San Luis de Colotlán jail, where he remained for the duration of the Colotecos' governance of the Colotlán Frontier.[41]

In another incident that won no friends among the region's more pious inhabitants, Juanico Córdova's partidarios reportedly threatened the life of the cura propietario of Totatiche, Bachiller Don Isidro Espino. Espino, who had apparently been a vocal opponent of Córdova's "public games," had come to the nearby pueblo of Acaspulco to fulfill his annual duty of confessing and celebrating the eucharist for the pueblo. Apparently, a member of the community who had committed an unspecified offense arrived to confess and be absolved. The indios of Acaspulco, however—"full of self importance" and bolstered by the protection of Juanico Córdova and Calixto Pacheco, according to the Spanish merchant giving the testimony—tried to apprehend the penitent. When Padre Espino attempted to defend the man, the Acaspulcanos "committed the grave offence of wanting to take the life of said Señor Cura." According to the witness, the indigenous governor of the pueblo "put his hand to his Knife to wound [Espino], another one of their persuasion lifted a plank, and another who was leading an ox formed a loop [with his lariat] to lasso him." According to the (apparently secondhand) witness recounting the incident, things could have ended badly for Padre Espino were it not for other "pious" indios who interrupted the threatened assault, and were then driven out of the pueblo along with Padre Espino.[42] Although threats against the lives of clergymen were not uncommon in late colonial New Spain, the fact that Juanico Córdova, and not Felipe Villar, was seen as the source of political authority on the Frontera de Colotlán surely influenced the actions of the Ascapulcanos.[43]

Juanico's attitude toward other non-Spanish groups and the ethnic status of his close associates provide additional evidence of the fluid nature of ethnic status, religion, and social relations during the period of the Colotecos' control over the Frontera. For example, during Juanico's "government" of Colotlán Fray José Antonio Navarro—head of ongoing Franciscan evangelization efforts in the nearby gobierno of Nayarit—applied for help from the viceregal government "to prohibit the indios from going from this territory to Colotlán."[44] It appears that these members of indigenous communities to the west—where the ongoing process of reduction to missions or incorporation into Spanish society was in full swing—viewed the area under the Colotecos' authority as an opportune cultural refuge. In fact, Juanico and the Justiciales of the three barrios of San Luis de Colotlán wrote a letter to Don José Duval del Valle—lieutenant of the Huejuquilla area and technically subordinate to the Capitán Protector (Governor) of Colotlán—asking him to "set free . . . various indios [from the] pueblos of Soledad and Tenzompa" and allow them to return to the *cavecera* (Colotlán). They added that this request was in support of the effort against Villar, whom the letter hoped will be sentenced to "an overseas prison" for life, for being "a suspicious troublemaker and a disturber of the peace and tranquility of these frontiers," and "for the fraud that Villar committed."[45] Juanico's intervention in this incident reflects his effort to fulfill a good patron's responsibilities to his supporters. Observers from Mesquitic (one of the Colotecos' allied pueblos) would later testify that part of the reason they followed Juanico's lead was his ties to the interior pueblos.[46] As further confirmation of this phenomenon, the captain of the detachment of Cataluñan Volunteers based in the presidio of Nayarit wrote to Lieutenant Duval on February 4, 1781, just after the arrest of Juanico and the Colotecos, directing him to order the Justicias of the pueblo of Asqueltan and its immediate vicinity (supporters of the Colotecos) to "hand over some indios from Nayarit that are hiding there."[47]

The story of Diego Ramos provides further indication of the atmosphere that prevailed while the Colotecos controlled Colotlán. One of the mulatos advenedizos who had found a home in the Colotlán region, Ramos had killed Colotlán's *diezmero* (tax collector) in a drunken swordfight some fourteen years earlier. After eight months of imprisonment the capitán protector set him free on the occasion of a general amnesty celebrating the birth of the prince. Ramos then served as the capitán protector for seven years and five months without receiving any salary. When Juanico and the Colotecos began their efforts to raise money and establish political control over the Frontera, they commissioned Ramos as a "collector of rents" in some of the nearby pueblos. Ramos collected contributions (cattle, for instance) from the indios flecheros and *cofradias* of a given community. He then sold them and passed the proceeds along to Juanico Córdova, with the understanding that the contributions would support the ongoing lawsuits "relating to the Frontera." Although it is possible that the Colotecos' integration of Ramos into their operations developed as a carryover from his prior service to the "powers that be," it seems likely that—as in the case of other castas, such as the Pocos—Ramos supported the agenda of Juanico and the Colotecos.[48]

Honor, Respect, and Personal Allegiance

The explanation for *how* Juanico Córdova managed to demand both the material resources and the social allegiance of so many of the inhabitants of the Colotlán Frontier—not only the indio fronterizo communities, but also less assimilated indios from the west and castas like Diego Ramos—goes beyond his parentage and family connections. Although these factors certainly helped to position him in a mediatory position in Frontera society, other prominent mestizos lived in the region without ever attaining a status on par with Córdova's. And although it might seem counterintuitive, it is clear that a number of communities, such as Asqueltan, reacted to Juanico's forceful assertions of authority by acquiescing to his demands for money and acknowledging him as the preeminent political power in the Frontera. As stated, the key lay with personal loyalties. Whatever Juanico's faults, many of the indio flechero militiamen saw him as an hombre fronterizo. He had fought with them in the campaigns to pacify the more rebellious, unassimilated pueblos to the west. He had carried weapons and did not shy away from the use of force to achieve his purposes. This element of military service and frontier machismo drew from both Spanish and indigenous cultural traditions that valued strength and warriorlike valor.[49] He had been instrumental in removing the unpopular Governor Villar and led the effort to ensure that he never returned. He organized and participated in cockfights, horse races, and other public games, all popular among the members of frontier society. And his relatively loose approach to race and religion suited many members of fronterizo society better than that of previous Spanish authorities. However, Juanico's efforts to enforce the boundaries of accepted behavior toward women suggest that his appeal as a strong, macho leader included strict attention to proscriptions about gender.

Other records from early 1780 suggest that Juanico's appeal extended to fronterizo women, and they confirm the dual nature of male honor as both virulent and protective. Don Gregorio Manuel de Fernández, indio Cacique of the barrio of Tochopa, in San Luis de Colotlán, was one of the three principales called by Calixto Pacheco to bring twenty pesos to the comisionado in Tlaltenango to help assure the position of the Colotecos' faction after the death of Governor Mendez de Lievana.[50] Some months later, in 1780, Don Gregorio imprisoned Alexandro de la Cruz, an indio flechero who had mistreated his wife and "failed to fulfill some obligations that all of the militiamen must do." De la Cruz's imprisonment had evidently been sanctioned or even instigated by Juanico Córdova, and the unfulfilled obligations may have referred to Córdova's fundraising efforts. Nevertheless, other evidence suggests that monetary gain formed only one part of Córdova's motivation in imprisoning men like de la Cruz. As other scholars have shown, social power in New Spain relied as much on maintaining order and exercising control over gender relations as it did on control over wealth.[51] Juanico imprisoned a number of men who stepped outside the accepted boundaries of gender behavior, in most cases conjoining both a social and financial penalty.[52]

In the case of Alexandro de la Cruz, Don Gregorio decided after the passing of an unspecific amount of time that the prisoner should be reconciled with his wife. However, when the Cacique freed de la Cruz and began to escort him back to his home, Juanico accosted the two on the road and gave Don Gregorio a blow with the flat of his sword; he forced him to return de la Cruz to the jail, and, in the words of Don Gregorio, flouted Don Gregorio's "authority and pious judgment."[53] Instead of making an enemy of Don Gregorio, however, Juanico's actions reinforced his status as a strong figure of authority. As will soon become apparent, despite his clear umbrage at Juanico's intervention, Don Gregorio continued to support the Colotecos in even the most drastic of their actions in the struggle for control over the pueblos of the Frontera.[54]

Conquering a Pueblo

By the summer of 1780, Juanico Córdova and the Colotecos had firm control over Colotlán and had successfully garnered material support from most of the larger pueblos of the Frontera. Challenges to their authority, such as the hasty appointment of Don José Manuel de Aguallo as Teniente General de la Frontera by Jerez's Alcalde Antonio de Jauregui, and the independent behavior of some of the pueblo principals, as in the case of Don Gregorio Manuel de Fernández, had been removed or contained, and the Colotecos were marshaling an impressive inventory to finance their case against Villar, other litigation in favor of the Frontera, and their own political ambitions.

The pueblos of Huejúcar and Santa María and their small satellite communities (*Rancherias*) remained a notable exception to these circumstances. Huejúcar, in particular, presented a significant obstacle to the Colotecos' ambitions. In light of the recent political developments, the principales of Huejúcar had petitioned the auditor general in Mexico City to remove their pueblo from the jurisdiction of Colotlán and place it under the authority of the more Spanish-oriented villa of Jerez.[55] To support their request, they cited their pueblo's prior service to the Crown in the subjugation of Nayarit and included a statement from a Spanish vecino [falsely] testifying to the fact that Huejúcar and Colotlán were of more or less the same size and "of equal merit."[56] In addition to this clear declaration of autonomy from the Colotecos' authority, they do not appear to have contributed to Juanico's fundraising efforts. Furthermore, the social strife between the verdadero Comun and the rowdy and racially diverse Pocos had intensified to the point that Juanico Córdova, Calixto Pacheco, and Antonio Ramirez wrote to the Principales and Comun of Huejúcar and asked them to permit the Pocos to move to San Luis de Colotlán. Their stated purpose was to procure "the greatest pacification, tranquility, and peacefulness" of the Frontera, "so that [the Pocos] do not offend Your Honors in any way, nor Your Honors do anything against them." The Colotecos proposed that the Pocos could cultivate their crops in the vicinity of San Luis de Colotlán, and that "Your Honors should not interfere with said Pocos nor they with Your Honors."[57] By proposing to shelter the Pocos, the Colotecos were reaffirming and enhancing their status as sources of power in the Colotlán Frontier.

As the letter's demands indicate, the leaders of Huejúcar's verdadero Comun had prohibited some or all of the Pocos from sowing their maize on the pueblo lands.[58] Now, rather than changing this stance in response to the request from the "Apoderados de la Frontera," Huejúcar's principales apparently imprisoned some of the Pocos in the pueblo jail. In response, Juanico and the Colotecos publicly proclaimed in June 1780 that the Huejucareños were "rebellious Villareños," disobedient subjects "aligned against the Capital [of San Luis de Colotlán]." This terminology reflected the Colotecos' familiarity with the language of power relations in the Spanish Americas. The Conquest model for understanding social allegiance—still active in the Colotlán region through the not-too-distant conquest of Nayarit and the recent participation of the indios flecheros in the subjugation of unruly western pueblos—is very evident in the Colotecos' proclamations, as they presented themselves as the representatives of the rightful "cabecera Conquistadora" who would now have to punish a disobedient subject pueblo. They cited the Huejucareños' "lack of loyalty" and stated that Huejúcar must be made to comply with its obligation to "respect, obey, and acknowledge to this its *Capital Cavesera* that all the pueblos are conquistados, and that [Huejúcar] will be Punished to the extent that their criminal offenses warrant." The Colotecos ominously frame this response as coming from the principales of San Luis de Colotlán "and all of the militares of the obedient pueblos."[59] Then, rounding up indios flecheros from San Luis de Colotlán, Mezquitic, Nostic, Totatiche, Asqueltán, Temastián, and Apozolco, the Colotecos marched on Huejúcar to enforce their authority in the most direct manner possible.

Taking up arms and violently assaulting a neighboring pueblo was a serious matter, and even Juanico Córdova appeared to have some doubts about the matter in the days leading up to the attack. In addition to indio flechero militiamen, the Colotecos recruited local *vecinos* (Spanish residents) from San Luis de Colotlán to participate in the assault, as well, and one of these men, shopkeeper Bernabe Rentería, later provided insight into the decision-making process. He stated: "Being one day in his [Renteria's] store with said Juan Vicencio, [Juanico] asked Renteria to declare himself with respect to the attack on Huejúcar, and that Rentería counseled that he should not do such a thing, since they had no competent judge to accompany them, nor superior order for it [the assault]; and that it would be better to wait for a communiqué from México to Colotlán . . . to sort out the matter, and that Calixto Pacheco arrived at that point, and while Córdova remained quiet Rentería renewed the conversation, in the hope that they would remain calm and peaceful; but that immediately said Calixto got up out of the seat that he was in, and full of fighting spirit and fury said to Juan de Córdova that he did not have to worry what anyone thought; that here there was no person whose opinion mattered more than [Juanico's] uncle Don Antonio Fernández de Córdova; and that Rentería was not worth anything."[60]

Rentería's account makes clear the significance of personal ties and connections in matters of social standing and political—and in this case military—authority. It is highly unlikely that Juanico Córdova would have claimed the dubious position of "Apoderado de todas las Fronteras" in the first place were it not for his uncle's social status. But Rentería's account also reveals more about the role of Calixto Pacheco in these events. While Juanico's family connections in the Spanish section of Frontera society contributed to his authority, Calixto's voice carried significant weight in the region's indigenous communities, as seen earlier in the case of the idolatries of Asqueltan. The collaboration of both of these men provided the Colotecos with an extensive range of cultural proficiency and social influence, allowing them to attain the level of power that was now culminating in the mobilization of the military force of some two-thirds of the Colotlán Frontier's indio flecheros. The Colotecos also enlisted various "renters, Spanish neighbors, and other people of mixed race" for their assault on Huejúcar, including the Pocos, who accompanied them in the battle.[61]

Many of the men who would follow the Colotecos in their attack must have known that Spanish authorities in neighboring districts, and in Guadalajara and Mexico City, would not easily stomach a rampaging army of indio militiamen so close to the silver mining districts of Bolaños and Zacatecas. Yet either their allegiance or deference to the Colotecos' authority evidently trumped any reservations that they had. For Spanish vecino Bernabe Rentería—who would, himself, march on Huejúcar with Juanico and Calixto—intimidation and fear of resisting the Colotecos's demands seem to have served as his motivation. As soon as it was possible he obtained permission to leave the invasion force and return home.[62] For Don Gregorio Manuel de Fernández, the indio Cacique of San Luis de Colotlán's barrio of Tochopa who

Juanico violently prohibited from releasing an abusive husband from jail, the motivation for participating in the invasion stemmed from understandings of honor and respect. Don Gregorio later plainly stated his reasons for joining the Colotecos in the assault: "so that they would not take me for a Coward, I resolved to accompany them."[63]

In late June 1780 Salvador Mendoza, indio flechero soldier of the pueblo of Huejúcar, was working in a *chilar* (chile field) in his pueblo lands when he saw his wife come running to find him. She told him that "all of the Tropa armada from Colotlán was there," and Mendoza ran to the village church where he took refuge with all of the other soldiers of Huejúcar.[64] As a witness from inside the church later testified, "Don Juan de Córdova came riding up on a horse [and] with great malice and hatred and with shouts told us that he was very capable of getting us out of the church." Córdova then proclaimed that "no order from his Excellency [the viceroy] was necessary (even though he did have one) but that it was enough that he [Córdova] said so, and that what he was going to do to [the Huejucareños] would stand in any tribunal." The Colotecos then laid siege to the church, and Juanico encouraged the several hundred indios fronterizos accompanying him in a loud voice, shouting, "War against all of these people who are disobedient to the Capital, and in the Name of the King Carlos III I order that this tower [of the church] be brought down." The observer goes on to point out that this proved that Córdova's "vengeance was not against us [the Huejucareños] but against the Temple of God . . . since ordering the destruction of it was certainly a Barbarity that not even Idiots would have ever done."[65]

The attackers then began shooting through the windows of the church with bows and guns, such that "the choir of the church became cloudy with the smoke," and the bells of the church rang from the sound of the arrows hitting them. The siege lasted for three days, during which time Juanico Córdova prohibited the people of the pueblo from bringing the defenders any food or water. Huejúcar's Teniente de Cura, Don José Iturriaga, fearing a massacre, advised the besieged Huejucareños to remain in the church.[66] Eventually the attackers stormed the church using ladders and entered the choir, throwing some defenders from the tower onto the ground, shooting others with arrows, and stabbing some with knives and swords. One of the defenders, Laurio Morillo, a veteran of the expeditions against the rebellious western pueblos and an outspoken *Villareño*, as mentioned, had predicted that "the King would order the execution of Córdova and his Caudillos." When the attackers entered the church, two of the Pocos reportedly stabbed Morillo five times, mortally wounding him.[67] The Colotecos then pillaged the church, sacked the "papers of the [pueblo] archive in order to avenge the Pocos,"[68] and seized somewhere between two hundred and four hundred indios flecheros and principales of Huejúcar and brought them back to San Luis de Colotlán where they put them in irons.[69]

Juanico and the Señores Colotecos most likely attacked Huejúcar to avenge the Pocos and discipline a noncompliant subject pueblo; otherwise, they risked a significant loss of the authority and status that they had claimed. In violently assaulting a neighboring pueblo, killing and imprisoning key enemies, and sacking and pillaging the church and pueblo archive, Juanico Córdova and the Colotecos had finally overstepped their authority in a manner that would no longer be ignored by neighboring Spanish elites and the colonial government. Immediately after the attack Padre Iturriaga, Huejúcar's Teniente de Cura, wrote to the ecclesiastical authorities in Guadalajara requesting that order be restored to the Frontera, that the perpetrators of this "sacrilege" be punished, and that the pueblo church be rebuilt.[70] Included in this outcry was a statement from Laurio Morillo's widow, María Geronima, who charged that "Córdova and his Company" had ordered her husband's killing at the hands of the *inquilinos* (tenants) Manuel and Fermin Reyes Tranquilino. María also alleged that the attack arose out of a desire to avenge the Pocos and at "their urging."[71] She directly refutes Juanico's claims to represent the rightful authority of the king and viceroy, stating that the invaders entered and attacked Huejúcar "without showing us Commissions [or demonstrating] that they had been authorized as competent judges; since their authority was only in their mouths."[72]

Reordering the Frontera

Responding to the outrage of María Geronima and Padre Iturriaga, on August 9, 1780, the bishop of Guadalajara, El Reverendisimo Señor Maestro Don Fray Antonio Canal, ordered Bachiller Don Antonio Canal, vicar and Juez Eclesiastico of the pueblo of Colotlán, to go to Huejúcar to "reconcile" (or purify) the church from the "homicidal sacrilege" that Juanico and the Colotecos had committed there. They requested that Padre Canal put together an indictment against the "aggressors" and send it along with Juanico Córdova to Guadalajara to face an ecclesiastical tribunal. Padre Canal responded on October 5 that he had gone to Huejúcar and "reconciled the church . . . in conformity to the Ritual Romano," but added that "the apprehension of the perpetrator of the homicidal sacrilege committed in the church could not be accomplished without requesting the assistance of the Secular Arm." Canal informed the ecclesiastical authorities that, to that end, he was suspending the execution of their order "until His Execellency the Viceroy of New Spain names a person to exercise Royal Jurisdiction in these Fronteras."[73]

Either in response to subsequent pressures from the church, or in pursuit of their own interests, viceregal authorities and nearby Spanish elites soon moved to reorder the unruly Colotlán Frontier in a manner more to their liking. By early January 1781, Bolaños mining magnate Antonio de Vivanco had arrived on the scene with his Junta de Guerra and the non-indio militias of three surrounding districts of Bolaños, Aguascalientes, and Jerez. The viceroy had commissioned Vivanco as "Colonel of the Battalion of Urban Militia, Infantry, and Royal Dragoons of the Royal Mines of Bolaños, and of the light companies of the villa of Jerez and of Aguascalientes with their respective jurisdictions; sole and absolute Chief of the Indios Flecheros from all of the pueblos of the Demarcation of said Frontera [of Colotlán]."[74] By mid-January Juanico Córdova and a number of his close friends and associates had been arrested, and Vivanco had set about the task of collecting evidence to condemn the Colotecos and restoring Spanish authority in the region. Unfortunately, no documentation exists as to the circumstances of the Colotecos' capture, or whether they or their indio flechero allies put up any resistance. What is clear is that neighboring Spanish vecinos wasted little time in supplying the Junta with damning testimony of the Colotecos' "scandalous," "illicit," "impious," and "rebellious" activities.[75]

The statements and testimony collected by Vivanco's Junta de Guerra uncover even more interesting aspects of the nature of social relations in this period, in terms of both the perceptions of neighboring Spanish vecinos and officials and of the opportunities that had been briefly presented to the indios and castas of Colotlán during the Colotecos' regime. Antonio de Jauregui, the Alcalde of Xerez, who had initially tried to circumvent Juanico's claim to power by appointing the ineffectual José Manuel de Aguallo as Teniente General de la Frontera, had already submitted his own report to the viceroy before Vivanco's Junta arrived in San Luis de Colotlán, decrying the "seditious and notably scandalous commotions" caused by the Colotecos. Jauregui reiterated his testimony to Vivanco, claiming that despite Jauregui's efforts to inform Juanico that he was overstepping his authority, Córdova "insisted on resisting, [and] inflaming the indios." He wrote that some "nine hundred indios" had participated in the attack on Huejúcar, and cautioned that the Spanish residents of Xerez, Tlaltenango, and the surrounding area "fear a general uprising from which fatal results could originate." To confirm this sentiment, he attached letters from other Spanish residents.[76] Summing up, Jauregui cited the interpueblo divisions of the region and stated that the Frontera de Colotlán had "never been more turbulent than at present, [with] four or five pueblos that follow the party of those of Colotlán, commanded by Juan Vicencio de Córdova and Calixto Pacheco. The rest of the pueblos have no other authority than the powerful arm of V.C., by whom they are liberated from the oppression and repartimientos [of] those of Colotlán."[77]

The ethnic nuances and complexities of Juanico's mestizo status and the Tlaxcalan conqueror-settler identity of the indios fronterizos are lost in Jauregui's report, as is the at least tacit incorporation of some Spanish residents and laborers into the Colotecos' faction. In claiming that Córdova and Pacheco's collection of pueblo resources for the lawsuit against Villar constituted *repartimientos*, Jauregui essentially charged them with having usurped a status to which they were not entitled. Throughout the account he described both Juanico and Calixto Pacheco as "indios" and their supporters as unruly "indios bárbaros" who must be pacified by "the means of Arms and Troops."[78] In fact, Jauregui's testimony represented a level of ethnic apprehension among neighboring Spanish onlookers that nearly approached that of whites in slaveholding communities in the broader circum-Caribbean or Spanish inhabitants of the Andean region during this period, although news of the Great Rebellion of Tupac Amaru II would not have reached them at this point.[79]

The testimony of other Spanish residents and officials expressed a similar sense of ethnic conflict, although most lacked Jauregui's sense of pending calamity. Miguel de Ortega, a thirty-year-old Spaniard who had a ranch at Patagua, near the pueblo of Temastian, recounted a conflict with Juanico Córdova and indios flecheros from the pueblo that further demonstrates the nature of the Colotecos' relationship with the indios fronterizos. Following his rise to power in 1780, Juanico had ordered Ortega to come to the pueblo of Temastián, but Ortega, considering himself subject only to the alcalde mayor of Jerez (Jauregui), did not answer the summons. One day Córdova and "various indios" from Temastián came to Ortega's house while he was away, and as he tells it, they "approached [the house], and my wife and family, and made her give them twenty pesos in cash, taking with them two mules, a Cow that had just given birth, and an ox." According to Ortega's wife, Juanico said that they took this property "as a punishment for not having obeyed his command."[80]

What happened next reveals an underlying and fundamentally more ominous type of dispute that would continue to surface in the next three decades after the imprisonment of the Colotecos. A few days later an unspecified number of indios flecheros from Temastián came by Ortega's ranch, "to oblige him to pay rent for the land in which he had settled." Ortega portrays this demand as unjustified, arguing that it was issued "despite his having long ago satisfied his obligation [for the land] to the owners of the Hacienda of Juanacatique Ordoñes, who had always *also* been recognized as the owners of said land." Faced with armed indio militiamen, Ortega was forced to concede to the pueblo's demands, but he put the blame on Córdova, from whom he feared "some criminal act, as [Córdova] was accustomed to do, validating himself with a multitude of authorities that he always claimed resided in his person, having been conceded to him by the viceroy."[81] The competing claims to ownership of the land reveal lines of social tension, or social "fault lines," that are discussed more extensively in the next chapter. For now, suffice it to state that Juanico Córdova's successful manifestation of authority stemmed in part from his ability to tap into deep-seated concerns of the region's indigenous communities and, perhaps more important—as in the case of Ortega's rent—provide a mechanism for them to act on these matters. The Junta de Guerra took it upon themselves to remove this mechanism, restoring property to individuals like Ortega and attempting to bury these underlying conflicts under the guise of redressing the offenses of the Colotecos.

After arresting Juanico Córdova, Calixto Pacheco, and two of their closest associates among the principales from their allied pueblos, Antonio Vivanco and his Junta de Guerra set about officially reestablishing order on the Colotlán Frontier. With large holdings in the silver mines of Bolaños, Vivanco had a vested interest in diffusing a potentially explosive social situation in Colotlán, and the Colotecos' partisan pueblos basically surrounded the mining district and provided a buffer from less assimilated indigenous communities to the west and northwest.[82] Despite being backed by militia forces from Bolaños, Aguascalientes, and Jerez, Vivanco chose a somewhat more accommodating method to defuse the tensions that had arisen during the Colotecos' governance of Colotlán. Maintaining an appearance of objectivity, he did not immediately free the prisoners from Huejúcar who had been jailed in San Luis de Colotlán since the attack the previous summer, but waited until the after the collection of testimony from all of the involved parties.[83] The Junta published an edict directed at the indios flecheros, promising recompense for the "extortions" collected by Juanico for the Villar litigation and announcing a return to pre-Coloteco social relations. They confiscated the Colotecos' property to finance this policy, noting that the wives and children of Juanico, Calixto Pacheco, and the others would be given charitable relief from Vivanco's personal coffers. In this manner, Vivanco and the Junta sought to establish their own authority in the eyes of the fronterizos, by restoring communal harmony and personally ensuring the welfare of dependent groups. The Junta members were careful to ensure cooperation by coupling the redistribution of the Colotecos' property with ongoing interrogations that threatened further arrests of any additional troublemakers.[84] Most of the Colotecos' former allies chose to cooperate with Vivanco and the Junta, readily agreeing that Juanico Córdova and Calixto Pacheco, in particular, had been the instigators of the recent events. Their testimony, coupled with the statements of the Spanish vecinos and the beleaguered Huejucareños, provided the Junta with an unambiguous condemnation of the Colotecos. Upon completion of the report, Vivanco added his own summary of the events, along with a strong condemnation of the actions of the Señores Colotecos, and forwarded it to Mexico City along with the prisoners and a strong guard.[85]

The Crimes of the Colotecos According to Antonio de Vivanco

"I must tell Your Excellency

. . . Of the disorders and illegal acts that there have been, in some places of the Frontier belonging to my military command: Of the little or no subordination that has been given, to many Ministers, priests, and Doctrineros, who have been charged with the education and teaching [of the *indios fronterizos*]: Of the little obedience that they have had to some of the superior resolutions of His Excellency the Viceroy, opposing the execution of these resolutions with false pretenses [. . .]: Of not permitting the Lieutenants and commissaries of the Royal Tribunal of the Acordada to carry out their work in the pursuit of Thieves: Of allowing all sorts of People of ill repute to live in the pueblos, sheltering them from the places they come from: Of not punishing robberies and continuous insults in the Frontera as they should: Of requiring undue contributions from the *indio flechero* soldiers in order to foment and cover up their iniquities: Of the persecution that many *indio* soldiers have received for their loyalty to the government, and for resisting said contributions: Of the poor natives, who are exiled from the Frontera, and from their homes and Lands so as not to suffer the insatiable wrath with which the principal Cabecillas—disturbers of the peace and public tranquility—persecute them: Of the scandalous and Public Cohabitations permitted by said Cabecillas: of the effusive and continuous intoxications: Of the prohibited Games, encouraged to the point of people losing their Clothing . . .

Of those from Colotlán having the gall to eject Don José Manuel de Aguallo, Lieutenant General of the Frontera from the pueblo, after he was provisionally commissioned by the Alcalde mayor of the villa of Xerez . . . and threatening his life so that he had to move to the pueblo of Santa María two leagues away. . . . Of having destroyed and consumed a large part of the goods of the Cofradías.

> . . . Of there not being a single rancher, Spaniard, or other class of Person located in the district of the Frontera who they have not persecuted and bothered, with [requests for] contributions and threats of throwing them out [of the Frontera] unless they consent to their demands: Of their not permitting the passage of travelers to the Royal Mines of Bolaños or other parts, without first mistreating them, and denying them lodging and assistance, even though more [travelers] are passing by there than usual . . .
>
> And lastly, keep in mind, as I do, the Mark of Rebels with which the *colotecos* are viewed and even treated by their neighbors, as they are drawing attention to their actions against the whole society and Public tranquility, and thus they are recalling the memory of the insurrections that they committed in the past century and beginning of the present one, against two Captain Protectors, whose lives they took for wanting to reduce them [to encomiendas], with the shameful practice of annually placing a cross in the place where they Assaulted the latter as an Example, with the entire pueblo gathered in front of the Casas Reales, in sight of the Captain Protectors that have succeeded them, until a few years ago when one of the Parish Priests prohibited it: And also remembering that they marched to invade the Royal mines of Bolaños not too long ago, arriving in sight of them with banners and War chests, trying to take with them a number of Mine and Hacienda workers, Natives of the Frontera, who were working in them, a feat that they accomplished under the threats that it merited the Force of War, and the Royal [mines] has not since been able to counter this. I, desirous of giving the best and purest service to the King our Lord, for whose purposes I am ready with my life, and all my fortune, to secure for Your Majesty by whatever means possible the peace and quiet of these lands, which up until now have been threatened with ruin because of the little subordination in which the Frontier Indians have lived, . . . have arrested the principal ringleaders and initiators of unrest, the list of whom I have in my power, and will attach to this dossier and will dispatch them under arrest with the necessary guard to the Capital of México, and at the disposition of Your Excellency, the costs of which I am willing to suffer out of my own fortune in courteous service to the King . . .[86]

In their summary of the turbulent events of the past couple of years, the Junta made a point to charge Juanico's uncle, Don Antonio Fernández de Córdova, with complicity in Señores Colotecos' offenses. As a Spaniard of high social standing who had helped remove Governor Villar, Don Antonio presented a threat to the Junta's efforts to reorder the Frontera de Colotlán. The Junta de Guerra was well aware of the weight his opinion carried with the indios flecheros, and it took pains to state, or perhaps even overstate, this to the viceroy: "All of the indio flechero soldiers [have great respect for him], and do not do anything, nor obey in any manner whatsoever, without his advice and consent, and [there are currently] more than two thousand indios quartered in the Plaza of this pueblo."[87] Consequently, it chose to eliminate any possibility of Don Antonio serving as a strong alternate authority to the function of the Junta, by placing him on the top of the list of cabecillas to be arrested and sent to México. They then arranged to pardon Don Antonio and allow him to keep his property in return for his commitment to "live from now on calmly and peaceably, without interfering in the Government of the Frontera using any title whatsoever, nor making even the smallest overture to the indio soldiers [of the Frontera] that might serve to incite restlessness, discord, or disturbances." To ensure the public nature of Don Antonio's submission to the will of the Junta, on January 15, 1781, he was brought before the assembled Junta de Guerra and principales of the Tlaxcala barrio of San Luis de Colotlán, who had been among the most fervent supporters of the Colotecos, and directed to place his hand upon the sword of one of the members of the Junta and swear to the aforementioned terms, adding that "as a Loyal vassal of the King our lord, he was disposed to comply, and obey [it] in all parts."[88]

With royal authority, in the form of the Spanish mining and ranching elites of the neighboring districts, having been reestablished, the nearly two-year period of relative fronterizo autonomy came to a close. It would be another thirty years before the children and grandchildren of the Colotecos would attempt to reorder the Frontera. Juanico Córdova, Calixto Pacheco, Juan Rivera, and Juan Lozano were sentenced to four years' imprisonment and permanent exile from the Colotlán Frontier. The viceroy sent Juanico to work on public projects in Puerto Rico and the others to San Juan de Ulua.[89] All were freed as a result of a general pardon three years later upon the birth of Prince Ferdinand. They were allowed to move to Guadalajara but were still forbidden to return to Colotlán or even to communicate directly or indirectly with the indios of the Frontera. They did not comply and soon were traveling back and forth to the region and hiding out in the interior pueblos. In 1785 Lieutenant Colonel Don José Sarachaga attempted to arrest Juanico Córdova for breaking the terms of his exile and pardon. When Sarachaga claimed that he was operating on Vivanco's authority, Juanico replied that he would "in no way recognize the authority of that man as his superior or judge."

The Señores Colotecos and Fronterizo Authority

At this point it is worthwhile to reflect on Juanico Córdova's letter from the Aguascalientes jail to his uncle Don Antonio. This was his first opportunity to communicate since his arrest, and by this point he seems to have accepted his fate with a grudging fatalism. The most striking aspect of his letter was the way in which he portrayed himself as well as his friends and fellow prisoners as fronterizo martyrs who "defended" the Frontera, and who were now suffering for the "sacrifice" they made for the "ungrateful" pueblos and "slumbering Señores de Repúblicas." The Señores Colotecos' authority—having ever been "only in their mouths," as the widow Morillo put it—had now "flown away" with the arrival of the Junta de Guerra. In a very real sense what was an accusation for Señora Morillo serves as a powerfully accurate description of what took place in Colotlán during this period. The political power and authority of the Colotecos had never been sanctioned by the viceroy, and although they made a tenuous claim to having been appointed "Apoderados of the Frontera," such a title carried no official weight beyond their abilities to convince their fellow fronterizos of its significance. Yet, for a significant amount of time, they managed to do just that.

While it lasted, the Colotecos' control over the Frontera pueblos stemmed from their ability to serve as an outlet for fronterizo concerns, and as an ostensible mechanism for taking action against the officials, vecinos, clergy, or even fellow indios who obstructed fronterizo goals. To be sustained, authority in late colonial New Spain needed both external and internal underpinning. The authority of Governor Felipe Villar had crumbled when he lost a sufficient amount of support *within* the Colotlán region despite having been granted official status by the external power source of the viceroy. The Colotecos also lost their authority as a result of their failure to amass sufficient support within Frontera society. One might speculate that outside forces would have eventually acted without instigation, but the Colotecos' inability to garner the cooperation of the pueblos of Huejúcar, Santa María, and their satellite communities led to the incident that marked the beginning of the end for Juanico Córdova and his friends.[90]

In addition to requiring support from local constituencies and a claim to some perceived external authority, assertions of political power in the Colotlán region often took on ethnic undertones. The Señores Colotecos appropriated a Conquistador identity, sheltered less assimilated indigenous groups, and cultivated growing casta constituencies like the Pocos. Both the Colotecos and the loyal pueblos like Huejúcar drew upon the mystique and imagery of the Tlaxcalan colonists' heritage. For Jerez Alcalde Mayor Antonio de Jauregui and like-minded vecinos, this cultural power struggle entailed the expression of Spanish fears of race war and attempts to portray the indios fronterizos as dangerous bárbaros needing containment. Whereas Jauregui could paint Juanico Córdova as an "indio" stirring up a potential indigenous uprising, within the region itself Juanico and his indio ladino companion Calixto Pacheco utilized Juanico's familial connections with local Spanish elites to gain more support for their objectives. In the end, both perceived status—who you were—and perceived purposes—whose interests you served—determined levels of support within the region.

Alternately "defending the rights and privileges" of the indios flecheros, exploiting his authority to raise funds, supporting indigenous land rights over those of Spanish vecinos, and cowing community members with the threat of violence, Juanico was a decidedly flawed champion of fronterizo interests. In fact, he could be viewed as an early example of the *caudillismo* and *caciquismo* that would become so prominent throughout Latin America in the nineteenth century. Finally, and perhaps most important, these events provide a means for accessing the histories of numerous individuals and groups who have not yet found a place in the historiography of late colonial New Spain. Castas like the Pocos present an obvious example, exercising considerable mobility after having left other regions to come join fronterizo communities, enjoying both their fueros and the cultural flexibility of Frontera society.[91]

The case of the Señores Colotecos demonstrates an important stage in the development of fronterizo identity in the Colotlán region. Identity must always be defined in relation to others, and the events of this narrative indicate a general alignment along lines of fronterizo versus outsider. These insider-outsider lines were not based strictly on race, but on sociocultural identification.[92] A number of nonindigenous newcomers were accepted and integrated into segments of Frontera society: free blacks, mulatos, sympathetic creole military leaders, some poorer Spanish laborers or tenants, and some priests. Others—newly arrived Spanish vecinos, antagonistic landowners, priests, and officials who disrupted the accepted fronterizo social order—created resentment and resistance. Either group could be associated with, or be seen to represent, Spanish colonial authority within the Frontera de Colotlán; in fact, both groups usually sought—and sometimes fought—to do so. Those aligned with the fronterizos usually achieved only fleeting success, as was the case with Juanico's Colotecos. By 1810 the fronterizos would convert their resentment of the second group (the outsiders) into participation in the war for independence.

3

The Countess and the "Insolent Indians"

José Manuel Lopez y José Calzada, the same individuals who were expelled in the year of 1795 are bringing in more livestock every day, with such insolence and arrogance that they have commanded the vaqueros of the Lady Countess to remove the livestock that are pasturing in that place, because [they say] the pastures are theirs, and the hacienda has robbed them.

—José Rafael de Molina, agent of the Countess of San Mateo de Valparaiso, requesting that possession of the Ameca Valley be restored to her

Agrarian conditions have served as one of the key explanations for rebellion in studies of late colonial Spanish America. The relationship between an hacienda owned by the Countess of San Mateo de Valparaiso and the "insolent" indios of San Andrés del Teúl provides an opportunity to examine a late colonial land conflict in the Colotlán region, one that goes beyond broad correlations between systemic agrarian pressures and social unrest. On the surface this was a land conflict between an indigenous pueblo and a wealthy hacienda. Underneath, it is clear that personal relationships played a key role in the conflict, in which social divisions often broke vertically along lines of loyalty rather than horizontally along lines of social class. Spanish officials played a key role in sustaining or challenging these relationships, but both the hacienda and the pueblo of San Andrés del Teúl circumvented the legal process at times. Their conflict over land use confirms the common argument that changes in agrarian production contributed to late colonial social conflict. More importantly, it shows *how* these economic stresses eventually led to insurrection: through the forming (and breaking) of personal relationships, loyalties, and social bonds on the local and regional level.

Land and Loyalty on a Late Colonial Frontier

During the colonial period the pueblo of San Andrés del Teúl was situated at the northern tip of the Frontera de Colotlán (see figure 2.1).[1] Like many of the other indigenous pueblos in the Colotlán region, the Teulenses claimed exemption from taxes and tribute by right of their intermarriage with the descendants of the Tlaxcalan colonists and their own service in the frontier militias. At times, residents or officials from neighboring districts objected to these privileges.[2] Conflict over the exemptions did not arise as a late colonial consequence of the Bourbon reforms. As other scholars have documented, indigenous communities in many parts of New Spain rapidly learned to navigate the protocol of the Spanish legal system to petition for redress, beginning almost immediately after the Conquest.[3] The indios from San Andrés, for instance, complained to the viceregal government about challenges to their exemptions, probably through the governor and captain general of Colotlán, just after the turn of the eighteenth century. In 1704, the viceroy commanded the justicias of the surrounding settlements "where the naturales from [San Andrés del] Teúl sell their seeds and fruits" not to "charge them alcabalas, storage fees, nor other undue privileges."[4]

Neither were conflicts over land in this region purely a late colonial phenomenon. The Teulenses had long claimed ownership of a plot that had been assigned to the Franciscans for their spiritual welfare in 1696, and in 1720 the viceroy directed the district governor of Sombrerete to allocate the property to the "naturales fronterizos of the pueblo of San Andrés del Teúl . . . giving them possession [of it] and any other territory that is clearly theirs or that of their ancestors."[5] It seems that the Franciscan fathers were making use of the land without providing the associated spiritual instruction.[6] The Teulenses recognized that charges of other parties in the colonial social order–in this case the Franciscans—not fulfilling their obligations could effectively get the attention of viceregal authorities. Also in 1720, the viceroy appointed Don José de la Campa Cos, Sombrerete cattleman and relative of the rich mining family of Campa Cos, as Captain Protector of the pueblo of San Andrés "and the rest of that [jurisdiction]."[7] His jurisdiction would have included the pueblo of Nueva Tlaxcala, which by this point was surrounded by the Spanish, mestizo, casta, and ladino settlers of the Sombrerete district who worked in the mines or associated cattle ranches. Both Nueva Tlaxcala and San Andrés del Teúl remained subject to the governor and captain general of Colotlán, and José de la Campa Cos would have functioned as one of the governor's lieutenants.[8]

The population of the canyon region around Colotlán had grown substantially over the seventeenth century, recovering from postconquest losses as corn and livestock production escalated to meet the growing demands of the Zacatecan mining centers.[9] In the next few years the indios of San Andrés del Teúl appealed to the viceregal government for protection against the encroachment of haciendas and individuals "dispossessing" them of their lands. Specifically, the pueblo cited land in the Ameca Valley, situated over the mountains to the west.[10] The role of Captain José de la Campa Cos in these early disputes is unclear, but the estate of his uncle Don Fernando de la Campa Cos, Count of San Mateo Valparaiso, an immensely wealthy mining magnate and hacendado, would play an important role in the history of the pueblo of San Andrés.[11]

Bonds of loyalty clearly existed between the Count and the Teulenses, perhaps as a result of their participation with him in the "pacification" of the neighboring sierra of Nayarit, where unevangelized Coras persisted until forced into Jesuit settlements in 1722. Indios flecheros from San Andrés and the other pueblos of Colotlán took part in the undertaking.[12] In the succeeding years, the Count's Hacienda of San Mateo began to make use of the grazing lands in the Valley of Ameca, apparently with the consent of the pueblo of San Andrés, who "assented to this, for the great love that they professed [toward the Count], and the benefaction that they received from him."[13] Don Fernando, for his part, established a benefice in the valley for the use of the indios of San Andrés, who made only sporadic use of the lands there, "extracting mezcales . . . and fishing in its river." No record of any litigation or dispute regarding the land in the valley exists for the period of the relationship between the Count and the pueblo of San Andrés (from 1722 until his death in 1742). It seems likely that Don Fernando protected the Teulenses' use of the valley, and they apparently made no objection to his using it for grazeland.[14] After the Count's death, the benefice fell into ruin.[15]

By 1777 San Andrés del Teúl and Nueva Tlaxcala had become part of a separate parish with its own benefice based in San Andrés, served by a *cura doctinero*.[16] The fact that parish was administered by a member of the regular clergy would make them an exception in a religious environment increasingly controlled by the secular church. The Teulenses would later claim to have "managed to have him appointed" by promising to support the priest from the proceeds of their lands in the Valley of Ameca: "In our pueblo resides a cura doctrinero, who administers the Holy Sacraments to us, and when we managed to have him appointed, it was with the condition that if his *obvenciones*[17] did not reach four hundred pesos, we would have to make up the difference, the work of the Church, Sacred ornaments, and other necessities for the Holy mass being our responsibility. [We could meet these expenses] without injury to our families because we paid the costs, so useful for our spiritual welfare, from the rents of the lands that we possess, [including the lands in the Valley of Ameca] and from the shearings and croppings from the mountains in those places."[18] The pressing needs of maintaining this obligation would play a key role in the relationships between the pueblo of San Andrés, a local Spanish official, and the Count's daughter.

Showdown at Corralitos

By 1795, Don Fernando de la Campa Cos had been dead for more than fifty years, and his youngest daughter and heiress, Doña Ana María de la Campa y Cos, Countess of San Mateo de Valparaiso, was an elderly widow interested in putting her huge estate in order before passing it on to her heirs.[19] Doña Ana María's deceased husband, Miguel de Berrío y Zaldívar, Marqués del Jaral, had been one of the largest landowners in the viceroyalty.[20] Memory of San Andrés's ownership of the lands in the valley had ostensibly been lost, and the Countess counted the Valley of Ameca among the lands of the Hacienda of San Mateo, one of the Countess's principal estates and residences.[21] In early 1795, a number of young men from San Andrés entered parts of the valley, bringing in some five hundred head of cattle and planting corn. Discovering tenants there, they informed them that any rent should be paid to them rather than to the hacienda.[22]

In response, the Countess obtained an order from Don Juan Antonia de Evia, the *subdelegado* of the villa of Fresnillo—a district to the east of San Andrés where the Hacienda of San Mateo was located—for restitution of the lands and protection of her ownership of them.[23] In March 1795, before the lands could be "repossessed" by the Countess, the governor of Colotlán, Josef Asencio de Uriarte, weighed in on the issue. As commander of the indio flechero frontier militias, and ostensible protector of all of the indigenous pueblos in the "frontiers of Colotlán," Uriarte ordered Subdelegado Evia to have Don Vicente Montoya, lieutenant (*Teniente*) of the Valley of Valparaiso—the location of the Hacienda of San Mateo—take the declarations of witnesses regarding the matter.[24] The indios of Colotlán had a long history of dealings with a governor of the Colotlán Frontier, but at this point the positions, and corresponding individuals, of subdelegado and even teniente were relatively new. Under the new system, the pueblo of San Andrés fell under the jurisdiction of the teniente of nearby Nueva Tlaxcala, Don Juan Francisco Servín de la Mora.[25] At the time of this dispute over the Ameca valley, Servín de la Mora would have held his post for only a couple of years at the most, and the extent of his authority, as interpreted by the pueblo, would not have been well established. Likewise, living as he did in Nueva Tlaxcala, the teniente had not yet accumulated much understanding of and familiarity with San Andrés and its concerns.

In December 1795 Lieutenant Montoya of Valparaiso and representatives from the hacienda, led by "the servant" Don José Marta la Marripa, summoned Lieutenant Servín de la Mora and the leaders of San Andrés to one of the disputed locations in the valley, known as Corralitos.[26] According to the Teulenses, this was done "with the pretext of inspecting the lands of the Hacienda [of San Mateo]." In reality, the representatives of the hacienda had called the meeting to eject the indios from the valley. All accounts of the incident agree that upon arrival Montoya and the men from the hacienda informed the indios that the valley belonged to the Countess, expelled all the pueblo's herders and farmers from the valley, drove out all of the Teulenses' livestock, and instructed the tenants to recognize the hacienda as the landlord, rather than the pueblo.[27] According to the principales of San Andrés, the men from the hacienda also confiscated the corn planted by young men from the pueblo. The principales also claimed that their supposed protector, Lieutenant Servín de la Mora, joined with the party of the hacienda in denying the pueblo's right to the valley:[28]

> The *Teniente* did not make any effort to defend us; he was joined with those that made up the party of the Hacienda, and all of them told us that from that day forward that Valley would remain a part of the Hacienda of San Mateo. With this ease they have stripped us of these lands, after such an ancient period of ownership. But what will astonish the pious heart of Your Excellency the most is that they proceeded so inhumanely against us that certain youngsters who had planted there with good faith, [thinking] that those lands belong to the pueblo, and [the cornfields] being already full of ears, [the fields' owners were forced to leave without the corn], and the *Teniente* allowed the Hacienda to take [the corn], leaving the fields, [that had been] cultivated with sweat and the work of those pitiful individuals, abandoned, and leaving [the youngsters] and their families in the worst hunger and necessity, imposing grave penalties if they cut even one single stalk.[29]

Soon after the encounter at Corralitos, José Rafael Molina, the Countess's agent, wrote to the viceregal authorities concerning the dispute, reporting the testimony of seven witnesses—"four Spaniards, two mestizos, and a Coyote"—who claimed that the Countess had always been in "calm and peaceful possession" of the lands of the Valley of Ameca, and that there had never been any interruption in her ownership. According to Molina and the Countess's witnesses, during the previous year the indios of the pueblo of San Andrés del Teúl had "undertaken the novel act" of entering various parts of the valley claiming to be the owners. Molina noted that "this is not because of any necessity for lands because they have there in their pueblo [something like] 8 leagues, mostly unpopulated and without use." He went on to suggest that the true reason for the indios' use of the Valley of Ameca was "to hide their robberies . . . which can not be discovered except by those that have knowledge of said Valley." The witnesses then proceeded to corroborate various thefts.[30]

According to Molina, the Countess's "ancient" land right in the Valley of Ameca was just as completely justified as was the lack of necessity of the valley on the part of the pueblo of San Andrés. Molina used the charge of "robberies and scandals," along with the claim that the Teulenses "gave no justification whatsoever, and only displayed various documents that do not touch on said lands," to justify their expulsion from the valley in December. He then demanded the restitution of one year's rent for the pastures in which the indios' five hundred or more cattle had grazed, and reiterated the failure of the Teulenses to produce proof of ownership, "even though it is easy for them to obtain such information."[31]

Molina's petition was remitted to the *asesor general* in Mexico City, who passed it on to the fiscal protector, who advised the viceroy on July 6, 1796, that the Countess "be restored in her possession of the sites that she complained were taken by the indios from San Andrés del Teúl of the Frontera de San Luis Colotlán," and that "said Naturales should pay for the pastures that their livestock ate in said places." He added, however, that the response of the pueblo should be heard with regard to the Countess's petition, and suggested that they be informed of such by means of a dispatch to the governor of Colotlán. On July 15, 1796, Viceroy Branciforte concurred, giving the Teulenses one month from notification of the proceedings to respond.[32]

Petition of the Teulenses

In November 1796, Juan Guillermo, Bernabé Antonio, Juan Marcos Perez, the principal officials—alcalde, *alférez*, and alguacil mayor, respectively—from San Andrés appeared before Governor Uriarte of Colotlán to discuss the matter, "in the name of our Republic, town council, and común." Their citing of these institutions indicated the pueblo principales' familiarity with Spanish terminology for signifying rationality and the capacity for good self-government, important factors to establish to bolster the pueblo's position in the eyes of the higher political authorities. The principales then proceeded to explain the origin of the conflict from the pueblo's point of view. According to the pueblo's elders, the lands in the Valley of Ameca that the villagers used for pasture and planting from time to time had always belonged to San Andrés. It was true, the elders said, that the Hacienda of San Mateo, owned by the Countess of San Mateo Valparaiso, had run cattle in the valley since the days of the Countess's father, Don Fernando de la Campa y Cos, but this was always with the pueblo's permission. The principales stated that "this Valley borders the Hacienda de San Mateo, and we and the owners of [the hacienda] have enjoyed the Valley in good harmony and agreement, and according to what our elders tell us, the owners of San Mateo have had this use [of the valley] by consent of the pueblo."[33]

In their complaints to Governor Uriarte—and in their subsequent petition to the viceroy—the principales of San Andrés focused their attention on the offenses of Lieutenant Juan Francisco Servín de la Mora. The intensity of their anger at the lieutenant stemmed from his apparent rupture of the patron-client bond that operated on the pueblo level to defend common interests. To highlight his transgressions, they charged him with mismanagement of the *caja de comunidad* (community treasury). They referred back to their view of the king's ostensible purpose for establishing the *cajas de comunidad*, "so that the rents from the lands would be locked up in them, maintaining a corresponding *libro de asientos* (record book) so that the most scrupulous and valid account of entries would be kept, [. . . so that] we would have aid in calamitous times of pain or barrenness." According to the principales of the pueblo, Servín de la Mora had not kept adequate account of the caja de communidad, "[never having kept the libro de asientos to this day, nor having constructed the caja de comunidad, receiving money without account or rationale."[34]

As a second charge, the Teulenses claimed that soon after his appointment Servín de la Mora had installed his own relatives and friends "under the pretext of being renters" for a small stipend, and that he denied the indios access to their own "lands and mountains." He also prohibited them from cutting wood, while at the same time "selling wood as he pleased."[35] The Teulenses pointed out to Uriarte that Servín de la Mora had failed to protect and represent them against the agents of the Hacienda of San Mateo.[36] In their statement, which was to be forwarded to Mexico City along with Uriarte's report, the Teulenses lamented their wretched situation, and listed a number of requests.[37]

THE PUEBLO'S DEMANDS

- The appointment of an impartial judge to examine the *Caja de Comunidad* and *libro de asientos* for signs of impropriety.
- The removal of Juan Francisco Servín de la Mora from his position as *Teniente* of Nueva Tlaxcala.
- "The freedom to name as counsel the Person who suits us, and seems appropriate to us."
- "The freedom to extract wood from our mountains, as much for the Church as for the relief of our pressing needs."
- "That the Community funds be rationed out to those of us who work in the service of the Church or in the construction of casas Reales, and that [funds] for ornaments be taken from them [the community funds]."
- "That we be protected in the possession that we have had of the Valley of Ameca, until the matter of ownership be settled by legal ends."
- "That the corn that the Hacienda harvested from the cornfields [*milpas*] of those poor youngsters who planted in that Valley, with the good faith that they could do so, be paid to them."

- "Finally, humbly prostrate at the Feet of Your Excellency we implore you to order that we nor any other child of our pueblo not be bothered or disturbed because of this business."
- "That lastly the said Don Juan Francisco Servín de la Mora be found responsible for all of the legal and personal costs of this business, and for the setbacks and damages that we have incurred as a result."

As a postscript to their petition, the Teulenses asked the viceroy "that the implementation of these provisions not be delegated to any one of the *vecinos* [non-Indian residents] of Nueva Tlaxcala who are of the faction or persuasion of the Lieutenant against who we complain." They singled out Don Felipe del Villar Gutierrez, resident of the nearby pueblo of Nochistlán, to the southeast of Colotlán. According to the Teulenses, Don Felipe, who had formerly served as governor and captain general of the Frontiers of Colotlán, was an "impartial disinterested subject of integrity."[38] This postscript may have been added after the death of Governor Uriarte, who died sometime after January 1797, since they noted that "as the new Governor has not arrived yet, no one else would be more appropriate for this commission." Uriarte's death did not bode well for the pueblo of San Andrés del Teúl. While Uriarte had clearly served as a valuable patron of the pueblo, Pedro Trelles Villa de Moros, the new interim governor, had previously served as corregidor of the royal mines at Bolaños, a position that had traditionally come into conflict with the interests of the indios of Colotlán. Most recently, he held the post of oidor in the audiencia of Guadalajara. He did not arrive in Colotlán until sometime after August 1797.[39]

Lament of the Pueblo of San Andrés del Teúl

> From all that is explained here, the characteristic insight of Your Excellency will recognize that we are the oppressed ones. . . . Our Church, half of which is covered in hay, threatens ruin: it finds itself nearly without ornaments. They impede us from exercising the rights to fish, gather mescales, and cut wood. They violently strip away our lands, without any semblance of justice regarding the lands over which we have had immemorial possession, and the Teniente who should defend us is our greatest tormentor, and lastly, having suffered the greatest outrages, costing us uncountable labor, reduced with the greatest scarcity to a small portion of bread, left with only the sustenance of ourselves and our tears: we see with the greatest pain that, in breach of the pious dispositions of our beloved sovereign; the Teniente Don Juan Francisco Servin de la Mora, his relatives, and allies enjoy our lands and mountains, squander their harvests and produce, and take from

> us all hope that their provisions will be of use to us in the calamitous times of sickness or barrenness, without validating our situation to the Governor, because the Teniente Servin de la Mora has more than enough ability to persuade him that our complaints and clamors are the effects of a malicious suspicion. We have received many other offences from this man, in the handling and administration of justice; but as our objective is only that he not return to govern us. . . . We remit to silence that which we have found in him, stating only that he be separated from us.[40]

Governor Uriarte's Report

Before his death in early 1797, Governor Uriarte forwarded the pueblo's petition and his own statement to the viceroy. In his report, Uriarte unmistakably sided with the Teulenses, with a few caveats. After a brief review of the libro de asientos and caja de comunidad, he found no fault with the bookkeeping of Lieutenant Juan Francisco Servín de la Mora, who had been appointed by Uriarte's predecessor. Records of all of the rents on the pueblo's lands, "with individual specificity of the People that pay them," were included since the cajas de comunidad had been established in the Colotlán region in 1793. The entries for withdrawals and returns of the community funds had been approved each year by the priest, scribe, and principales of San Andrés. Uriarte made note of the fact that, notwithstanding their recognition of their own signatures approving the accounts, the indios of San Andrés "remained convinced of the falsity of his [Servín de la Mora's] accounts." Additionally, Uriarte found no substantial proof of the lieutenant's alleged abuses—exploiting the pueblo's timber and natural resources while denying access to the Teulenses, themselves—with regard to the use of the pueblo's "lands and mountains."[41]

He did concur, however, with the indios' claims regarding the Hacienda of San Mateo's seizure of the Valley of Ameca. Having reviewed the documents produced by the principales of San Andrés, and reports of the actions of Vicente Montoya, the Justicia of Valparaiso, Uriarte deemed the pueblo's claim of ownership valid. Interestingly, he also commented that it was apparent that Montoya's "passion had assisted him in the fulfillment" of the indios' expulsion from the valley. Concerning the testimony of the Countess's seven witnesses who cited the Hacienda's "ancient" possession of the valley, Uriarte responded that "the word of not a single [one of them] is trustworthy for these impartial depositions, since all of them are servants of the Hacienda itself, who without a doubt have failed to tell the truth." Alternatively, Uriarte noted that the Teulenses' ownership "is consistent, and can be substantiated."[42]

Whereas Governor Uriarte had found no fault with Servín de la Mora's accounts, he strongly disapproved of the lieutenant's failure to support the indios in their confrontation with the party of the hacienda at Corralitos. Uriate asserted that, as the Teulenses' official protector, Servín de la Mora should have protested the treatment they received at the hands of the Countess's servants. Uriarte did not accept the lieutenant's excuse that he had been afraid of "the passion" with which Lieutenant Montoya and the Countess's servant Don José Marta la Marripa "had been going around," and the governor informed the viceroy that he had "seriously reproved" Servín de la Mora. "To avoid complaints, procuring peace and calmness," Governor Uriarte ordered the lieutenant to "cease in the commission of Justice that he [had] obtained." In his final remarks, Uriarte advised that, as the *Teulenses* had requested, an impartial person pass judgment on the land issue.[43]

Conclusion of Governor Uriarte's Report

> With regard to the taking of land that the Hacienda of San Mateo has done to them in the Valley of Ameca, which can be termed violent, there is no doubt according to my information that they [the indios of Teúl] mourn with just cause. . . . The lament of the Indios of San Andres is continual, no grounds appear in this gobierno whatsoever for the excesses [supposedly committed by them] in order to cover their wrongdoing, attributed to them by the partial witnesses of the Hacienda, who want the Valley of Ameca. [The Hacienda's] justifications according to their reports seem clear, but in order to prevent protests and to achieve the serenity of these [indios], I propose, if it has superior approbation, that the marking and naming of the ownership of the lands of said Hacienda de San Mateo and said pueblo proceed through impartial people, to permanently make it clear with legitimate titles: This is what I can inform Your Excellency of, in virtue of the superior decree: Colotlán, January 31 of 1797.
>
> Josef Asensio de Uriarte[44]

Return to Corralitos

Throughout the next few months, the dispute remained mired in red tape, as the *Fiscales* of the viceregal court recorded the matter and requested further reports from the Countess. In June 1797, Viceroy Branciforte approved his advisers' recommendations and disregarded Governor Uriarte's conclusions. The viceroy ordered that, in lieu of there being no substantial evidence for the complaints against Lieutenant Servín de la Mora, the lieutenant be restored to his position with full payment of his salary that had been in arrears, "for the damages and expenses that he has incurred, from the undue and unjustified separation from his office, stemming from those false complaints of the Indios." Following the advice of the *Fiscal de lo Civil* the viceroy instructed the new interim governor of Colotlán to "also make clear to [Lieutenant Servín de la Mora] that he is equally restored in his honor and reputation, which could have been damaged with the cessation of his position by mandate of the Governor [of Colotlán]." The interim governor was also to condemn the indios "for their rashness and falsehood," to notify them that "if in the future they return to behaving with such dishonesty, they will be punished as forcefully as the case merits," and to "warn them to treat the said Lieutenant with the respect that they are obliged to give."[45]

By fall 1797, Pedro Trelles Villa de Moros, the interim governor of the Frontiers of Colotlán, had arrived to take up his post and had faithfully carried out each portion of the viceroy's instructions, including the restoration of Lieutenant Servín de la Mora to his position. Although no official decision regarding the ownership of the Ameca Valley had been recorded, the valley had been under the ostensible control of the Countess's Hacienda of San Mateo since the expulsion of the Teulense herders and farmers in December 1795. Nevertheless, in September or October 1797, José Rafael de Molina, the Countess' agent, wrote to the viceroy yet again. Apparently José Manuel López and José Calzada, two of the "youngsters" from San Andrés who had been driven out of the Ameca Valley in 1795, had returned to Corralitos, one of the disputed locations in the valley, bringing with them some eight hundred to a thousand cattle and four hundred goats and sheep. They compelled the Countess's vaqueros to remove the Hacienda's cattle from the area, declaring that the Countess had robbed them of their rightful lands. According to Molina, this occurred just as the Señora Countess "believed that with the measures undertaken and the restitutions that were made to her the indios of San Andrés were pacified and contained, reducing their boundaries and limits."[46] As Molina put it, "Following the ancient custom of the Indios, they have let pass more than two years and have begun to reenter the very same summer pastures from which they were expelled, bringing in more livestock every day." Molina also charged the Teulenses with kidnapping servants of the Hacienda who "discovered their robberies."[47]

MOLINA'S ACCUSATIONS

> "The same individuals who were expelled in the year of 1795, are bringing in more livestock every day, with such insolence and arrogance that they have commanded the vaqueros of the Lady Countess to remove the livestock that are pasturing in that place, because [they say that] the pastures are theirs, and the hacienda has robbed them. Their

objective isn't only the use of the lands, but to have a lair in which to hide their mayhem and wickedness, they have returned to these places with the greatest insolence and disrespect."[48]

"They go unpunished for this and similar excesses because their Protector does nothing but what they want because of the insolence that they display and the fear that he has of them, which is leading to more pride and determination every day as a result of the impunity they experience, they go on being more insolent and arrogant each day, and it will reach the extreme of a gang of bandits being formed that will rob and assault all of the Haciendas in the vicinity, because nothing gives men more determination and confidence in their crimes than to see themselves go unpunished. The Lady [Countess] is not only interested in the restitution of the land that has been plundered yet again, but also in . . . getting some enemies who constantly [give her problems] off of her back."[49]

Evidently the relationship between the Teulenses and Lieutenant Servín de la Mora had changed since his reinstatement. Molina reported that now the lieutenant "does nothing but what [the Teulenses] want because of the insolence that they display and the fear that he has of them." Molina went on to request that the indios—principally José Lopez and José Calzada—and their livestock be expelled immediately from the Valley of Ameca and removed to their pueblo. Additionally, Molina declared that the Countess would no longer simply be satisfied with the restoration of her possession of the valley. She now asked that a separate indictment be drawn up "to investigate the robberies that the Indios of Teúl commit, interrogating the common thieves."[50] In response to the Countess's petition, Viceroy Branciforte—through the fiscal protector —ordered the Justicia of Valparaiso in November 1797 to restore the disputed property to the Countess, and to begin a separate inquiry into the other "excesses" of the Teulenses.[51] The justicia was to question witnesses regarding "who the delinquents are and the location of the pasajes and places where they have gone," and to report back to the viceroy.[52]

The next record of the dispute came two years later, and, although the situation had escalated somewhat, the Countess's agent Molina was still demanding justice in relation to the "robberies, insults, and [illicit] introductions [of livestock] by the indios of Teúl," who continued to make use of the Valley of Ameca. Molina reported in August 1799 that the Teulenses had been "expelled time and time again [from the valley] in 1798 and 1799," but that they kept coming back. He now charged them with stealing livestock and hiding in the rough country in and around the valley, stating that "they are professional thieves and they do not have any other occupation with which to maintain themselves [except for] robbery and pillage." Perhaps even more audaciously, the indios of San Andrés had begun to give—or what is more likely, sell—permission for other individuals to bring livestock into the Valley, giving them documents "in which [the Teulenses] title themselves '*Jueces Superiores* and *Justicias mayores*.'" Molina viewed this practice as a "clear manifestation" of the "pride and effrontery" the indios of San Andrés had acquired as a result of going unpunished for so long.[53] However, considered in light of Juanico Córdova's similar use of titles and documents in the previous chapter, it is clear that the indios fronterizos had a tradition of employing such tools and made use of them when it served their purposes.

Lieutenant Servín de la Mora still held his position of supposed authority over the pueblo. But, according to Molina, the lieutenant's fear of the Teulenses had, if anything, increased, leaving him unable to act to restrict their activities. In a petition to Pedro Trelles Villa de Moros, still serving as the interim governor of the Colotlán Frontier, Molina stated that Servín de la Mora "does not dare to do anything, [being] afraid of the insolence and insubordination of the Indios, and that they will carry out the threats that they were going to kill him and would not obey him." He went on to state the Countess' proposal "regarding the interest of her haciendas, and that of public and State justice, that the thieves who are apprehended [...] be punished severely." According to Molina, "If the impunity continues, and they see that they are not punished as they deserve, then as soon as they are expelled they will return to entering [the Ameca Valley], since, notwithstanding the threats of the Most Excellent Señor Your Excellency's predecessor concerning obedience to the Teniente, they despise him. [The Indians of Teúl] will be ungovernable, and be made powerful, causing great havoc."[54]

Servín de la Mora also wrote to the interim governor, excusing his seeming inaction with the explanation that "no one in that immediate vicinity would lend a hand to help."[55] It does appear, though, that two of the Teulenses had been imprisoned as a result of the Countess's prior accusations, although it is not clear who apprehended them. José María Calzada, "their general," was still on the loose and had been spotted hiding out in the valley "with a considerable number of stolen livestock."[56] Molina must have known that the level of organization of the Teulenses' actions—such that observers identified key leaders as "generals"—and the effectiveness of their intimidation of the lieutenant would increase the likelihood that Villa de Moros would consider them a threat to the peace and stability of the region.

Molina subsequently pressed the new viceroy, Miguel José de Azanza, to authorize Governor Trelles Villa de Moros to take charge of the case and finally put things in order—from the Countess's point of view. "It is necessary, therefore, to pursue the case through all possible means [in order to] teach them a lesson, " Molina said, "and for that [the case] must be entrusted to an authorized and respected Judge who can restrain the insults of the indios; and there is no other than the Governor of the Frontier, himself." According to Molina, the Countess sought "the conclusion of [this case] in which it is necessary to send the principal ringleaders to prison, and to take their confessions and everything."[57] She asked that the Teulenses "confine themselves to the boundaries of what belongs to them, . . . and that they not enter into her lands, nor insult or provoke her managers and servants, nor steal her livestock." Molina also mentioned that the warrant given to one Rafael Cisneros by the Teulenses, granting Cisneros the right to run livestock in the valley, needed to be seized. On August 27, 1799, the viceroy agreed to the Countess's petition and ordered that Governor Trelles Villa de Moros take charge of the case in the manner specified by Molina.[58]

The only other documents referring to the dispute between the Countess and the pueblo of San Andrés simply show that, by 1802, two other indigenous communities in the Colotlán region, Tlalcosagua and Huejúcar, had also claimed rights to lands allegedly owned by the Countess.[59] Residents of these two villages jointly petitioned Governor Trelles Villa de Moros to join their claim to the one from San Andrés, and appealed for justice in the matter. They asserted that the Countess' Hacienda del Cuidado had "usurped, little by little," land that was theirs. The governor seems to have been at least minimally sympathetic to their plea.[60]

Late Colonial Land Disputes and Social Fault Lines

Throughout all these events, local relationships served as the most significant venues and the most direct reasons for social conflict, feeding on and subsuming disputes over land and labor, or broader economic and political issues. Population growth and the corresponding rise in the value of land obviously stimulated the dispute over the Ameca Valley. But it is unlikely that the conflict would have escalated to the degree it did had the Countess's father still been living during the 1790s. The story of the Teulenses' disputes with Lieutenant Servín de la Mora and the Countess of San Mateo Valparaiso confirms some of the received historical wisdom concerning the role of demographic patterns and agrarian trends in producing insurrection.[61] Nonetheless, the Teulenses' struggles with the Countess reveal a history of land conflict that is itself as unruly as the "insolent" indios of San Andrés.

Throughout their conflict over the valley, the Teulenses recognized specific bonds of allegiance, whether on their part or that of their adversaries.

The "party of the Hacienda," composed locally of the vaqueros, servants, and *majordomos* of the Countess's estate, and controlled by the Countess of San Mateo Valparaiso, were obviously aligned with the elite landowning class of "miners and merchants."[62] Lieutenant Don Juan Francisco Servín de la Mora and his "relatives and allies" clearly served as another faction in the pueblo's orbit. In their 1796 petition, the desire of the pueblo of San Andrés to get rid of Servín de la Mora superseded even their effort to legitimate their claim to the lands in the Valley of Ameca. The Teulenses recognized that the lieutenant served as the agent of a different community from that of the pueblo, or even the Countess, for that matter, and were especially adamant that none of "the vecinos of Nuevo Tlaxcala who are of the faction or persuasion of the Teniente" be given any power over them.[63] They had been intermittently using the valley in times of hardship throughout the eighteenth century, and, in their eyes, it was only with the "offenses" of Servín de la Mora that things fell apart. Regardless of the actual significance of the lieutenant's actions—or inaction—relative to their claim to ownership, they place the blame on his shoulders, rather than accusing the Countess, the governor of Colotlán, or some other powerful figure.[64]

The governors of Colotlán play an important role in the relationships depicted in the narratives of both this chapter and the previous one. The significance placed on the office was demonstrated most poignantly by the annual planting of the cross in front of the governor's residence in remembrance of the two prior holders of the office who died during indigenous revolts. Remember that the governor of Colotlán also served as commander of the frontier militias of Colotlán, in which men from all of the Frontier pueblos participated. A single office whose place among the social fault-lines could depend heavily on individual character, background, or preference, different governors received varying degrees of support from different pueblos and factions. The indios fronterizos from San Andrés del Teúl, Tlacosahua, and Huejúcar tended to view the governor of Colotlán as a traditional patron. Governor Josef Asencio de Uriarte certainly functioned in this manner, as his favorable report and dismissal of Lieutenant Servín de la Mora show. Don Felipe del Villar Gutierrez, the former governor of Colotlán recommended by the Teulenses as an "impartial disinterested subject of integrity," also bears out this interpretation. While the Colotecos and their allies in many of the "pueblos de abajo" had taken significant measures to oppose Villar, the Teulenses joined Huejúcar and Santa María in supporting Villar. As the case of the Teulenses' relationship with Don Fernando Campa Cos, the Countess's father, demonstrates, other local military leaders could also fit into this role, particularly for those indios flecheros who had served with them in combat.[65] As discussed in the next chapter, during the 1810 insurrection Padre Miguel Hidalgo himself took on the task of appointing a new rebel governor of Colotlán, opting for a prominent creole with wealth and standing in the vecino community rather than someone closely aligned with the fronterizos.[66]

Any analysis of social relations would be incomplete without acknowledging the role of religion.[67] The Teulenses themselves underscored the connection between their obligations to keep the church in good repair and the priest's fees up to standard, and the—consequently—legitimate need to utilize the resources of their *tierras y montes*, including the Valley of Ameca. In other pueblos of the Colotlán Frontier, parish priests served as mediators, protectors, and even instigators in the relationships among pueblos and Spanish officials during the years preceding the insurrection.[68] During the insurrection local clergy would play an important role in the region, which would remain very much a bastion of pro-church sentiment throughout Mexican history.[69]

Late colonial demographic pressures such as the growth of creole settlements, the expansion of large estates, and the growth of mining communities presented new challenges to the socioeconomic efforts of the Teulenses and similar indigenous pueblos. However, alliances, enmities, and interpersonal social relationships ultimately superseded any structural pressures, economic or otherwise. In a similar vein, we should not reduce the indios of San Andrés del Teúl to simply "the oppressed ones," as they deemed themselves in their 1796 lament to the viceroy and the governor of Colotlán. As the events of these narratives show, the members of the pueblo of San Andrés experienced considerable success in utilizing the Valley of Ameca, with or without official approval, during the course of their struggle with the extremely wealthy and powerful Countess of San Mateo Valparaiso. Just as humans across the social spectrum have done throughout the centuries, the Teulenses pursued their own agenda in their own interest and that of their community, seeking powerful allies where possible, and working through both official channels and extralegal means as the opportunity arose.

4

The Revolutions of This Canyon

> The more than 5,000 Indian archers brought from the region of Colotlán by the priest . . . Calvillo seemed to have not experienced three hundred years of Spanish domination, as they were armed and dressed just as in the wars of the conquest.
>
> —Description of Padre Miguel Hidalgo's troops on the eve of the Battle of Puente de Calderón, January 1811

The indios fronterizos of Colotlán experienced the war for independence as a very local and personal struggle. In characterizing their role in the early phase of the Mexican independence struggle, José Atanacio Desiderio, Laureano Perfecto, and other Indians from Tocatique, a small pueblo of around 250 people to the south of San Luis de Colotlán, said they were participating in "the revolutions of *this* canyon."[1] They were also careful to point out the insurgent commander under whom they served, stating that they "went around with [Francisco] Toral." At least thirty-nine men from the pueblo of Totatique fought with Toral, and various others fought with other commanders. This would have included almost the entire adult male population of the pueblo.[2] They were joined by Frontier Indians from all over the Colotlán region, including those five thousand Indian archers mentioned above.[3] This contemporary reference to the Conquest is telling, as these rebels were participating in the dismantling of the colonial world that their indio conquistador ancestors had helped to create.

This chapter examines the social contours of the insurgency's outbreak in the Colotlán region. The ethnic composition of the insurgents, among both leaders and rank and file, are evident in a rich set of records from the initial period of insurgency. Patterns in the mobilization, organization, recruitment, and mobility of the rebels can also be identified. The insurrection in the Colotlán region had strong roots in the Frontier's indigenous past, and pueblo leaders and local personalities were able to capitalize on it in 1810. This indigenous quality of the insurrection grafted into the larger "Hidalgo Revolt" as local rebels aligned themselves with creole commanders whose political connections outside of the Colotlán region represented a measure of external authority. Nevertheless, a considerable gulf—largely ethnic in its origins and its consequences—existed between the aims of the vast majority of the rebels and the creole elite leadership. The inhabitants of the Colotlán region overwhelmingly joined the initial, more socially charged stage of the insurrection. Ethnicity, status, and social networks fueled this participation, and also shaped the outcome of the war, which left the indios fronterizos without many of the protections and privileges they had sought to preserve throughout the colonial period.

Independence and the Gente de Pueblo

Spain's empire in the Americas began to crumble in 1808, as creole elites in many regions formed self-governing juntas in response to the French usurpation of the Spanish throne. In the autumn of 1810, however, a different challenge to Spanish dominion arose in New Spain, in a series of rebellions sparked by Padre Miguel Hidalgo's famous *Grito de Dolores*.[4] After a disastrous defeat at the Battle of Puente de Calderón in January 1811, Hidalgo's numerous forces scattered throughout the viceroyalty, and royal forces captured and eventually executed the principal leaders later that year. To the extent that a proto-national rebel leadership existed, its reins were taken up by a second priest, José María Morelos, who continued to field an army against Spanish forces until his capture and execution in 1815. However, in a basic, strategic sense, the Spanish regime managed to suppress the initial wave of popular rebellion that had erupted in 1810 through the use of brutal military reprisals and the large-scale issuing of royal and ecclesiastical pardons. While popular rebellion continued in the form of guerrilla bands that achieved sporadic success over the next few years, the insurgents would never again attain strength equal to that of the initial Hidalgo period, and New Spanish independence was only achieved in 1821 when a substantial element of New Spain's conservative creole elite changed their position on independence following a liberal turn of events in New Spain.[5]

The origins of the forces unleashed in the Hidalgo Revolt differed from region to region, and historians are now beginning to demonstrate the drawbacks of conceptualizing these events as a national "movement," or even a broad, widespread reaction to imperial policies, structural change, or demographic and agrarian pressures.[6] The Bourbon reforms of the middle and late eighteenth century, extensive in scope, and often cited as the primary source of colonial unrest, clearly altered labor patterns, land ownership, local-level politics, and other traditional aspects of New Spanish society in ways that sparked resentment toward the *peninsular*-dominated imperial regime all over the viceroyalty.[7] In the cases of many of the rebels who took up arms against the Spanish, however, the roots of popular grievance extended far back into the colonial period. As has already been shown, in Colotlán these roots drew from a fertile and diverse cultural soil that had developed into a fluid indio fronterizo identity, while at the same time preserving strong traditions of indigenous strength and status in relation to the Spanish world.

The 1810 insurrection presented the fronterizos, along with much of the rest of rural, indigenous New Spain, with an opportunity to recover and defend this status and these traditions from the erosions of late colonial reforms and political transformations. Historians are recognizing that these efforts were in fact more preservative than politically radical, and that the aims of insurgent peasants and villagers differed significantly from those of creole elites.[8]

For historians interested in developing a comprehensive picture of the transformation of the colonial Atlantic World into an ostensibly modern and national Western Hemisphere, the stories of the insurgents from Colotlán matter. The social underpinnings of the independence struggle in New Spain contain important implications that extend beyond the history of Mexico, or even Latin America, into broader debates over the meaning of subversion, social conflict, and revolution in the Atlantic World.[9] Focusing on the outcomes of the independence wars, rather than the aims of the participants, scholars have tended to characterize the Spanish American wars for independence as relatively unrevolutionary.[10] Historians of both the Latin American and North American wars for independence have struggled to extend their focus beyond elite ideology and include the role of the popular classes in the wars of independence.[11]

Historians have given more attention to a series of episodes in the late eighteenth century that illustrate the nature of popular rebellion. Although they range from tax riots to restorative ethnic rebellions, these episodes of violence and protest are typically described as "precursor" revolts.[12] Urban tax riots took place in many areas in response to tax reforms instituted in 1765, most prominently in Quito. During the final years of the American Revolution in 1780 and 1781, the Comunero Revolt erupted in New Granada in response to the imposition of new tobacco and poll taxes. In a more violent rural uprising that foreshadowed the Hidalgo phase of independence in New Spain, José Gabriel Condorcanqui (better known as Tupac Amaru II), a mestizo descendant of the last Inca ruler, led a large group of both mestizo and indigenous rebels against colonial authorities until his capture and execution in 1781.[13]

From 1776 on, Spanish officials believed that Britain's loss of its North American colonies posed a threat to royal authority in the Spanish territories. Soon after the conclusion of the Tupac Amaru II revolt, as General George Washington prepared to besiege Yorktown, a Spanish official warned the king that "if it has not been possible for Great Britain to subdue this part of the North, located rather near to the Metropolis, what prudent person can fail to fear an equally reckless tragedy in the . . . extended dominions of Spain in these Indies?" The writer, prescient in his connection of the possibilities of a conjunction of indigenous and creole interests, went on to point out the continued threat of ethnic violence in Spanish America: "the uprising of the Indian Túpac-Amaru originated from the excesses of the corregidors and other bureaucrats in Peru, and gathered such a large number of adherents that it became formidable, costing many casualties, and much effort and expense, to defeat him. . . . If it had not been for the greed of some of his captains, who turned him in, the flame of this conflagration would not have been put out, and if the rebellion would have garnered the support of a leader of high status among the whites I am persuaded that it would have been very difficult or impossible to suppress. . . . It is still not known if the evil has been extinguished or if, when we least expect, it will resurface with unstoppable violence."[14]

Predominantly rural insurrections like this one differed from the urban-centered riots, which were directly sparked by tax reforms. But both strains of colonial conflict—reaction to reform and socioethnic tension—would form an important part of struggles for independence.[15] One of the most interesting aspects of the Señores Colotecos' contentious bid for power in the 1780s, for example, is that it exhibits *both* types of this social friction. Analysis of the 1810 rebellion in Colotlán demonstrates important continuities from this episode that carry through into the independence period. Such an analysis also confirms the importance of placing interpretations of structural and broader political tensions in the context of local social and ethnic realities.

Conflicts among settlers, soldiers, slaves, and Indians should not be separated from any of the principal revolutionary narratives. Even though some scholars of North America have addressed the deficiency, a fundamental recognition of the role of native communities in our histories of the independence period still lies ahead.[16] The creole elite's political dominance of the independence movements has often obscured the role of the gente de pueblo.[17] In this vein, then, our attention now shifts back to the Colotlán region at the moment of the insurgency's inception.

Assembling an "Indiada"

The 1810 insurrection commenced in Colotlán with a communal marshaling of the powerful symbolism of the Frontier's indigenous past.[18] News of Hidalgo's rebellion in Dolores reached the Colotlán region in late September 1810, and according to an early-nineteenth-century account of the period, "the greater part of the population, and especially the indigenous class, appeared to be very much in favor of the cause of Independence, the excommunication proclaimed by Bishop Cabañas of Guadalajara having failed to restrain them."[19] In fact, it appears that the Cura of San Luis de Colotlán, Don Cayetano Ibarra, decided not to publicize the edict in response to threats from local indios that "they would violently take him down from the pulpit."[20] The current governor of the Frontier, Don Gregorio Perez, ordered the urban vecino militia companies of the Colotlán Frontier to active duty and alert, stationing them in the cabecera of San Luis de Colotlán, the companies of indios flecheros having been officially "extinguished" in the 1790s.[21] Indios fronterizos and those castas who had joined their communities still remained a part of the militia in these pueblos—although not those of surrounding districts like Jerez—but the status of indio flechero militiaman had been eliminated, and creole officers now officially headed all of the units.

At this point, Padre Pablo José Calvillo, teniente de cura of the pueblo of Jesús María in Aguascalientes, arrived in San Luis de Colotlán. Calvillo, whose life and role in the insurrection are discussed in more detail in the next chapter, had served in the parish of San Luis de Colotlán and also in nearby Tepechitlán and Teúl in the Tlaltenango district. Son of an elite creole family from Valle de Huejúcar, Calvillo counted many of the creole militia officers among his friends, and he had close ties to indigenous leaders. On a Saturday evening in late September 1810, "a multitude of Indians" met at Calvillo's home in San Luis de Colotlán, "under the pretext of a dance."[22] Then, in a manner reminiscent of the annual cross-planting procession that had served as a warning to countless Frontier governors over the course of most of the eighteenth century, Calvillo led "a multitude of people, armed with bows and arrows, slings, clubs, and machetes," in a march on the Casas Reales. This time, however, the crowd did not stop with a symbolic cross-planting and warning of the tenuous nature of the governor's authority; they actually besieged the residence, demanding the surrender of some thirty-two Spaniards who had sought refuge there. The militia companies, "having been seduced by Padre Calvillo," did not resist these actions. The following morning the militias formed ranks in the plaza, where the Indians had gathered to demand the head of Governor Perez. When the governor ordered the militias to open fire on the crowd, the militiamen responded "that they were no longer on his side," and the officers commanded the troops to disperse. Storming the governor's residence, the Indians took custody of the imprisoned Spaniards and apparently killed Governor Perez.[23] In succeeding days, many of the indigenous inhabitants and former militiamen reorganized themselves into insurgent military companies. According to one source, when some of the militia officers refused to join the rebels, the corporals and sergeants assumed command of their units.[24] It is clear that the allegiances of the creole officers split. At least three of the lower-ranking officers joined the insurgents.[25] Governor Perez's Ayudante Mayor, Lieutenant Don José Ygnacio Alegria, in fear for his life, was later forced to flee the city in disguise.[26] After disbanding (and substantially incorporating) the vecino Frontier militias and imprisoning local Spanish-born vecinos (also known as *Europeos* or *gachupines*), the insurgents pillaged their homes and stores and in a few cases killed some of the more unpopular Europeos.[27] The word in the region was that "all of the ranches and towns up to the valley [of Tlaltenango] and Huejuquilla [in the district of Colotlán] are in open rebellion."[28]

Correspondence among royalist commanders and insurgent leaders, trial records, pardon documents, and other sources allow us to piece together a large portion of the subsequent story of the rebels from Colotlán. The general course of events is apparent for rebels all around the region, but more specific observations can be made based on the later depositions of 629 insurgents who laid down their arms following an *indulto* edict published on April 6, 1811, in Tlaltenango.[29] A large majority of these men identified their home village or pueblo and the insurgent captain for whom they fought. Many others identified their ethnic status, and some their former social position or occupation before the outbreak of the insurrection. Some even provided information concerning the way in which they entered the ranks of the rebels. In all, I have identified from one to 74 individual insurgents for each of 72 different insurgent leaders from the Colotlán region, in addition to 36 other insurgent leaders for whom I have not found evidence of specific followers. Evidence of their actions and social status, along with data about the origins and ethnicity of their soldiers, provide important new information about the social bases and composition of the insurgency.

The insurgent mobilization spread throughout the entire Colotlán region, and, at least initially, included both sides of the factious interpueblo dispute from the 1780s.[30] The families of the Señores Colotecos from Chapter 2 figure prominently among the names of the local rebel leaders from San Luis de Colotlán, with one "Florentino Pacheco" serving as a *capitán particular* for one of the pueblo's companies. "Don Victoriano Cordova" held an even higher position as *Gefe* of rebels from various pueblos, and may have also been the insurgent leader identified as "El Coloteco" by some indigenous rebels.[31] The resurrection of this identity in 1810 reveals connections to previous traditions of revolt that accompanied the independence-era social conflict. In another similarity, the forces from the former "loyal pueblos" from the 1780s (Huejúcar, Santiago, and Santa María de los Angeles), were all led by Don Marcos Escobedo—the creole teniente of the pueblo of Tepechitlán—in addition to men from Tlalcosagua who had also aligned themselves with Huejúcar in the lawsuits against the Countess of San Mateo Valparaiso since 1802.[32] Although he would later accept the higher rank of *Mariscal*, Padre Calvillo initially took the title of chaplain. His connections with both the indios fronterizos and the creole families of the surrounding districts imbued him with significant influence during the course of the insurgency.

The ethnic distribution of rebel soldiers and the statements of individual insurgents show that the impetus for, as well as control over the process of, rebel mobilization in the Colotlán Frontier originated from the indio fronterizo leadership of the region's pueblos. Each of the three former vecino militia officers who formed insurgent companies—Vicente Nales, Manuel Campos, and Miguel Guizas—led vecino insurgents. There is no evidence that any indio rebels served under these three men. Instead, in the days following the dispersion of the vecino militias and the imprisonment of the local Europeos, the indigenous leaders of most of the Frontier pueblos appointed indigenous captains to lead the military forces of their communities. For instance, José Gregorio Lopez, a vecino from Tlaltenango, reported that "he was a Soldier of the Indians of Colotlán by force, and that he participated in the first uprising in that same pueblo."[33] Aparicio Cervantes, an indio from Tlaltenango, stated that the Justiciales of his pueblo had appointed him as Capitán of a rebel company.[34] This indicates a deliberate political process on the part of the fronterizo pueblo leadership in support of the rebellion. Aparicio's status was more of a rule than an exception, as there were at least twenty-six identifiably indigenous insurgent leaders/captains/officers in the Colotlán region, and others whose ethnic status is unclear.

Indigenous rebels from the Colotlán region overwhelmingly followed indigenous officers into battle, even if those officers had, themselves, established links to the creole-dominated rebel hierarchy. Nine of the companies of rebels from the Colotlán region for which sufficient documentation exists were composed of all indigenous troops, with the exception of two groups that each had one non-indio soldier. Indigenous captains led at least eight of these groups, three of them using the non-Hispanic aliases of El Coloteco, Tlemole, and Chano.[35] The ninth was captained by a "cabecilla José Pinedo" of indeterminate but likely indigenous ethnicity. All of Captain Pinedo's men were indios from the pueblo of Teocaltiche, and a Juan Pinedo had served as an indio flechero militiaman with Juan Vicencio Fernández de Córdova.[36] Francisco Toral and a Colonel Suarez, two creole or mestizo officers, were also listed as leaders by more indigenous than nonindigenous rebels. It is possible that these officers recruited indigenous men to fight directly under them. However, as both of these men were higher-ranking officers who commanded the allegiance of various companies of insurgents, it is more likely that those rebels who identified themselves as soldiers of Toral and Suarez would have served under a lower-ranking indigenous captain who, in turn, reported to one of these two.

The data support the premise that the vast majority of the Colotlán region's indigenous population mobilized during the initial phase of the insurrection. Of the 802 named insurgents, 119 (15 percent) were identified as Spanish or Hispanicized vecinos and 297 (37 percent) as indigenous (indios or naturales); the ethnic status of the remaining 386 (48 percent) remained unspecified or unclear. These data are leader-heavy; the lowest-level insurgents or *soldados razos*, as some called themselves, are underrepresented in the sample relative to their share of the insurgent population as a whole. This stems from the fact that observers—whether royalist military officials, witnesses to insurgent activities, or scribes recording pardons—tended to focus more attention on cabecillas (leaders of rebel groups) than on their insurgent followers. Factoring out the 108 insurgent leaders from the sample, the remaining 694 insurgents break down into the following ethnic categories: 271 indios (39 percent), 90 vecinos (13 percent), and 333 unknown ethnicity (48 percent). If we only consider those insurgents for whom a specific ethnic status is identifiable, 71.4 percent were indigenous. This number meshes well with statements by contemporary observers, who used terms like *indiada* to describe the rebels in the Colotlán region, and who commented on the native dress and use of bows and slings by the fronterizo insurgents.[37]

Thus, the evidence from the Colotlán case supports the notion that rates of indigenous participation in the Mexican wars of independence were higher than has been recognized. In the first instance, Colotlán most assuredly *was* a heavily indigenous region in the early nineteenth century, and the significant participation of its indigenous communities is consistent with (and in fact may even surpass) revisionist estimates of the proportion of indio rebels relative to the population as a whole.[38] With regard to the twentieth-century nationalist vision that Mexico's predominantly indigenous identity had already succumbed to mestizaje by the independence period, it is also clear based on the evidence from Colotlán that distinctions between indigenous and nonindigenous inhabitants remained throughout the decade of the independence struggle, as local creole and Spanish military commanders' descriptions of the Colotlán insurgents attest.

The claim that "Indians were . . . underrepresented in the ranks of the insurgent leadership, *even at the local level in areas marked by a heavily Indian ethnic composition*," is more dubious.[39] It should be clear from the mobilization process in the Colotlán Frontier that indigenous leaders *did*, in fact, form a substantial part of the insurgent ranks, including positions of leadership. The fact that only 26 of 108 insurgent leaders in the Colotlán region were identifiably indio might seem to bear out the traditional view that Indians were underrepresented. But the ethnicities of 53 of the remaining leaders are unspecified, and it is likely that many of them had family ties to the indigenous communities of the region, whether or not they were entirely indigenous themselves. This is clearly evident in the case of those "notable" fronterizo families who had driven the 1780 to 1785 efforts to assert local, indio flechero control over the political structure of the Frontier—Córdovas, Pachecos, and others—and who stepped into leadership roles during the initiation of the 1810 insurgency. Additionally, the indigenous principales in pueblos all across the Colotlán Frontier actively fostered the insurrection in the region by appointing indio captains to positions of military authority and instructing members of their pueblos to follow them. Table 4.1 lists information on individual insurgent commanders with 394 individually identified followers. As the table shows, creole captains drew insurgents from a more diverse geographical area into their companies, while indigenous captains tended to lead men from one or two pueblos, at the most. This undoubtedly corresponds to the generally higher ranks achieved by the creoles, but it also stems from the fact that indigenous leaders drew their authority from the pueblo común from which their men were drawn.

Insurgent leaders (including pueblo principales) were not above forcefully impressing people into military service. However, a surprisingly small number of rebels from the Colotlán region said they were forced to join the insurgency. Out of 802 insurgents, only 115 claimed to have been forced to join the rebels. Of these, 67 were indigenous, 18 were vecinos, and the ethnic status of 33 was unknown.[40] Those indigenous rebels who did claim to have been pressed into service may have been following a long tradition of employing "self-exculpatory claims" to navigate the colonial legal system.[41] Given the paternalistic colonial view of indios' status as political actors, such excuses were more likely to be accepted when offered by indios, who were thought to be less competent, and thus less culpable, than were creole vecinos. Members of indigenous communities could play on these assumptions to avoid punishment, claiming that insurgent commanders had led them astray.

Overall, a small percentage of insurgents made claims of having been pressed into service. However, such a pattern does seem evident among natives of Tlaltenango, the site of the mass pardons in April 1811. There, 46.5 percent of the insurgents made such claims. These 67 rebels included 52 indios serving under two indigenous captains, one individual of unknown ethnicity, 14 vecinos who listed a number of different insurgent culprits as having impressed them, including "60 indios from Colotlán," and Daniel Camarena, cited for a similar activity in the neighboring canyon of Juchipila.[42]

Table 4.1. Insurgent Commanders with Ten or More Identifiable Followers

Title	Name	Named Insurgents	Indios	Vecinos	Unknown Ethnicity	Pueblos Represented
Creole Commanders						
Coronel	Ysidro Torres	74	2	21	51	10
Coronel	Francisco Toral	57	36	4	17	8
Coronel	Suárez	34	18	9	7	11
Coronel	Padre Ramírez	16	1	4	11	7
Capitán	Atanasio Estrada San Martín	16	0	5	11	5
Capellán/Mariscal	Padre Pablo José Calvillo	13	1	0	12	4
Capitán	Pedro López	12	0	5	7	6
Indigenous Commanders						
Capitán	Diego Jacovo (El Chano)	46	45	1	0	2
Capitán	Francisco Sánchez (El Tlemole)	35	34	0	1	2
Unknown	Patricio Flores	21	21	0	0	1
Capitán	José Pinedo	12	12	0	0	1
Commanders of Unknown Ethnicity						
Comisionado/Capitán	Gorgonio Marquez	32	4	6	22	7
Capitán	Doroteo Serrano	16	1	7	8	4
Unknown	Mauricio Fregoso	10	1	4	5	3

Source: Data from multiple archival and documentary sources. See Note 23 on the Insurgent Database in the Introduction for a detailed explanation.

The case of one rebel shows that forcible conscription could also begin as voluntary participation. A local indigenous sergeant told José Tiburcio, an indio from Tlaltenango, that "they were going to the Rancho de los Llamas to take some Souls, [but that] it turned out that they funneled him into going to the uprising of Totatiche."[43] Tiburcio's case shows that some insurgents may well have expected to raid local haciendas, rather than assaulting towns and participating in more large-scale military action.

As it turned out, thousands of rebels from the Colotlán region were soon to do just that. During October and early November 1810, most of the indio captains aligned their companies with those of creole officers (comisionados) appointed by insurgent commanders from outside of the region with connections to the core leadership, such as Rafael Iriarte. In this manner, the creole higher command funneled the indigenous insurgents from Colotlán into their political agenda, while the fronterizos, just as they had done in the past, utilized alliances with a few key creole/vecino patrons to leverage their own actions and efforts against powerful adversaries, both within the region itself and in the vecino towns and large estates on the periphery of the Frontera. In early October the intendant of Zacatecas, Francisco Rendón, fled the city, and the Count of Santiago de la Laguna took command and brought his personal retainers to bolster the defense of the city. However, when the Count's emissary to Iriate, José María Cos, joined the insurgents instead of returning to Zacatecas, the Count withdrew to Guadalajara along with many of the city's more prominent Europeos. Iriarte's men, including some several thousand poorly armed rebels from the Colotlán region, occupied the city of Zacatecas without a fight in early November.[44] They then traveled to San Luis Potosi to support the insurrection in that city before returning to Zacatecas later in the month. Meanwhile, Iriarte organized parties to plunder royalist haciendas and instructed the captains from Colotlán to make their troops drill, parade, and practice loosing arrows in an attempt to create a more disciplined and effective army.[45]

By the early part of December the rebels from Colotlán had traveled to Guadalajara, which the muleteer and hacienda administrator José Antonio Torres, also known as "El Amo Torres," had captured on November 11, and where Hidalgo's army regrouped before its disastrous defeat at the Puente de Calderón.[46] Once again, during December and the first part of January, Padre Calvillo and the other rebel commanders from the Colotlán region devoted their time to preparing their forces for battle against the royalists. It is at this point that an unknown observer made the remark about the indios fronterizos from Colotlán seeming to have not "experienced three hundred years of Spanish domination," and being "armed and dressed just as in the wars of the conquest."[47]

The Colotlán Insurgents in the "Dialogue of the Deaf"

During this period in Guadalajara, the rebels from Colotlán must have experienced the excitement and idealism of the large insurgent army. When Calvillo and his men arrived, Hidalgo's army numbered around thirty-six thousand, with more arriving daily.[48] Backed by so many followers, on November 29 Hidalgo issued his first printed decree from the balcony of the royal palace, announcing the abolition of slavery and Indian tribute, the reduction of the alcabala and other taxes, and the elimination of governmental monopolies on tobacco, playing cards, and other items. The rebels from Colotlán would have appreciated these edicts, as the dispute over tribute exemptions and issues of taxation, labor, and production had provoked conflicts in Colotlán throughout the late colonial period. However, Hidalgo's edicts should not be construed as representative of the political objectives of the insurgent creole elite leadership. In fact, both these radical proclamations and the ensuing execution of many Guadalajaran Spaniards contributed to a growing alienation of Hidalgo's officers and many Guadalajaran creoles from the movement.[49] More significantly for modern Mexican history, a fundamental disconnect existed between the aims of the vast majority of the rebels and the higher-level creole leaders. This divergence of rebel philosophies was described by historian Eric Van Young as a "dialogue of the deaf," in which a predominantly indigenous Mexican peasantry fought "in defense of embattled communities they conceived as antecedent to, and in some sense existing outside of, the colonial state," while the creole leadership sought to transform the colony of New Spain into a native-born elite-centered vision of an independent nation.[50] The Colotlán case supports this view, as the inhabitants of Colotlán could not have known that eventual independence would bring about a sweeping departure from the past rights and traditions they fought to resecure.

Even Padre Hidalgo, for all of his radical pronouncements and appeal to the popular classes, remained apart from indigenous concerns in terms of social relations with creole elites in the Colotlán region. While in Guadalajara, Hidalgo decided to fill the vacant post of Governador de la Frontera de Colotlán with a suitable insurgent member of the creole elite. Rather than choosing any of the region's creoles who had aligned themselves with the insurgent indios, such as Ysidro Torres, Padre Pablo José Calvillo, or Francisco Toral, Hidalgo chose Don José Ramon Alegria, a wealthy miner from Real de San José del Yermo, in the Juchipila district. Don José Ramon was the father of Lieutenant Don José Ygnacio Alegria, who had fled Colotlán after the outbreak of the insurrection, and had received erroneous news that "the indios had wounded or killed his son." Upon hearing that his son had successfully escaped in disguise to Guadalajara, Don José Ramon traveled to the city. He discovered on his arrival that Padre Hidalgo, "feared and respected by the Authorities, Military Units, and Community," had control of the city, and Alegria felt it necessary to present himself to this "Gefe de los Insurgentes."[51]

Having been informed that Alegria was "a longtime resident of Tlaltenango," Hidalgo had Don José Ramon sit by his side, and spoke at length with him about the situation in Colotlán. This conversation led to Hidalgo "handing over the Governance of those Frontiers [. . . to Alegria . . .,] conferring upon him "the rank of Lieutenant Colonel." During the course of his later statement to the royalist authorities, Alegria made other meaningful comments that highlight the ethnic subcontext of social divisions in the early phase of the insurgency: "In that time it was necessary to condescend to everyone, and an Official of my seniority had to take the rank of Lieutenant Colonel, despite many prisoners, blacks, and riffraff with colonels' chevrons. This is the surest proof that I only accepted a false rank out of fear and in order not to give insult, since I could have easily acquired the rank of Brigadier, or after serving for a month that of Field Marshall."[52] Alegria never assumed command of the Frontera, as Hidalgo changed his mind and chose another (unspecified) person for that position, giving Alegria "a greater appointment." The new position also went unfilled, as Alegria "left the city under diverse pretexts" and took refuge "far from the city" until March 1811, when royalist control over the Guadalajara area had been more firmly reestablished. Nevertheless, Alegria's case shows that the "national" insurgent leadership, including Hidalgo, remained substantially out of touch with the social situation in Colotlán.[53]

The Limits of the Revolutions of These Canyons

On January 17, 1811, Hidalgo's massive rebel army confronted the more disciplined and much smaller royalist force commanded by Brigadier General Félix Calleja in the Battle of Puente de Calderón. The insurgents from Colotlán participated amid the confusion and chaos of the rebel army's disastrous defeat. According to one account, the indigenous insurgents from Colotlán loosed their arrows from the front ranks under the protection of the rebel artillery. Yet, when a fateful royalist cannonball exploded a pile of ammunition in the midst of the rebel army, followed by a bayonet charge by Calleja's royalists, the rebels fled the field and the battle ended in a rout of Hidalgo's army.[54] The dispersion of Hidalgo's forces and subsequent splintering of the insurgency is well-known. The core leadership of the rebel army fled northward in different groups, with Padre Hidalgo's group passing through the

Colotlán region before his eventual capture at Monclova, Coahuila. After the defeat, some of the insurgents from Colotlán returned to their homes and others joined in assaults—described variously as either "sackings," "uprisings," or "wars"—on the principal towns of Bolaños, Jerez, Juchipila, and Teúl. These outlying vecino towns, plus San Luis de Colotlán, Tlaltenango, and the vast majority of the interior pueblos, remained insurgent territory at this point.[55]

The testimony of the insurgents from the Colotlán region suggests that indigenous rebels were more likely than nonindigenous insurgents to remain closer to their homes. Before the Battle of Puente de Calderon, this only held true for Colotlán to a limited degree, as large numbers of the indios from Colotlán traveled to Zacatecas, San Luis Potosi, and later to Guadalajara before the fateful confrontation on January 17. Still, a number of insurgents apparently never left the region, and after the Battle of Puente de Calderon most remained within the Colotlán region, only occasionally venturing outside the canyons to attack towns in neighboring districts. Sufficient data exist to track the mobility of 223 insurgents. Of those who were identifiably indigenous, 53 percent operated within 60 kilometers of their place of residence. By contrast, only 38 percent of vecino insurgents operated within that distance.[56]

Examination of the insurgents from Colotlán also allows for correlations to be drawn between the geographical origins of insurgents participating in a given raid. For example, before heading south to Guadalajara and the Battle of Puente de Calderon, insurgents sacked the mining center of Bolaños and imprisoned the Europeos they found there. Twenty of the thirty-three participating insurgents identifiable in the historical record were from the mountain village of Atolinga and small communities nearby, less than twenty-five miles to the east of the mines.[57]

Despite the fact that Hidalgo's insurgent army had disintegrated into quarreling factions after the defeat at Puente de Calderon, similar raids continued in February and March 1811, as local insurgent bands reasserted control over the canyons and pueblos of Colotlán region following the dispersal of Hidalgo's army. These events aroused the enmity of the royalist general José de la Cruz, who had been named president of the audiencia of Guadalajara and military commander for all of Nueva Galicia after the Battle of Puente de Calderón. From Guadalajara, Cruz wrote to a subordinate officer, Colonel Rosendo Porlier, that "in the area of Tlaltenango and Tiul [*sic*], along the route from the frontier to Colotlán there are warnings of growing movements [of rebels]. Tonight I am writing to Zacatecas so that a division will head out toward Colotlán, and if the commander of the troops from Durango carries out the plan as I have asked, I am determined to send another [division] from here, and catch this rabble, led entirely by priests, between two fires."[58]

Although numerous other rebel cabecillas were operating in the region at this point, Padre Calvillo had taken on the title of "Field Marshal" and now drew most of the attention. On March 8 and 9 General Cruz characterized the insurgency in Colotlán as an indiada (a substantial indigenous uprising) organized by "that rogue" Padre Calvillo, who continued to "enlarge his revolutionary gang near Juchipila." Cruz informed Porlier that "the moment I receive an answer from Zacatecas I will try to send out a force to annihilate it."[59] Lieutenant Colonel and interim intendant Don José Manuel de Ochoa had retaken the city of Zacatecas after the Battle of Puente de Calderon. Ochoa subsequently appointed Juan Joseph Zambrano to command the city's garrison, and in response to General Cruz's request, Zambrano sent out the royalist priest José Francisco Alvarez to form one wing of the two-pronged attack on the rebels in the Colotlán region. Padre Alvarez, cura of la Cienega de los Olivos in Nueva Vizcaya, was to secure "the canyon of Tlaltenango and the pueblos of Colotlán" with one hundred men and two cannons. Zambrano also placed much of the blame for this continued resistance on "Padre Calvillo and his henchmen, who have been in those pueblos agitating them and making common cause."[60] After the return of Porlier's company to Guadalajara, Cruz sent out Comandante Don Pedro Celestino Negrete "with a strong division," to form the second wing of the attack on Colotlán.[61]

Padre Álvarez staged his march on the Frontier from the royalist-leaning villa of Jerez, accompanied by a detachment of local loyalists under the command of two members of the Jauregui family, who had been prominent supporters of the Junta de Guerra from Chapter 2. On March 25 the royalist force passed through the pueblo of Huejúcar, after first having sent them an "exhortation"—most likely an offer of pardon accompanied by a demand to peacefully submit to the royalist forces—from the Hacienda of Las Víboras, about five miles north of the pueblo near the village of Tepetongo. He reported to Calleja that "the cunning and malice that always arises with these [indios] led them to join with their brothers the rebels of Colotlán and the other pueblos of the frontier." Álvarez "nevertheless took an equal determination to write to [the inhabitants] of Santa María, Santiago, [San Luis de] Colotlán and its attached pueblos, from which I received no answer whatsoever, aside from the verbal message from the indios correos [Indian messengers] that they were forming the cabildo to receive me, according to a credential that they brought from the cura of [San Luis de] Colotlán.[62] This cura, Padre Don Cayetano Ibarra, apparently tried unsuccessfully to encourage the indigenous insurgents to "receive [Álvarez' force] in peace."[63]

"On the 26th I entered Santa María, which was in worse condition and without any inhabitants." The next morning at around 10 a.m., when passing through the pueblo of Santiago about a mile from San Luis de Colotlán, Álvarez saw "a numerous column of indios" occupying a prominent position covering the left side of the road, another column in the center, and cavalry along the right side of the road, "armed with bows, slings, guns, and other ranged weapons." Álvarez sent a message requesting the rebels to surrender, but, as he reported it, "from the heights came the loud cry of 'Viva Nuestra Señora de Guadalupe,' upon which I opened fire with the cannons and rifles." Álvarez's order to attack the rebels' center and right flank failed as a result of the "endless amount of arrows and rocks" launched by the insurgents. The barrage knocked Padre Álvarez off his horse and wounded the royalists' chaplain Don Francisco Inguanzo [from Jerez], both of whom were escorted back to Jerez by twenty men, while the remaining royalist officers led their men in a withdrawal to the pueblo of Santa María, where they were attacked by yet another force of around 150 mixed rebel infantry and cavalry. This resulted in a full-fledged retreat to Jerez, during which the royalists saw yet another group of some five hundred insurgents scaling the mountains between Huejúcar and Tlacosagua. Álvarez's forces did manage to make it back to the villa of Jerez with 26 prisoners, 12 of whom the royalist priest ordered shot on the spot. He sent the remaining prisoners to the insurgents with news of the March 21 capture of Hidalgo, Allende, and other key rebel leaders in Coahuila.[64]

Álvarez's message may well have had the desired demoralizing effect, as the insurgents' fortunes took a turn for the worse when they met Pedro Celestino Negrete's forces a little over a week later, on April 7, 1811. The day before this battle, Negrete, who later became one of the three members of the governing triumvirate of Mexico after the overthrow of Emperor Agustín Iturbide, had publicly offered a royal pardon in the pueblo of Tlaltenango, eventually resulting in the surrender of 343 insurgents from around the Colotlán region (although mostly from the Tlaltenango and Juchipila valleys).[65] Continuing northward to San Luis de Colotlán, Negrete's troops defeated a group of 4,000 rebels, reportedly killing more than 1,500 and driving many others to flee into the canyons and interior sierra of the Frontier. As the rebel soldiers fled into the nearby hills, Negrete's troops followed, killing whomever they could overtake.[66] News of this battle delighted royalists throughout western New Spain. Back in Guadalajara, General Cruz celebrated the battle on April 10 with a "triple salvo of cannon" and a public announcement extolling the victory.[67] In the canyons of Colotlán, some of the insurgents "escaped to the mountains, others were pardoned."[68]

Negrete's defeat of the Colotlán rebels on April 7, 1811 and the subsequent acceptance of royal pardons for hundreds of the region's rebels dealt a major blow to the insurgency in the Colotlán region. Individual insurgent leaders of different ethnicities continued to wage guerrilla war on the Spanish regime throughout the decade, but with only sporadic success. The insurgency would never again exhibit the widespread popular participation and sweeping social connotations of this early period, although the interior canyons of the Frontier would remain a refuge for rebels and bandits for years to come. The rest of the decade would bring an intense struggle over both social and political loyalties, as individuals and communities balanced social and material goals, allegiance, and security; this is the focus of the next chapter.

During this period, the status and privileges that the fronterizos had sought to recover or protect continued to fade into the past, unable to survive either the late colonial reforms of the Spanish regime or creole conceptions of race and property in the formation of a new nation-state. However, colonial configurations of community and social relations on the local level did not diminish as quickly. Despite the use of grand rhetoric by prominent insurgent and royalist elites—"The Unjust Cause," "the Patria," and the "True Faith," among others—and even despite the powerful symbolism of the Virgin of Guadalupe and other images used as unifying forces, indigenous and non-indigenous insurgents in the Colotlán region had treated alignment with the rebels in the same way they viewed other late colonial social action. Family, pueblo-level community, ethnic identity (including that of indio fronterizo), patron-client relations, and other local relationships continued to supersede any adherence to broad proto-national identities or patriotism.

5

Power and Pardon in the Independence of Mexico

> I was the head leader of those Bandits, I convinced all of those inhabitants to join the group, and I persuaded them to the defense of the unjust cause, and with such a motive entered into various actions, from which more deaths than I can number have resulted; but for which I weep and will weep for the rest of my days.
>
> —Confession of Padre Pablo José Calvillo, December 1811

In late 1810, in the colonial town of Irapuato in the Guanajuato region of New Spain, a royalist military officer strode down a line of eighty-five rebel prisoners, counting off every tenth man. Royalist soldiers separated out those prisoners unfortunate enough to be designated. While the other seventy-seven prisoners watched, the eight men pulled from the line were placed before a firing squad and shot. All of the prisoners had been sentenced to death for having broken the terms of a viceregal amnesty. However, in light of the prisoners' "repentant" demeanor and their declarations that insurgent leaders had forced them to violate the pardon, royalist authorities decided to execute "only those designated by fate," repardoning the rest.[1] Although the practice of *diezmando*—counting off every tenth man to be executed—might seem the most remarkable aspect of this incident, it is not difficult to imagine that the indulto real, or royal pardon, loomed larger in significance to the seventy-seven prisoners who did not have to face the guns that day.[2]

Only a few months had passed since September 1810 when Miguel Hidalgo's call to arms touched off the massive social rebellion that spread rapidly and sporadically around the viceroyalty. This might seem a short span for rebel prisoners to have been pardoned, recaptured, and pardoned yet again, but beginning in October of that year, Viceroy Francisco Xavier Venegas and a host of other New Spanish officials and royalist military commanders began issuing an extensive array of amnesty and pardon decrees in an attempt to cope with the rebellion. When Viceroy Venegas offered to pardon Hidalgo and fellow insurgent commander Ignacio Allende in February 1811, they replied "Pardon, Your Excellency, is for criminals, not for the defenders of the Patria."[3] Unfortunately for the insurgent cause, this defiant stance was not the rule. "Thousands upon thousands" of Mexican insurgents did accept the royal pardon, clearly altering the course of the independence struggle.[4]

For historians, the paper trail left by the pardon process provides a way to trace the effects of the independence-era conflicts on Mexican social cohesion. Loyalties, more so than any other social, economic, or political currency, would determine the course and eventual outcome of the independence struggle. Personal, local-level networks of patrons, clients, clergy, parishioners, and families by turns implicated, mediated, and otherwise influenced individuals' relationship to the insurgencies, and to each other. Conversely, the heightened ethnic tensions, fears of caste war, and general chaos caused by the violence and lawlessness that prevailed in many regions strained personal and local social relations in the colony. As seen in the case of Padre Pablo José Calvillo and the indigenous communities of Colotlán, this unrest often pitted family loyalties against fealty to the Crown, and religious conviction and social convention against political allegiance.

The Pardon Process

The use of the indulto real in New Spain began well before the early-nineteenth-century wars of independence, one of many successful transplants from medieval Iberia. Van Young refers back to the Hapsburg era before the eighteenth-century, when "the primary attribute of sovereignty was judicial power and a manifestation of that power the gift of absolution." The Crown's use of pardons, he observed, stemmed from "vestige[s] of older (Hapsburg) Spanish styles of governance," in which pardon served as a "manifestation" of the monarch's judicial power; and as a result of the practical limits of coercive military force and repression.[5] It is clear that granting the indulto to wayward colonial subjects in New Spain began as early as the sixteenth century, as evidenced in a 1595 record approving the pardon of three indios from Totolapa who had been exiled.[6] Other documents from the seventeenth century confirm that the Hapsburg rulers of Spanish America did, in fact, utilize the pardon as a means of reconciling disobedient subjects to the empire. However, it was not until the increasing conflicts of the late eighteenth century—brought on in part by intensified Bourbon efforts to reform the mechanisms of imperial power—that the practice came into frequent use in New Spain.[7] As more and more subjects resisted the imposition of new decrees and ordinances, the Bourbons found the indulto to be a useful way to mitigate the sting of the new measures. When late colonial conflicts blossomed into violent warfare after the Napoleonic crisis, the indulto became the primary means of reconciliation between insurgents and the crown.

Both sides in the Mexican independence struggle appealed to long-standing bonds of allegiance to the king. Hidalgo and his fellow insurgent leaders proclaimed the centuries-old mantra of colonial Latin American rebels: "death to bad government, [but] long live the king!" and as long as the French ruled in Spain, the insurgents' claim to be fighting for the imprisoned Bourbons could be sustained.[8] Meanwhile, the royalists framed the conflict in terms of fidelity, order, and honor, portraying theirs as "the Just Cause" (la Causa Justa). Decrees of blanket amnesty for any rebel who would lay down his or her arms began almost as soon as the fighting had begun, and were usually explained in terms of the "generosity" and "benevolence" of Ferdinand VII, without mention of the obvious military expediency that lay more directly behind such proclamations.[9]

On October 15, 1810, just over a month after the initiation of the rebellion, General Felix Calleja promulgated a viceregal decree pardoning "those repentant insurgents who abandon the detestable faction that they have followed."[10] During the subsequent ten years, the viceroy, regional governors, and military commanders issued numerous decrees, rarely in concert with one another. This led to widespread confusion as to who was eligible for a pardon at any given time.[11] Questions and controversies arose as to what exactly the indulto constituted, and who could confer it. Although viceroys Venegas, Calleja, and Apodaca periodically clarified the official pardon policy, numerous individual commanders and governors often acted independently. In 1815, for instance, Viceroy Calleja confirmed a local royalist captain's pardon of *indio* José Ricardo Damian, "so as not to undermine" the captain's decision, but admonished the commander not to overstep his authority by dispensing other pardons.[12] Yet royalist officers like Pedro Celestino Negrete clearly acted with the official authority of General José de la Cruz in using pardons to stifle the rebellion in Nueva Galicia, as in the case of the several hundred rebels who came in to the pueblo of Tlaltenango to accept Negrete's April 6, 1811, indulto.[13] As Van Young intimates in *The Other Rebellion*, the pardon process was necessarily an imperfect mix of wholesale bureaucratic decree and strategic military practice.[14]

After their initial pronouncement in Mexico City, pardon decrees issued by the viceroys were forwarded to the regional capitals for publication in the principal plazas, and further distribution to the pueblos under regional jurisdiction. Subdelegados (royal district governors) were charged with ensuring that the edicts were displayed prominently in their districts. In a typical example decreed by Viceroy Calleja in June 1814, rebels wishing to accept the offer and apply for pardon were to report to a regional commander of royalist military forces, turn in their weapons and horses, and find a person of known loyalty to give surety for their behavior. As in the case of most pardon decrees, a time limit was specified—in this case thirty days after publication of the edict—after which unrepentant rebels would "forever" lose the opportunity to reincorporate into civic society as a loyal subject (or at least until the next pardon decree). The pardoned individuals (indultados) were to live "calmly and peacefully, subject to the laws of the pueblo they choose for their residence."[15] Given recent scholarship on mobility restrictions and gender, it is safe to assume that the reassertion of the king's paternal authority was implicit in this common restriction on the mobility of the former insurgents.[16]

Although a number of decrees included statements promising forgiveness of past sins, these and other restrictions suggest that indultado (pardoned) did not equal *absuelto* (absolved).[17] Offers of pardon also periodically took place after royalist military victories, when it was assumed (correctly) that the defeat of a prominent local rebel leader would encourage former insurgents to throw in their lot with the royalists. In these instances, rank-and-file rebels would often simply answer a few stock questions, usually including their name, pueblo of origin, and name of the individual they followed. They would then be listed on a pardon roll, given a paper (*cédula*) attesting to their pardoned status, and set free. This was the case in the Tlaltenango pardon of April 1811. Pardoned former rebels who had lost their cédulas had to submit a formal petition to have it reissued.[18] Confusion over these cédulas could result in controversy at times, such as in the case of José Lionicio, who a royalist commander sent back to Mexico City as a prisoner because "he could not tell if the indulto certificate that [Lionicio] had presented was valid." After verifying the validity of the cédula, authorities in the capital set José Lionicio free and opened an investigation "to determine the motives" of the royalist commander.[19] Still, such suspicions were not always unfounded, as in the case of three rebels captured in Irapuato who were found to have "surreptitiously solicited a pardon certificate."[20] In another instance, a group of enterprising rebels even stole preprinted "packets of blank amnesty forms."[21]

Over time, as royalist commanders found it especially difficult to persuade particular insurgent commanders to accept a pardon, they would imprison the wives or *amasias* (lovers) of the rebels in order to force them to lay down their arms. The cases of the wife and amasia of insurgent leader Vicente Vargas are illustrative of this type of female involvement in the insurgency. In 1817 Monica Salas, Vargas's wife, was imprisoned in the Casa de Recogidas La Magdalena, in the city of Puebla. Her two daughters and two granddaughters were confined as well.[22] It is unclear whether Monica had expressed any rebel sentiment herself. Vargas held a high rank in the rebel forces, and the imprisonment of his family was probably an attempt to persuade him to accept a royal pardon. He did so on January 22, 1818, and his wife, children, and grandchildren were set free.[23] While one can only speculate as to the reasons for Vargas's "redemption" of his wife and children, Spanish officials would not have been blind to gendered conceptions of male honor in such situations. Many Mexican men would have considered it dishonorable to allow the women of their family to suffer disgrace on their behalf. In a similar case, María Luisa García Carrasco, wife of rebel José Pioquinto Urtado, was held along with Juana Dolores Delgadillo, who a royalist official disparagingly referred to as the "amacia [*sic*] in general of all those rebels that frequent the pueblo of San Felipe." The two were imprisoned until José accepted a pardon, at which time María Luisa was freed. Juana Dolores somehow escaped en route to Mexico City.[24] The practice of confining women because of their family ties became more prevalent after 1814.[25] This skillful manipulation of family and personal bonds by royalist commanders—confining women as leverage to draw their insurgent family members into the pardon process—demonstrates a recognition on their part that personal and local loyalties often trumped broader allegiance.[26]

In addition to confining female family members, in a number of instances royalists successfully incited intrainsurgent betrayal through the strategic granting of pardons. Two rebels from San Angel named Vazquez and Calderón delivered insurgent lieutenant colonel Miguel Gonzalez to royal authorities, having been promised a pardon in return. Gonzalez received a sentence of eight years in San Juan de Ulúa prison in Veracruz.[27] In another interesting case, a royalist sublieutenant, Ignacio Oliden, robbed his captain and fled to the insurgents "to escape the penalty for his crime." Oliden then made a deal with royal authorities in which he turned in an insurgent commander named Rueda in exchange for a pardon, with the stipulation that he return the captain's belongings.[28] However, bargaining for pardons could be dangerous, as a number of prospective rebel turncoats discovered when they were promptly jailed after coming in to accept a pardon.[29]

Pardon judgments often included prearranged stipulations and conditions, and royalist and insurgent military commanders alike were not above haggling during such negotiations. Many fit the pattern described in the Oliden case, in which pardoned rebels were ordered to repay plundered money and goods. Such suits included money, papers, horses, and other items. In one interesting suit, Don Gregorio Martinez, the surgeon for a regiment of royal dragoons, appealed for the return of his books and medical instruments, taken by Miguel Espinosa, a rebel who had since been pardoned. Perhaps to strengthen his case, Don Gregorio noted that Espinosa "with his [lack of] knowledge is practicing to the detriment of the sick and wounded."[30]

Other common conditions of pardon included banishment of the rebel from his home pueblo (as in the case of the Señores Colotecos), exile from the Americas, the necessity of a chaperone, and parole-like restrictions such as a prohibition on the use of firearms. Tomás Hernandez, a former insurgent prisoner who petitioned the viceroy for a forgiveness of the remaining time in his five-year sentence for "having cut off the tongue of a royalist named Macedonio," received a pardon on the condition that Macedonio forgive him for the offense.[31] For the large number of indultados who had deserted the royal army, restricted pardon often meant a return to the regiment.[32] José María Alcala, a talented gunsmith, received a pardon as a direct result of his useful occupation. The pardon stipulated that Alcala work in a specific factory.[33] On other occasions, officials confiscated the belongings of the pardoned rebels or their families, or imposed fines. A pardoned man living in Puente de Ixtla unsuccessfully petitioned for an exemption to the civil penalty applied to him for having fenced goods for the rebels. Authorities also denied the request of a pardoned deserter who had held the rank of lieutenant in the royal army that he be paid his salary, which was then in arrearage.[34] Don Manuel Carvajal was fined five hundred pesos for sheltering a rebel priest who had escaped confinement in the Convento del Carmen and who eventually fled the colony.[35]

Members of the Catholic clergy are heavily represented in the indulto records. Of some 491 cases from the AGN, 69 relate specifically to clergymen, and several of these cases involved group pardons of more than one priest. In a number of other cases, priests acted as mediators or arbitrators in the process of extending offers of pardon to insurgents, and royalist officials granted many loyal priests the right to give or withhold amnesty.[36] At times, the granting of this privilege to individual clergymen caused conflict between the priest and local officials, as in the case of Padre Don José Ignacio Muiz, whose application for the privilege of being a "pardon-dealer" met opposition from the subdelegado of Ixtlahuacán, in the Cuquío district of Nueva Galicia. Officials in Mexico City decided to grant Padre Muiz's petition "in spite of [the subdelegado's claim] that Muiz would abuse the privilege."[37] Despite opposition, over the course of the insurgency the Catholic Church managed to maintain—and even enhance—its position as a mediator of power and allegiance through its role in the pardon process.

At times, the mediatory position of priests caused them to fall under suspicion. Such was the case of Franciscan friar Don Pedro Ronda, brought up on charges of treason after he said mass in the presence of a group of insurgents to whom he was supposed to have been presenting an amnesty edict. Luckily for Ronda, he was pardoned after managing to demonstrate that the rebels had arrived after he started the mass. This indicated that he had not specifically said it for them, which would have been a tacit moral approbation of their cause.[38] In another case fiscal teniente Cayetano Payes filed a complaint that the priest Don José Mariano Mantecón had made a deal with one of the judges in a case against four men accused of treason, resulting in the pardon of the accused.[39] In at least one instance, a priest rescued condemned insurgents from the firing squad by persuading a royalist commander to postpone the execution until the details of a recent viceregal pronouncement could be determined.[40] Officials placed other pardoned rebels under the supervision of loyal clergy in a type of conditional parole.[41]

The church influenced the indulto process in other ways, as well. When captured insurgent Vicente Miranda managed to forestall his pending death sentence by entering a church in Oaxaca and claiming religious asylum, the ecclesiastical *cabildo* of the city took up his case. Although the court eventually decided against Miranda, enough time had passed that he had been pardoned in the interim.[42] In another example of civil-ecclesiastical conflict over jurisprudence in Oaxaca, church authorities forestalled the execution of former parish priest and rebel lieutenant colonel José Ignacio Couto by arguing with military authorities over whether the prisoner should be defrocked before confronting the firing squad. In the meantime, Couto escaped and applied for pardon. His request having been denied, he remained in hiding until the general amnesty in September 1820.[43]

The significance of the battle for priestly loyalty was certainly not lost on the royalists, who frequently went to great lengths to regain the allegiance of insurgent clergy. A number of documents contained messages from royalist commanders promising safe passage, good treatment, and pardon if the rebel priest came in voluntarily.[44] After the initial "Hidalgo" phase of the revolt, a large number of priests began to reaffirm their loyalty to the Crown and apply for pardon. The factors driving this trend included a division among the rebel leadership between clergymen and creole military officers, and the propaganda onslaught waged by the church hierarchy and viceregal government, including excommunication bans against the insurgents. Indulto records confirm the effectiveness of the threat of excommunication, as in the case of José Manuel Carrera, a parish priest from the pueblo of Nopala, who had joined the insurrection at the beginning of the Hidalgo phase. After being defrocked and excommunicated, Carrera applied for and received a royal pardon.[45]

A number of rebel priests volunteered to fight for the royalists to demonstrate their renewed loyalty.[46] In one extraordinary case, two Franciscans from San Luis Potosí joined the insurgency together in November 1810 as the initial phase began. After their capture in 1811, one of the men, Friar José Vargas, died in prison. Spanish authorities exiled the other, Melchor Saenz, to Havana, but pirates captured his ship en route. Saenz, who had exacerbated his crime by publicly stabbing a portrait of royalist general and future viceroy Felix Calleja, somehow managed to make his way back to San Luis Potosí, where he promptly applied for pardon and offered his services to the royal army.[47] Royal officials sometimes accepted such offers and allowed clergymen to lead royalist units against the rebels. In other cases, though, they denied priests' requests for military service out of respect for the ordained status and vows of the clergymen.[48]

Not all pardoned priests accepted their return to the good graces of the Crown with expressions of overt loyalty. In 1818 Subdeacon Ignacio María Ordoño, a rebel priest imprisoned since 1814, "proffered [insults] toward various authorities" upon notification that he would be pardoned and set free. Although this resulted in a new round of litigation, Ordoño was eventually released. In another instance, the head of the Augustinian order in Mexico City ordered that an Augustinian friar who had been pardoned after fighting with the rebels in Zacatecas be required to return to the capital and rejoin a monastery, "so that the public order would not be disrupted."[49]

The difficult challenge of maintaining a semblance of public order remained a principal concern of the viceregal government throughout the independence period. Time after time, the pardon process provided a mechanism for intracolonial social bonds to be reknit. In 1814 inhabitants of the pueblo of San Mateo de Piñas denounced their own parish priest as an insurgent. Royal authorities removed the priest, Brother José Manuel Ordoño, from his post and brought charges of treason against him. Three years later, authorities reopened the case, noting "the difficulties that have arisen in the pueblo . . . due to the lack of a parish priest." Ordoño, having since been pardoned and having maintained good conduct, was then restored to his position.[50] Such examples of social reintegration would prove indispensable to the eventual compromise establishing Mexico's independence.

The mitigating factors that influenced the granting of pardons, in which the outcome of someone's petition often depended upon their previous social status, kinship ties, or patronage, further demonstrate the role of the indulto as a reintegrative force. The imprisoning of women as a result of their own actions, rather than those of a husband or lover, show how mediating circumstances could affect the pardon process. Women who convinced royalist troops to desert were commonly sentenced to death, even as early as 1811. If they were found to be pregnant, however, their sentences were either postponed until the birth of the child, or they were pardoned altogether. Such was the case with Juana Barrera, Mariana Anaya, and Luisa Vega, who were arrested in October 1813 after they attempted to convince troops from a royal infantry regiment in Tula to desert. Ignacio Inarra, a soldier in the regiment, denounced the women to his commander. All three were sentenced to death, but the executions of Juana and Mariana were suspended due to their pregnancies, during which time they were confined in the Casa de Recogidas. After giving birth, they were pardoned. It is unclear whether Luisa was shot.[51]

Other mitigating factors also aided the causes of pardon applicants. Prisoners who were ill or disabled often petitioned successfully for pardon, as in the cases of ten prisoners in Mexico city who were *inútiles para trabajar*, and of "disabled" prisoner José Mariano Reyes.[52] A number of prospective indultados, including many who had been condemned to death, benefited from the birth of Spanish Princess María Isabel Luisa in 1817, after which proud father Ferdinand VII proclaimed a mass amnesty.[53] When it served the royal interest, however, penitent rebels could be excluded from mass pardon decrees, as is evident in the case of Tomás Vargas and "the other four hundred and forty-seven insurgent prisoners brought from Tulancingo and destined to work on the *zanja cuadrada*," a waterway surrounding Mexico City. The Tulancingo region was predominantly indigenous Otomí, a factor that may have influenced Viceroy Calleja's decision to deny the prisoners' appeal to be included in the most recent indulto.[54]

Nevertheless, despite the viceroy's unwillingness to pardon the men from Tulancingo, it is evident that pardons could extend to indigenous rebels. In January 1811, Viceroy Venegas issued an edict stating that indios would have the same rights as Spaniards, including the indulto.[55] Just as with non-Indians, justice could be slow for some indio petitioners, especially when there were extenuating circumstances. In 1814, authorities imprisoned Bartolome Sánchez, indigenous governor of the "república de indios" of Juchitán, along with varios indios of the pueblo, for having appropriated the goods of two "gentlemen" passing through Juchitán en route to Guatemala. Sánchez's pardon application was not granted until 1818.[56] In another case, Viceroy Venegas pardoned an entire pueblo of indios on the condition that they not return to their town (which happened to have been demolished by the royal army).[57] Indigenous women also made use of the indulto, as in the case of Ines Feliciana, who claimed in 1812 that she had been falsely imprisoned, solely on suspicions of having accompanied the insurgents.[58]

Family members weighed in on many decisions, particularly fathers petitioning for mercy for their sons. In one case, a father found it necessary to apply for the pardon of his eleven-year-old son who had "escaped" from a rebel band.[59] Mothers, brothers, and wives also applied in the stead of their family members, as did some royalist officers for wayward subordinates. Some of these petitions were denied, but the efforts of family members could be crucial. Royalist troops executed Francisco Trevio, an insurgent captured in 1818, but after a long period of litigation they pardoned his companion, José María Noriega, citing "the services his wife had rendered for the royalists."[60]

A number of cases note the presence of a powerful sponsor or character witness, demonstrating that patronage networks and important allies could be useful in efforts to obtain pardons. When notables like the bishop of Puebla, a royalist colonel and general, and other "honorable" people weighed in on pardon cases, the results tended to favor the applicant.[61] Not surprisingly, the successful indulto petitions of individuals who had held lofty positions themselves before the rebellion also show that status aided the pursuit of a pardon.

Ultimately, the pardon process functioned as the most important means of reconciling a diverse range of New Spanish rebels, including clergymen, women, foreigners, royalist deserters, indios, and other castas (people of non-European ancestry), with the rest of New Spanish society. Reincorporating these individuals into their respective positions in the social hierarchy also removed alternative sources of outside authority, such as Padre Calvillo, from the rebel ranks, thereby reinforcing social norms and stifling more popular, class-based expressions of rebellion. Without this mechanism, the social divisions exposed in the popular phase of the revolt would have never been repaired, and the royalist counterinsurgency would have diminished. As one observer present in New Spain from 1816 to 1818, remarked: the "main body of [royal forces in Mexico] was composed of pardoned insurgents and disaffected Creoles."[62] It would be these same individuals who, in 1821, would form the basis for the *Ejército Trigarante* (Army of the Three Guarantees) and the independence of Mexico.

Curas, Cabecillas, and Partisan Pueblos

A return to the Colotlán region confirms that concerns over status, ethnicity, and personal relationships guided the shifting loyalties of the post-Hidalgo phase of the independence period. To distinguish these features of the independence struggle, it is necessary to expand our focus to include the predominantly creole middlemen who often served as insurgent leaders. The shifting loyalties of many of these individuals dramatically altered the course of the insurrection, yet historians have paid little attention to them. Their stories confirm the importance of family connections, the reciprocal honoring of obligations as a means of garnering and maintaining respect and status, and the tension between identification with the concerns of indigenous communities and those of creole vecinos. All of these issues are dramatically evident in the life of Padre Pablo José Calvillo. Despite eventually accepting both military and ecclesiastical pardons, Calvillo continued to struggle internally over his own divided loyalties.

Pablo José de los Dolores Calvillo Ximénez de Alvarado was born on March 2, 1772, and baptized in the chapel at Peña Colorada, his family's estancia (estate) near the small vecino community of Valle de Huejúcar, in the Juchipila valley, about thirty-five miles to the southwest of San Luis de Colotlán.[63] The Calvillos had come to the region after 1650, from Michoacán, and derived their wealth from ranching, agriculture and some commerce. Don Vicente and his wife both came from respectable creole families. In 1778, sixteen families numbering sixty inhabitants lived on the estancia, which formed a part of the larger Hacienda de San Nicolás, owned by Pablo's father, Vicente, and his brothers.[64] Pablo spent his early years on the estancia around the livestock and laborers of the hacienda.[65]

As befitted the youngest son and ninth child of a relatively well-to-do hacendado, and perhaps with the encouragement and support of high-ranking ecclesiastical relatives, Calvillo began preparing for a career in the clergy.[66] One of his uncles, Don Joaquín Calvillo, served as Pablo José's godfather and tutor, and was a respected clergyman in the region who had previously served as the royal commissioner (*comisario oficial real*) of the Bolaños mining district. Another kinsman, Bachiller José Antonio Calvillo, held the important position of rector of the Seminario de San Luis Gonzaga in Zacatecas during this period. *Bachiller* signified that the bearer of the title held a bachelor's degree. Still another relative, Don Luis Calvillo, served as a high-ranking church official at the cathedral in Valladolid. It is likely that Calvillo undertook some preparatory education in either Zacatecas or Guadalajara during his late teen years. He would have needed a bachelor's degree before taking advanced theological studies at the Seminario Tridentino de San José y Real Universidad in Guadalajara, where he was enrolled by 1795 at the age of twenty-three.[67] This seminary, located in what is now the *Museo Regional*, served as the principal training ground for parish priests and the future church hierarchy of central-western Mexico, along with the Colegio de Misiones in Zacatecas. The entrance requirements stated that students must be older than twelve years of age, "of legitimate birth, preferably poor, must know how to read and write competently, and must demonstrate their desire to serve God."[68] The "preferably poor" policy was not absolute, and the acceptance of the sons of moderately wealthy hacendados like the Calvillos into the school was, in fact, the standard practice.[69]

While studying at the Seminario Tridentino, Calvillo most likely stayed with relatives or friends of the family, as his name is not listed in the lodging lists of the seminary. He attended classes in "four principal subjects: grammar, rhetoric, philosophy, and theology; and four secondary subjects: doctrine, sacred scripture, sacred eloquence, and Mexican [Nahuatl] language."[70] Foreign (non-Spanish) students were not accepted in order to prevent any "heretical contamination" of the social structure.[71] Thus, if Calvillo became exposed to any of the more liberal ideological trends of the period it would have most likely been through his friends and associates in Guadalajara, rather than through the Seminario curriculum. Be that as it may, Calvillo was not alone among the seminarians in his later decision to join the independence movement. The rector of the seminary, Bishop Juan Cruz Ruiz de Cabañas y Crespo, would later complain in a report to the king of the "rotten and miserable" alumni who joined the insurgents.[72]

Calvillo achieved the status of *presbítero* (fully ordained priest) by early 1798.[73] He served in a series of assignments to the parishes of Juchipila, Ojo Caliente, Tepechitlán, Teúl, and San Luís de Colotlán, deepening his familiarity with the indigenous communities of the Colotlán Frontera.[74] In November 1808, a serious illness forced Calvillo to travel to Aguascalientes for treatment.[75] He would be plagued by poor health for the rest of his life. Upon his recovery the following year, he received an appointment as a *teniente de cura* (lieutenant priest) ministering to the Indian pueblo of Jesús María, in Aguascalientes.[76] It would be from this pueblo, two years later, that Calvillo would begin to raise an indigenous army to support Hidalgo's rebellion.

Founded in the late seventeenth century as a part of Spanish attempts to pacify and settle the area surrounding the villa of Aguascalientes, Jesús María contained 628 people, according to an 1808 census.[77] On January 11, 1810, the subdelegado of Aguascalientes, Don Bernadino Díaz de Cosío, started a disturbance in Jesús María. Don Bernadino, who would later serve as a prominent loyalist commander, entered the pueblo with an escort of four royal dragoons in order to punish several Indians who had demonstrated a "lack of respect and subordination toward a commissioner that [Díaz de Cosío] had sent to investigate the robbery of some [cattle]."[78] Roque Abarca, intendant of Guadalajara at the time and thus officially in command of the regiment from which Díaz had requested the service of the dragoons, documented the events in a report to the provisional magistrate in Aguascalientes. In a comment that reveals the prevailing social tension and late colonial Spanish attitudes toward even long-settled indigenous communities, Abarca wrote that "to go to a pueblo of indios, the number of troops he asked of me seemed insufficient."[79]

The Indians' response to the intrusion of Díaz and the dragoons was to "come out of the doors of the houses to see the novelty." However, when Díaz ordered his men to search the houses, an indigenous woman became angry and began "insulting [the subdelegate] with words," at which point

Díaz began to hit the woman. When a large group of Indian men came to her assistance, Díaz and his men barricaded themselves in a hallway. Padre Calvillo was able to resolve the dispute by persuading the subdelegate and his men to leave the town, accompanied by "the following insult from the indigenous woman: 'Ah such a good little subdelegado, I'd give him a punch that not even holy oil can cure!'"[80]

Whether the anger of the indigenous men arose from a proprietary view of the woman or from a communal urge to protect one of their own, it is certain that Díaz de Cosío impetuously crossed important lines of accepted behavior. In his report of the incident, even dragoon commander Roque Abarca placed the majority of the blame on the "impulsive" subdelegate.[81] The significance of Calvillo's role in the occurrence can be seen in his mediatory actions to de-escalate a possibly violent situation, rather than supporting the official prerogative of Díaz de Cosío. Calvillo evidently had sufficient moral authority to persuade his parishioners to allow the subdelegate and dragoons to leave unharmed. However, Calvillo's failure to support Díaz de Cosío earned the enmity of the subdelegate, and this would come back to haunt him a few years later.[82]

This incident in Jesús María occurred within a long-standing tradition of indigenous resistance, not necessarily to Spanish authority as a whole, but certainly to particular representatives of that authority in the Colotlán region. The Jesús María incident demonstrates the strained relations between Calvillo's parishioners and the government officials in the months before Hidalgo's *grito*. When Guanajuato exploded in revolt after September 16, parish priests throughout New Spain were faced with the conflicting interests of rebellious parishioners and official intransigence. Having grown up in a rural setting among a heavily Indian population, served his entire career in Indian parishes, and developed a close relationship with his indigenous parishioners, Padre Calvillo would soon serve as a link between the creole-dominated interregional insurgency on the one hand and the indigenous rebels from the Colotlán region on the other.

Subversive Priests and Parishioners

The role of clergy in the New Spanish insurgency has long been of interest to scholars of the period. Few deny the significance of clerical participation in these movements, as many of the most prominent insurgent leaders were parish priests.[83] Still, the number of clergy who supported the insurgency is widely debated.[84] Clearly, "contemporary witnesses" largely agreed the rebellion was "initiated . . . and sustained to a great extent by Creole members of the lower clergy."[85] Contemporary observers among the royalist elite may have failed to recognize any agency on the part of the mostly indigenous "followers" of rebel clergymen, thereby overemphasizing the role of the priest in "initiating" and "sustaining" the rebellion.

The predominant explanation for clerical participation holds that a "crisis of ecclesiastical privilege" brought about by the Bourbon reforms instigated widespread clerical resentment toward the Spanish colonial regime that led many parish priests, particularly those in more economically disadvantaged parishes, to foment rebellion among their parishioners.[86] Most historians holding this view would acknowledge a variety of other factors, such as the coffeehouse or *tertulia* ideals of admirers of the Enlightenment, the charismatic example and influence of Miguel Hidalgo, or the potent imagery of the Virgen de Guadalupe. Nonetheless, the pervasive encroachment of Bourbon regalism into the traditional domain of clerical prerogative and privilege is usually cited as the ultimate cause of clerical disaffection.[87]

But clerical participation in the insurrection cannot be explained solely in terms of resentment of the Bourbons' intrusion into church, state, and society. Socioeconomic status and position do seem to have played at least some role, as the majority of the higher-ranking church officials supported the Crown, while many of the insurgent priests, including Hidalgo himself, had experienced difficulty advancing or maintaining high rank in the ecclesiastical hierarchy. Van Young notes that clerical loyalty to the Spanish regime "cut across the church of New Spain along several axes," notably class, ethnic, ecclesiastic affiliation, and geographic divisions. Others have argued that a majority of the clergy remained neutral, and that regional trends can be detected in the participation of the clergy for or against the rebellion, with the clergy in the larger cities following their ecclesiastical authorities in supporting the Crown, and with the highest percentage of clerical insurgents coming from the ranks of the parish priests who served predominately indigenous parishes.[88] This characterization fits the evidence from Colotlán, where priests from the interior of the region were more likely to support the insurgents, while clergy from the towns of neighboring districts generally supported the Spanish regime. However, a number of clergy from the city of Zacatecas (both regular and secular) favored the insurgency.[89]

In building his argument that a smaller number of clergy supported the rebellion than thought, Van Young argues that many parish clergymen, even in rural areas, became relatively "distanced" from their parishioners due to conflicts over priests' economic entitlements, cultural heterodoxy, and assimilation, and clerical involvement in local politics, among other factors. This line of argument connects the depth of the relationship between priest and parishioners to the level of clerical commitment to the insurrection, and suggests that those priests who did develop close relationships with the members of their parish may have also developed a measure of affinity for indigenous grievances.[90] The case of Padre Calvillo supports such a view.

"I was the head leader of those Bandits"

Padre Calvillo's role in the initiation of the September 1810 insurrection in Colotlán has already been described in Chapter 4. He facilitated the gathering of a large number of indios fronterizos at his home, joined them in marching on Governor Perez's residence in the Casas Reales, and arranged for the transference of the Frontier militias' loyalties from the governor to the insurgent captains. Although he himself initially took the title of chaplain, by the Battle of Calderon Padre Calvillo had taken the title of Field Marshal and directly led the indios of Colotlán into battle. The day after their disastrous defeat at Calderon, Hidalgo and some of the other insurgent leaders escaped, traveling through northern Jalisco, southern Zacatecas, and Aguascalientes on their way north. Calvillo helped guide Hidalgo's portion of the retreating army through this region, as he was obviously familiar with the land and inhabitants. The fact that he guided and traveled with Hidalgo rather than Ignacio Allende and the others is significant, as it provides a clue as to where his sympathies lay in the division that had taken place within the rebel leadership. The retreating rebels wasted no time, arriving in Calvillo's old parish of Juchipila on the afternoon of January 18, 1811, and continuing on to Calvillo's home community of Valle de Huejúcar, where Hidalgo is said to have been welcomed with a cup of chocolate.[91] Here Calvillo left Hidalgo and the rest of the party, who continued north to meet up with Allende and the other surviving insurgent leaders.

The subsequent details of Padre Calvillo's insurgent career clearly reflect the importance of family connections in maintaining and transferring loyalties during this period. In February and March 1811 Calvillo traveled around the Colotlán region, coordinating rebel activities and leading guerrilla resistance against the royalists. These activities included a secret trip in disguise into Aguascalientes to round up support and meet with friends. While there he stayed at the home of his niece's husband, José María Medina, the son of another local creole family and administrator of the Hacienda de la Labor in the Valle de Huejúcar.[92] Medina had himself been commissioned "to apprehend Europeans" in the Valley of Huejúcar by the Count of Santiago de la Laguna, who temporarily served as the insurgent chief in Zacatecas. However, Medina took pains to avoid being portrayed as a fervent supporter of either side. In March 1811, Calvillo freed a group of prisoners from the jail in Juchipila and captured a group of royalists in Nochistlán. Calvillo turned the royalists over to insurgent leader Daniel Camarena, who promptly executed them.[93] As related in the previous chapter, royalist general José de la Cruz dubbed the activities of Calvillo and the Colotlán insurgents an *indiada* and determined to crush the insurgency in the region. Padre Calvillo and the Colotlán rebels defeated the first part of the two-pronged Spanish expedition to reconquer the region, led by the royalist priest padre Álvarez, but were then defeated by the second invading force led by Negrete in a battle at San Luis de Colotlán on April 7, 1811.[94]

Several hundred rebels from Colotlán accepted pardons after this defeat, including a number of the indigenous rebels who had fought with Padre Calvillo. An injured Calvillo, nursing wounds from a serious fall from a horse, took refuge in the mountains of Tayahua between Valle de Huejúcar and San Luis de Colotlán.[95] Documents from an indictment for treason against his nephew-in-law José María Medina reveal that Padre Calvillo also began to arrange for a royal pardon during this time. On June 19 a relative, Don Vicente Eusebio Alvarez del Calvillo, received a pardon from General José de la Cruz in Guadalajara.[96] Other insurgents soon became aware of the Calvillo family's shifting allegiance, resulting in a confrontation at José María Medina's home. On July 9 insurgent brothers Julian, Anastasio, and Francisco Najera came to Medina's residence along with "17 other men armed with rifles, pistols, and lances," shouting very denigrative words at Medina in relation to his perceived lack of adherence to the insurgent cause (and probably that of his extended family as well).[97]

Their accusations were not unfounded, and from July 19 to the August 5 Calvillo stayed at the home of José María Medina, "soliciting his Indulto with the obvious consent" of Don Felipe Pérez de Terán, the villa's subdelegado.[98] Calvillo and Medina used this time to arrange to betray a number of other insurgents to Subdelegado Terán, apparently in exchange for their own pardons and those of other family members and close associates. The falling out between other rebel leaders and the Calvillos and José María Medina grew to include rebel colonel José Rafael Lopez de Oropesa and the cabecilla padre Garcia Ramos, both of whom refused to enter pardon negotiations. As a consequence of this, and in conjunction with their own efforts to receive a royal pardon, Calvillo and Medina negotiated with Terán during the summer of 1811. Terán wrote the following letter to Padre Calvillo:

> Aguascalientes July 24 of 1811
>
> My esteemed Friend: The adjoining commission will certify to You that I merit [your] Confidence . . . as I will withhold from you none of the faculties at my disposal, providing you with them as a courtesy in this defense of the Just Cause. I live with the certainty that You will fulfill this duty with the efficiency it merits, as this is

the sure course of action to reestablish everything you wish and for the good result that is fitting. I hope that you will communicate to me in the sense that if you need any assistance from me I will come with the Troops under my command, whether to calm spirits or to persecute the evildoers.

I am Always Your True Friend, and Servant, Felipe Terán[99]

Terán also wrote to José María Medina at the Hacienda de la Labor, acknowledging receipt of a communication from Medina on July 27, and responding the following day assuring him that "I understand [what you said in your letter from yesterday], but there's no reason for concern because this Troop is well armed, full of Valor and filled with enthusiasm, and ready for any hardship or march when the hour presents itself."[100] Still uncertain of his status with the royalists, Padre Calvillo left with his nephew Don Miguel Calvillo in early August to try to bring fellow insurgent cabecilla Abad Miramontes and others in as prisoners. José María Medina later testified that Calvillo "did not want to assist the rebel Padre Garcia Ramos" in planning an attack on Aguascalientes itself, and that he (and presumably some of his men) met with Abad Miramontes and Flores and disarmed them, "robbing them of the money they had with them and treating them as Cabecillas." Calvillo also arranged for the Najera brothers, along with José Felipe Gonzalez and others, to be arrested by Terán, who imprisoned them in the Aguascalientes barracks.[101] Unlike that of José María Medina, the Najeras' role in the insurgency was unequivocal. Anastasio Najera held the rank of colonel in the insurgent army, Francisco Najera had attacked the royalist Manuel de Esparza with "an edged weapon" in January 1811, and all three of the Najera brothers had recently taken part in an assault on a nearby mine, the Real de Asientos, along with Gonzalez. A tribunal met to consider the evidence against the prisoners; each of them was executed—shot in the back and then hung from the gallows for two hours.[102]

On August 12, 1811, an insurgent army including substantial numbers of rebels from Colotlán under the leadership of cabecillas García Ramos, Abad Miramontes, Hermosillo y Oropresa succeeded in temporarily capturing Aguascalientes, forcing royalists under Subdelegate Felipe Terán and Padre Álvarez to flee to Zacatecas.[103] However, supported by royalist forces from Zacatecas, Terán and Álvarez soon retook Aguascalientes after a ferocious battle on September 2. According to an account by a royalist commander who took part in the battle, the royalists cut the hair of 300 to 400 captured Indian women and children (symbolic "pacification," as short hair signified Hispanicization), raped some of the women, and then set them free.[104] Subdelegate Terán, newly reinstated as the authority in the city, ordered between

135 and 150 captured rebels to be "hung, shot, whipped, and drawn and quartered." This "warning to the insurgents" included a number of indios from Jesús María who had fought with Calvillo from the beginning of his insurgency.[105] Terán also executed Albino Torres, "a famous and daring Indian who had effectively helped Padre Calvillo to encourage the indios of Colotlán and Nayarit to rebel."[106] Royal control having been reestablished in the villa of Aguascalientes, royalist commanders in Zacatecas sent an expedition to pursue those rebels who had escaped into the canyons of the Frontera."[107]

The brutal actions of the royalists in Aguascalientes seems to have shocked Padre Calvillo, who had refrained from handing himself over to the authorities up to this point. In March 1811 Bishop Cabañas y Crespos and the other prelates in Guadalajara had formally petitioned General Cruz to offer pardons to all of the priests who had been charged with participation in the insurgency.[108] Now, in September, Bishop Cabañas sent two priests from the Colegio Clerical San Felipe Neri as envoys to the region, charged with the mission of bolstering royalist sentiment in the region and conferring pardons to stop insurgent activities.[109] Several key rebel leaders who had joined the insurgency with Padre Calvillo in San Luis de Colotlán in September 1810 now came forward and accepted indultos. These included Francisco Cordoba on October 19, Don Francisco Rosales Toral on December 4, and Padre Calvillo himself on December 11. General Cruz pardoned another Toral on December 21, and on Christmas Eve, 1811 the Guadalajara *Junta de Seguridad* confirmed the pardon of Padre Calvillo's brother Don José Miguel Calvillo and a companion of his, Don José María Varela.[110]

Having secured a political/military pardon from General Cruz, Padre Calvillo now applied for reinstatement to the good graces of the church. His petition, the text of which is provided below, was furthered by the support of his family and important friends in Guadalajara, such as the Baron de Santa Cruz.[111] Josef María Moreno, the ecclesiastical judge and interim priest of the Valle de Huejúcar, helped to clear up an initial hesitance with regard to when Calvillo first heard about the excommunication edicts, certifying in a communication to the bishop of Guadalajara that health problems had delayed Padre Calvillo's appearance before the royal authorities until this time.[112] The Guadalajaran prelates accepted Calvillo's appeal, on the condition that he undergo reflective spiritual exercises and brief seclusion in a nearby monastery as a means of demonstrating his penitence.[113] After Calvillo finished his penance, he returned to his priestly duties. Significantly, Calvillo received an appointment to a parish in the town of Aguascalientes, rather than to any of the rural, indigenous parishes where he had previously served. He remained there for some two years until his past came back to haunt him. While walking the streets of the city in August 1814 he got into an argument and then a street fight with the fervent royalist Bernadino Díaz de Cosío, the same official who had caused problems in Calvillo's parish of Jesús María in January 1810. Unfortunately for Calvillo, this incident touched off a new round of legal proceedings and investigations that lasted until the beginning of 1815, when he was exonerated and sent to Zacatecas. Soon afterward, in March 1815, he was ordered to the Franciscan monastery in Guadalupe, outside the city of Zacatecas. He stayed there until bad health led him to be transferred to the Hospital de la Santa Veracruz in Zacatecas, where he died on April 6, 1816.[114]

The Confession of Padre Pablo José Calvillo

I, the parish priest Don Pablo Calvillo, citizen of this Bishopric, appear before your Lordship as I am best able and say: That as a result of my great weakness, and misery, I embraced the cause of insurrection in the beginning of the revolution, and even since then have used the title Chaplain of these Troops. Misery itself dragged me to the point of having accepted the imaginary title of Field Marshal and with this motive I proceeded toward my total ruin, committing the excesses of having commanded the taking of six lives by virtue of my crazy authority, and in effect this has been confirmed; just as the lives of six others have been taken by the weapons of the King our Lord (May God Save Him) as a result of having been turned in by me as dissidents, as proof of my repentance.[115]

I was the head leader of those Bandits, I convinced all of those inhabitants to join the group, and I persuaded them to the defense of the unjust cause, and with such a motive entered into various actions, from which more deaths than I can number have resulted; but for which I weep and will weep for the rest of my days.

In the time in which I was Chaplain I committed the disrespect of celebrating [mass] on nine occasions, and after I had already taken up arms I absolved two people, because of extreme necessity. I did not exercise any other Priestly functions, because even then in the middle of my sin, the God of Mercies wanted to instill in me the respect due to the Altar.

All of these actions along with the others that the unspeakable temerity of my conduct in those unfortunate circumstances could have caused, even though they horrified humanity, are due to compassion, and in the same manner I express them to your Lordship so that in the use of your goodness you might have the

> pity to lift from me the impropriety that I have incurred through [these acts], and restore me in terms of the power to freely exercise the functions of my priesthood. I confess to your Lordship that my repentance is sincere, and I equally proclaim that upon [the implementation of my pardon] I will practice the spiritual activities that your Lordship imposes upon me, and that my obedience to the orders of my Prelates will be so exact that not one bit of your decrees will be missed.
>
> I petition your Lordship in this manner in order that I might receive your goodness and mercy.
>
> Pablo José Calvillo[116]

"Upstanding men" and "Acuerados"

After the indultos of a number of important regional-level creole leaders like Padre Calvillo in late 1811, the insurrection in Colotlán no longer transcended the canyons in the form of assaults on medium to large villas and cities like Jerez, Aguascalientes, and Zacatecas. However, resistance within the region did not end with the pardoning of these leaders. The majority of the pueblos of the Frontera de Colotlán remained firmly in the hands of the indios fronterizos. It would take more than two years to temporarily reestablish a measure of Spanish control in the region. In November 1811 Don Manuel Iturbe é Iraeta, the new governor of Colotlán, was forced to establish his headquarters in Teúl down in the Tlaltenango valley, rather than in San Luis de Colotlán.[117] Ever since Negrete's troops left the Frontera after their victory over the rebels in April 1811, control over the cabecera pueblo had remained uncertain, reportedly because "no upstanding man wanted to take charge [as they were] scared of falling victim to banditry."[118] When wealthy vecino Don José Joaquín Velis tried to assume control over the pueblo, his former servant José Pineda, "who captained a gang of *acuerados* from all over the place without any political plan," took Don José Joaquín to the outskirts of the pueblo and decapitated him, taking his clothing for themselves. The term acuerados or "leathery ones" referred derogatorily to a lack of proper clothing or Hispanicization. When a royalist force eventually arrived, Pineda and his followers fled to the canyons of Asqueltán, where Pineda was captured and summarily shot. Pineda's head was placed on a pole where the road to Zacatecas exited the pueblo.[119] Throughout this account a distinction is maintained between the "upstanding" vecinos and the uncivilized acuerados.

Royalist officers generated numerous reports of patrols engaging rebel bands—often described as bandits—throughout 1812 and 1813. The bulk of the rebels in the Colotlán Frontera at this point, including Pineda's acuerados, appear to be indios fronterizos, although they sometimes joined with larger groups led by creole officers from the periphery who ventured into the valleys and canyons of the Frontera.[120] Tellingly, royalist officers continued to employ the term indiada to describe the insurrection in the region, as in the case of Subdelegado Felipe Terán of Zacatecas who reported that the rebel "ringleaders formed their mob of rogues" for a rebel assault on Teocaltiche and that "the Indiada of infinite pueblos from that territory [has no doubt] recognized that their resources are very weak when the upstanding men know how to oppose the infamous efforts of that rabble."[121] The royalists usually fielded detachments of 20 to 150 men, relatively well armed and equipped, while the insurgents often fought with bows, slings, machetes, and, to a lesser degree, firearms. The rebels in the Colotlán Frontier had little access to cannons, although on July 5, 1812, Padre Álvarez destroyed two forges that several hundred rebels were constructing at the Hacienda de San Pedro de los Villalobos in the Tlaltenango district.[122]

As these events indicate, the lines of allegiance during this period reverted to substantially ethnic ones, in the sense that insurgent or bandit-driven violence tended to be exercised by primarily indigenous fronterizos against well-to-do vecinos. Parish records from the municipal archive of the vecino villa of Jerez show a series of executions of indios from the pueblos of Huejúcar and Tlalcosagua in May, June, and July 1812, for instance.[123] Periodic royalist patrols would enter the region in punitive expeditions or to attack a particularly large gathering of rebel indiadas when such groups were pinpointed. Rebel bands were often identified with a given pueblo, such as "the Gang of Mamata," which Governor Iturbe é Iraeta proved unable to attack in January 1812 after he was wounded by a stone from a sling in a confrontation with rebels in Chimaltitán.[124] However, opposition to the Spanish regime was not uniform across the region, and after three years of violent struggle former divisions among the pueblos of the Frontera resurfaced.

By the summer of 1813 royalist assaults on the rebels of the Frontera had taken a toll on the inhabitants of the region, and most rebel bands had dropped in size from groups of several hundred to smaller bands of 10 to 150. Royalist patrols now sought out rebel leaders in the canyons and backcountry more often than in pueblos full of insurgent supporters. In 1813, the Huicholes of the western pueblos of the Frontera, who had supported the insurgency since its initiation in 1810, turned against an indio cabecilla named Antonio Cañas after he employed heavy-handed methods against some of their own people. When a group of 70 royalist soldiers under the command of Teniente Macedonio Padilla from Bolaños and 20 loyalist vecinos from Totatiche entered the rough country of western Colotlán and eastern Nayarit in pursuit of Cañas, some of his Huichol followers began to drift away rather than face the soldiers. To discourage further desertion Cañas had seven of them hung, leading to a riot among his own followers that resulted in Cañas fleeing through the sierra with only 20 followers left. Padilla arranged for a party of 50 Huicholes from the pueblos of San Andrés, San Sebastian, and Santa Catarina—on the Colotlán side of Huichol country—to pursue Cañas into the rough terrain to which he had fled. The Huicholes succeeded in capturing Cañas before he could fling himself to his death from a high peak; they also detained the remaining men, women, and children who were with him. Cañas's head was hung on a pole in the pueblo of Jesús María to discourage further Huichol participation in the insurgency.[125] In another interesting turn of events, the commander of a detachment of Iturbe é Iraeta's Colotlán militia who was then stationed in Jesús María was none other than Don Manuel Campos, a vecino from Coculiten and one of the original Colotlán militia officers who had joined Calvillo's insurgents in September 1810. Campos had subsequently received a pardon from Padilla and resumed command of his militia unit.[126] As of December 1816, he was still leading royalist expeditions against rebels in the region.[127]

The interpueblo differences from the period of the Señores Colotecos in the 1780s also reappeared during the later stage of the insurgency. In April 1816 an insurgent force led by a rebel leader known as Hermosillo attacked the pueblo of Huejúcar, forcing the royalist squadron quartered in the pueblo to take refuge in the church, much like the 1780 assault led by Juanico Córdova. This time, however, the attackers apparently could not overcome the defenders. Instead, they sacked the pueblo to punish the Huejucareños who "had declared themselves in favor of the royalist cause."[128] This identification of Huejúcar as a "loyal pueblo" harkens back to their support of Villar and conflict with the Señores Colotecos in the 1780s, and demonstrates that elements of the partisan demarcation of Fronterizo identities carried through to the later period of the 1810–21 insurgency.

These echoes of past fronterizo rebellion were further confirmed after a new royalist commander, Lieutenant Colonel Mariano Urrea, received an appointment to govern the Colotlán Frontera in late 1815.[129] Like his predecessor Iturbe é Iraeta, Urrea found the interior of the Colotlán region, including San Luis de Colotlán itself, threatening and unstable. He decided instead to base his operations in Tlaltenango. Padre Don Cayetano Ibarra, the cura of San Luis de Colotlán described in chapter 4 who had feared to publish the excommunication edicts against the rebels in 1810, had also relocated to Tlaltenango at some point during the insurgency, leaving the spiritual care of San Luis de Colotlán in the hands of his subordinate, Padre Tadeo Suarez of Mezquitic. Governor Urrea appointed Don Ysidro Díaz de León—

a vecino from the vicinity of Atolinga and another pardoned former insurgent like Manuel Campos—as his lieutenant, in charge of a small garrison in San Luis de Colotlán to "safeguard the vecinos in that area." However, when word came that a rebel force led by Rafael Oropeza was en route to attack the pueblo, Lieutenant Díaz de León fled the town "on his excellent horse," leaving a number of the local vecinos to take shelter in the Casas Reales. The insurgents then set fire to the buildings, and when the men inside tried to escape they were executed. One defender, Don Vicente Gandara, remained in the burning building until Oropeza agreed to grant him a pardon after Padre Tadeo Suarez begged the insurgent leader to be merciful.[130]

The telling aspect of these incidents lies in the fact that when Oropeza's insurgents left the pueblo, at least ten prominent local indios fronterizos left with them, including Jacinto Córdova, Antonio Córdova, and Cármen Lozano–whose names stand out as members of the Señores Colotecos families from Chapter 2. When these men later returned to their homes, Governor Urrea sent word from Tlaltenango to have them arrested and brought before him, at which time he had them shot.[131] Further insight into the allegiances of the fronterizos during these events lies in the participation of Don Anselmo Pacheco, governor of San Luis de Colotlán's indigenous barrio of Soyatitán and his son, Don Gregorio. These relatives of Calixto Pacheco from Chapter 2 were called before Urrea in Tlaltenango for their tacit support of the rebels and for letting the Casas Reales burn for "more than a month." Urrea set the Pachecos free after establishing that they had also "lent some aid to the [vecino] population."[132]

Circumscribed Loyalties

The insurgent and royalist leaders waging the war of independence in the Colotlán region did not just fight for control over territory, material resources, and political authority. They also struggled over the loyalties of the region's inhabitants. Pardons played a crucial role in the reassertion of royal authority in both Colotlán and the larger colony, serving as the "carrot" to the initially besieged but powerful "stick" of the royalist military response. The pardon process served as a reintegrative force, holding together many of the traditional relationships of the New Spanish social order during the tumultuous independence period. It thus provided a basis for the eventual consensus and compromise that resulted in an independent Mexico. Although pardons were ostensibly administered to reconcile the rebellious inhabitants of New Spain with their monarch, the more consequential result was to promote reconciliation *within* New Spain. This minimized polarization along lines of class or caste and prevented the success of a critical rupture or social revolution that might have driven a greater wedge between creole elites and the popular classes, thereby stifling the development of anything approximating a French or Haitian "Revolution." Mexican independence was achieved in 1821 only after former Mexican royalists dissatisfied with the restoration of the liberal Constitution of Cádiz in Spain negotiated a compromise guaranteeing the maintenance of the Catholic religion, (official) racial equality, and political independence but, significantly, *not* substantial social change.

In understanding this ultimate social consequence of pardons, it is important to recognize that the many, varied, overlapping amnesty decrees and stipulations led to a chaotic process. The diversity of the various parties issuing pardons undercut their military effectiveness. Indeed, based upon the stated intention of the Spanish viceregal government in issuing such widespread pardon decrees—eliminating armed resistance to royal authority and reincorporating wayward rebels by making them faithful subjects of the king—the pardon process achieved mixed results for the Crown. As the introductory anecdote demonstrated, even in the first few months of the decade-long rebellion many individuals who had violated the terms of one pardon were then offered a second. This seeming disorder and confusion allowed for a fluidity and flexibility that proved crucial to the secondary, and, in the long run, more significant result of the pardon process: the establishment of creole-dominated social relations. As local vecinos traded allegiance like currency, rebels were reintegrated into their respective positions in society through the pardon process. The creole intermediaries brokering these deals, including many former insurgents, would emerge as the ascendant political class in the years to come, while pardoned indigenous rebels were considered pacified and contained.

Epilogue

> The Commander of the Corps of the Colotlán Frontier, Urrea, was in agreement with me and complied well [with our plans for independence]. But I believe that they do not love him very much around here.
>
> —Pedro Celestino Negrete, former royalist commander and supporter of the Plan de Iguala, to Agustín de Iturbide, July 1821

In 1821, former royalist officer Agustín de Iturbide organized the creole compromise that finally achieved Mexican independence, albeit in a much less radical manner than would have been the case had Padre Hidalgo's followers managed to gain the upper hand militarily in 1810 and 1811.[1] Mass amnesties in 1817 and 1820 had resulted in the pardoning of a large number of imprisoned and active insurgents, and the possibility of achieving independence through insurgent military success seemed slim.[2] The restoration of the 1812 Constitution of Cádiz after a liberal revolt in Spain in 1820 initiated elections throughout New Spain for municipal councils (*ayuntamientos*) and provincial delegates to the Spanish Cortes. This marked the political mobilization of a large sector of New Spain's creole elite, even though the insurgency had stalled militarily.[3] After conspiring with the remaining insurgent leaders in early 1821, Iturbide formulated the Plan de Iguala, guaranteeing independence from Spain as a constitutional monarchy, the maintenance of Roman Catholicism as Mexico's official religion (thereby securing the ecclesiastical fueros of the clergy), and official racial equality, in the sense that no one could be excluded from political office on the basis of racial status.

These events reflected a majority consensus regarding independence, the role of the church, and a desire to eliminate the perquisites of peninsular status. The plan's success was more representative of the population's exhaustion and weariness from nearly eleven years of devastating warfare than it was of any broad political agreement regarding the government to be developed in the new Mexican nation. This diversity of opinion would lead to political strife and limit the effectiveness of the national government for decades to come. Furthermore, the Plan de Iguala effectively eliminated any vestige of political recognition for the traditional ethnic status of groups like the indios flecheros or other repúblicas and comunes of indios; an extremely important consequence of independence in regions like Colotlán.[4] Those scholars who have examined the political process during this early postindependence period have tended to argue that Mexico's indigenous population played an important role in electoral politics, but their political power may have been overstated.[5] The Colotlán case certainly presents a very different picture of this political transition.

"They do not love him very much around here."

The best record of the social composition of the postindependence political elite in the Colotlán region is a set of correspondence from the Colotlán, Fresnillo, Juchipila, Tlaltenango and Aguascalientes districts to the Ayuntamiento of Zacatecas recording the municipal-level electors in January 1821.[6] The lists reflect the political ascendancy of the region's prominent vecinos and conspicuously exclude any participation on the part of the indio fronterizo population. Instead, prominent royalists and a few former insurgent creole indultados formed the bulk of the electorate. Among them was José María Medina, Padre Calvillo's nephew-in-law, whose loyalties had undulated between Calvillo and the royalists during the insurgency and who had participated in the betrayal of the Najeras.[7] Medina and a relative of his served as electors for Valle de Huejúcar. By 1822 Medina was also serving as an officer in the newly created militia of the Gobierno de Colotlán under Iturbide's Mexican Empire.[8]

Ysidro Díaz de León was an 1821 elector from Tlaltenango. Díaz de León had joined with the insurgents for sixteen days during 1811 and subsequently received a pardon. As described in chapter 5, Governor Urrea later appointed him to serve as the lieutenant of the royalist garrison in San Luis de Colotlán, after which Díaz de León fled "on his excellent horse" when word of Oropeza's approaching rebel force reached the pueblo. Joining him in representing Tlaltenango were Don José Vital Magallanes and Don Juan Magallanes.[9] Don Vital was also an indultado, who had claimed in 1811 to have been violently forced to assist the insurgents when they occupied his valley.[10] Before the insurgency Don Juan had waged a long-running legal battle with the Indians of Tlaltenango, Tocatique, Sicacalco, and Teocaltiche, who all had maintained in 1803 that he and the Indians of the pueblo of Jalpa had prohibited them from cultivating their communal land at a site called Morones.[11]

A number of other electors, including Padre Tadeo Suarez, José María Alegría, Pedro de Vivanco, and the Padilla family, form part of this pattern of creole dominance during the transition from a colonial to a national political structure.[12] Antonio de Vivanco, head of the family and the first Marqués, served as commander of the Junta de Guerra that suppressed the Señores

Colotecos in the 1780s. His son-in-law José Morán, also known as the Marqués de Vivanco, joined Iturbide's Army of the Three Guarantees and then abandoned him after the 1823 Plan de Casa Mata.[13] Macedonio Padilla had been a signatory to an 1815 declaration of loyalty to the king, written on behalf of the mining interests at Bolaños, and it was he who led the royalist expedition against Antonio Cañas and hung the rebel cabecilla's head on a pole in the pueblo of Jesús María.[14] Not only were the indios fronterizos excluded from political power and representation of their communities in the new political order, but many of the men who did represent the Frontera pueblos had historically opposed fronterizo interests.

This is perhaps most evident in the fact that Don Mariano Urrea himself, still serving as the governor and military commander of the Colotlán Frontera at this point, directed the entire 1821 electoral process in the region.[15] As discussed in chapter 5, Urrea had executed a number of prominent members of San Luis de Colotlán's fronterizo families just a few years earlier. Roughly six months after the electoral juntas, military commanders from the Zacatecas and Aguascalientes region declared their support for Agustín Iturbide's plan for independence. Pedro Celestino Negrete, the royalist commander who had crushed Padre Calvillo's army at San Luis de Colotlán in April 1811, was one of the most important supporters of this plan and served as Iturbide's military commander for much of western and northern Mexico. Having just traveled through part of the Colotlán region on his way from Zacatecas to Aguascalientes, Negrete wrote to Iturbide on July 6 that "the Commander of the Corps of the Colotlán Frontier, Urrea, was in agreement with me and complied well [with our plans for independence]. But I believe that they do not love him very much around here."[16]

Vecino Political Ascendancy and Fronterizo Independence

The conspicuous absence of indios fronterizos from the ranks of these 1821 local political elites shows that independence in the Colotlán region marked the political attainment of vecino designs for the Frontera. It did not redress many of the concerns and conflicts that had originally spurred fronterizo participation in the insurgency. Since the early-colonial integration of the Tlaxcalan colonists into the region, the pueblos of Colotlán had combined indigenous strategies of resistance with service to the Spanish empire to preserve autonomy and create a special status as indios fronterizos. Following the successful conquest of Nayarit in the 1720s, neighboring land owners and Spanish officials had gradually encroached upon pueblo lands and attempted to abolish or ignore the privileges and freedoms that had traditionally accompanied Frontier Indian status. The establishment of the mining center of Bolaños heightened this cultural conflict, fueling vecino efforts to reduce the power of the fronterizo militias. Fronterizo leaders like the Señores Colotecos had attempted to assert local control over the Frontera and address the pueblos' concerns, adapting to new ethnic configurations such as the integration of casta newcomers into some Frontera pueblos. As the nineteenth century drew nearer, imperial reforms, increased demographic pressures, and changing late colonial conceptions of race exacerbated conflict with neighboring vecinos. These developments served to redefine the status of indio fronterizo along sharper cultural lines, more conducive to vecino interests.

During the insurrection, the indios fronterizos rebelled against wealthy Spanish landowners and merchants, but their alignment with creole leaders channeled insurgent activity in directions that did not always mesh with fronterizo aims. In a strategic, military sense, the Spanish won the battle for the loyalties of creole insurgent leaders when they suppressed the most dramatic phase of the rebellion and reintegrated many rebels into New Spanish society through the pardon process. As the decade of fighting wore on, the insurgency took on a more ethnic undertone, leading to the eventual destruction of the more virulent and locally driven strains of rebellion. With the defection of creole elites like Padre Calvillo, José de Medina, Manuel Campos, and others, the rebellion was pushed back into the Colotlán region and then smashed into pockets of rural resistance and banditry. Consequently, many creoles who had abandoned the insurgency returned to positions of power in the Frontera. By 1821 this resulted in a relatively unified creole elite on the one hand and a splintered and battered fronterizo population on the other.

The political reconfiguration of the Colotlán region that accompanied Mexican independence transformed what was once a center of indigenous autonomy into an official periphery. Split up among the new states of Jalisco, Zacatecas, Aguascalientes, and Nayarit, the fronterizo communities saw their recent enemies rise to powerful new positions in the postindependence era. The monopolization of political power in the hands of the creole vecino elite after independence did not mean that fronterizo power was eradicated, only that it was dispersed and delegitimized. Local protests and social unrest arose in the region in the decades after independence. The banditry that began with the suppression of the earlier phase of the independence struggle continued for generations.[17] In the midnineteenth century, local interests fed into the ability of regional caudillo Manuel Lozada to effectively secede from the national government and maintain regional autonomy in Nayarit and the Colotlán sierra for more than twenty years until he was captured and executed in 1873.[18] In fact, much of Mariano Azuela's classic novel of the Mexican Revolution, *Los de Abajo*, is set in and around the canyon of Juchipila, all along the eastern edge of the old Colotlán Frontier.[19] Future research on the people of the Colotlán canyons and sierra may confirm that vestiges of the indio fronterizo identity—the product of a rich and contentious colonial cultural legacy—survived well into the modern era. Nonetheless, the period leading up to and through Mexican independence transformed the indios fronterizos in the eyes of their neighbors, from the indigenous allies of the conquest and colonial era to the acuerados and bandits of the royalist resurgence and early 1820s. Having once preserved the privileged status of Indian conquistadors, they would continue to be labeled with the mark of rebels in the decades to come.

Glossary

alcabala Sales tax.
alcalde Town mayor.
alcalde mayor Royal district governor, based in a town or villa.
alférez Lieutenant.
alguacil mayor Constable.
alhondigaje Storage fees.
arrendatarios Tenant farmers or small ranchers.
asesor general Chief legal adviser.
audiencia High court.
ayuntamiento Municipal council.
bachiller Individual with a bachelor's degree.
cabecilla Ringleader or bandit chief; someone who instigates unrest.
cacique Hereditary indigenous chief; later used more broadly to refer to a rural strongman.
capitán general Military governor.
capitán protector Official charged with overseeing a given number of indigenous pueblos. The capitán protector of Colotlán functioned as the governor of the Frontera de Colotlán and also held the title of capitán general.
cabecera District capital (in this case, San Luis de Colotlán).
casta Person of a particular racial "caste"; most often used for individuals of mixed African, European, and Native American ancestry.
caudillo Personalistic local or regional strongman, especially in a military sense.
Chichimecs Generic Nahuatl-derived term used to refer to "unpacified" indigenous groups in central and northern New Spain.
cofradía Lay religious confraternity, often used to raise funds for celebrations and the indigent.

coima Kickback or bribe.

Colotecos Late colonial colloquial ethnonym for the people of Colotlán. See also "Señores Colotecos."

comisionado Individual empowered by political authorities to hold a certain position or carry out a specific task.

pueblo conquistador Conception of the pueblos of the Colotlán region as conquering populations according to the Conquest model.

comisario general Franciscan official with authority over provincials.

común A given community with certain inherent rights.

corregidor Equivalent of a royal district governor, based in a town or villa.

coyote Individual with three indigenous grandparents and one Spanish grandparent according to the casta system.

criollo (creole) Person of European or African descent born in the Americas; in New Spain usually referred to someone of Spanish descent.

cura Parish priest.

cura doctinero Regular priest ministering to a doctrina.

cura propietario Priest who has been granted a parish benefice for life.

diezmero Tithe collector.

doctrina Indigenous congregation of new or nonacculturated Christians.

encomienda Royal grant of the right to the labor or tribute of a designated group of indios

fiscal Chief legal counselor.

fronterizos Predominantly indigenous inhabitants of the Colotlán Frontier.

Frontera de Colotlán Territorial designation for the Colotlán Frontier, used by both Spanish colonial authorities and the inhabitants of the region and surrounding area.

fuero Privilege granted to a specific group exempting them from tribute or other obligations, sometimes (as in the case of the ecclesiastical fuero) granting immunity from prosecution in royal courts.

gremio Guild or fraternity.

gobierno Basic political district governed by a gobernador, often in frontier areas.

hacendado Owner of a large estate, or hacienda.

hacienda Large privately owned estate, with both livestock and agricultural production.

Huejucareños Members of the pueblo of Huejúcar.

indio Term used by inhabitants of New Spain for members of the indigenous population. This status connoted certain rights and responsibilities, including tribute and special legal status.

indios bárbaros Literally "barbarous Indians," referring to unassimilated or unacculturated, indigenous groups.

indios flecheros Indio militiamen. The term flecheros both signified the literal armament of the militiamen (bows and arrows) and categorized their auxiliary and irregular status in relation to standard militia companies.

indios fronterizos Literally, "frontier Indians." Sometimes translated as Indian frontiersmen. Signifies the special status of the inhabitants of many of the indigenous pueblos in the Colotlán area and other places designated frontiers. Also known as naturales fronterizos, they served as militia and settlers among other "unpacified" indigenous groups and in return enjoyed special privileges.

indios hidalgos Indian noblemen; the Tlaxcalan colonists who received special privileges from the Crown in return for settling in the Colotlán region.

indios ladinos Hispanicized, Spanish-speaking, acculturated Indians.

indios puros Individuals of purely indigenous ancestry, who could claim full status as members of an indigenous pueblo and república.

india Tlaxcalteca Indigenous woman descended from the Tlaxcalan colonists.

inquilinos Tenants.

instrumentos públicos Public records.

intendente Intendant; governor of a late colonial administrative district known as an ***intendencia*** (intendancy).

juez eclesiástico Designated ecclesiastical magistrate for a given parish.

jueces superiores Magistrates of the high court.

Junta de Guerra Council of war.

justicias District governors or their lieutenants, generically used for any wielder of imperial justice.

justiciales Officeholders of an indigenous pueblo.

ladino Hispanicized, Spanish-speaking, acculturated.

latifundios Large estates.

lobo Person of indigenous and African ancestry, who was more indigenous than African.

mezcales Maguey (or agave) plants. Used in the production of mezcal. The fibers are harvested to to make pita thread, utilized in the art of piteado, or embroidered leather. Colotlán has remained the center of this art form up to the present day.

mestizo Person of mixed Spanish-indigenous ancestry.

militares Military men.

mulato Person of mixed Spanish-African (or sometimes indigenous-African) ancestry.

mulato advenedizo Person of mixed Spanish-African ancestry with free status who joined indigenous communities in the Colotlán region. "*Advenedizo*" could signify "upstart," "immigrant," or newcomer.

naturales See *indios*.

New Spain Spanish viceroyalty, including all of Central America, present-day Mexico, and most of what is now the western United States.

Nueva Galicia (also New Galicia) Western portion of New Spain, including most of the present-day states of Jalisco, Nayarit, Zacatecas, Aguascalientes, and Durango.

obvenciones Fees paid periodically to parish priests.

oidor Judge of an audiencia.

padrones Census records.

partidarios Partisan supporters.

los Pocos "The lesser ones." Refers in this case to the minority faction of individuals (many of uncertain racial status) in the pueblo of Huejúcar and a couple of surrounding pueblos who supported the Señores Colotecos.

pasajes Literally "passages," used here to refer to places in the Valley of Ameca, similar to gaps.

peninsulars People of Spanish ancestry born in Spain.

principales Chief members of an indigenous pueblo, responsible for matters of pueblo government. Held pueblo-level office such as regidor, alguacil mayor, or gobernador.

provincial High-ranking Franciscan official.

protocolos Notarial records.

pueblo Indigenous town or village. Distinct from a villa or city in that it was directly subject to royal control, without its own charter.

pueblos de adentro Interior pueblos in the Colotlán region, usually to the west and south.

rancheria Unincorporated rural settlement, smaller than a pueblo.

Real Hacienda Royal Treasury.

reducción Relocation of indios to a fixed settlement.

repartimiento Allotment of forced indigenous labor.

república de indios "Republic of Indians," the political body of an indigenous pueblo, officially recognized by the Spanish government. The "Señores de Republicas" were the officeholders, with the "empleos de la Republica" being the offices themselves.

Señores Colotecos Literally, "the Lords of Colotlán," one of the titles used by Juanico Córdova and his fellow Cabecillas.

serrano Person from the highlands.

sitio de ganado mayor Unit of land, about one square league, considered appropriate for a cattle ranch.

subdelegado Governor of a subdistrict within an intendancy.

tobacco rents Income generated through the royal monopoly on the sale of tobacco.

teniente Lieutenant, deputy of a governor, either civil or military in nature, often given jurisdiction over a small territory of one or two pueblos.

teniente de cura Assistant to the head priest of a parish; could also be the chief priest of a smaller parish.

teniente general Lieutenant military governor.

Teulenses Inhabitants of the pueblo of San Andrés del Teúl.

tierras y montes Lands and mountains.

Tlaxcalans Allies of the Spanish during the conquest of Mexico. In 1591 several hundred Tlaxcalan families were sent to colonize various frontier areas of the viceroyalty (including Colotlán) to help acculturate unassimilated indigenous groups. The Tlaxcalans were granted various rights and privileges in perpetuity.

tochos Slang for indigenous people of Caxcán ancestry.

vaqueros Cowboys.

vara A measure of land. 1 vara equals .83 meters.

vecinos Property-owning citizens of a pueblo, villa, or city. In colonial Spanish America, the term was often used by indigenous communities to refer to Spanish, creole, or Hispanicized residents of neighboring settlements.

viejos Village elders, literally "old ones."

villa Relatively large and officially recognized and incorporated town.

Villareños Supporters of deposed Governor Villar.

Notes

Introduction

1. In November 2014, this campus, known as the Centro Universitario del Norte, publicized a new initiative to offer room and board, child care, and security in an effort to get more indigenous students to enroll in the university. "Buscan que más indígenas estudien in CUNorte," *El Informador*, Nov. 21, 2014.

2. Few scholars have investigated the role of indigenous identity during the Mexican independence period, even though ethnicity and cultural relationships are of great interest to scholars of Latin America. Among the important exceptions are Peter Guardino, *The Time of Liberty: Popular Culture in Oaxaca, 1750–1850* (Durham, N.C.: Duke University Press, 2005), and Eric Van Young, *The Other Rebellion: Popular Violence, Ideology, and the Mexican Struggle for Independence, 1810–1821* (Stanford, Calif.: Stanford University Press, 2001). Jordana Dym, *From Sovereign Villages to National States: City, State, and Federation in Central America, 1759–1839* (Albuquerque: University of New Mexico Press, 2006), examines the changing nature of pueblo governance during the independence period, although her study is focused on Central America. By paying special attention to local politics and mentalities, their work furnishes an important analysis of the lives of the popular classes in this period.

3. Material and structural explanations played an important role in the earlier literature on this period of Latin American history. Imperial reforms and agrarian pressures were often portrayed as the driving forces in the disintegration of Spain's American empire. Nancy Farriss provided an important transitional work for the development of the first of these two paradigms for explaining the revolts in *Crown and Clergy in Colonial Mexico, 1759–1821: The Crisis of Ecclesiastical Privilege* (London: Athlone, 1968). She argued that (primarily mid-to-late) eighteenth-century imperial reorganization known as the Bourbon reforms presented a threat that drove many parish priests to incite their parishioners to rebel openly against the viceregal government. In the 1970s and 1980s, a number of scholars began delving into the broader structural factors underlying the eruption of insurrection in 1810. Brian

Hamnett, for instance, concentrated on Bourbon-era socioeconomic factors, such as control over land and labor in *Roots of Insurgency: Mexican Regions, 1750–1824* (Cambridge, U.K.: Cambridge University Press, 1986), but he hinted at the presence of regional and even local variances when he suggested on page 202 that "the roots of insurgency . . . lay precisely in the localized tensions which the broader movement often subsumed." This history of the indios fronterizos is designed to shed further light on these "localized tensions."

4. Matthew Restall presented some of the principal themes of this new approach in *Seven Myths of the Spanish Conquest* (Oxford, U.K.: Oxford University Press, 2003). Chapter 3, "Invisible Warriors: The Myth of the White Conquistador," underscores the role of indigenous and African warriors in the process of conquest. The recent *Indian Conquistadors: Indigenous Allies in the Conquest of Mesoamerica*, edited by Laura E. Matthew and Michel R. Oudijk (Norman: University of Oklahoma Press, 2007), showcases new scholarship, demonstrating that the scope and variety of indigenous conquistadors were wider than conventional histories have recognized. The essays also question conventional narratives of conquest.

5. Examples of this "New Conquest History," many of which draw on indigenous-language source material, include Matthew Restall, *Maya Conquistador* (Boston: Beacon Press, 1998); Lisa Sousa and Kevin Terraciano, "The 'Original Conquest' of Oaxaca: Nahua and Mixtec Accounts of the Spanish Conquest," *Ethnohistory* 50, no. 2 (Spring 2003): 349–400; Stephanie Wood, *Transcending Conquest: Nahua Views of Spanish Colonial Mexico* (Norman: University of Oklahoma Press, 2003); John F. Chuchiak IV, "The Sins of the Fathers: Franciscan Friars, Parish Priests, and the Sexual Conquest of the Yucatec Maya, 1545–1808," *Ethnohistory* 54, no. 1 (Winter 2007): 69–127; Yanna Yannakakis, *The Art of Being In-between: Native Intermediaries, Indian Identity, and Local Rule in Colonial Oaxaca* (Durham, N.C.: Duke University Press, 2008); María Castañeda de la Paz, "Central Mexican Indigenous Coats of Arms and the Conquest of Mesoamerica" *Ethnohistory* 56, no. 1 (Winter 2009): 125–61; Ida Altman's *The War for Mexico's West: Indians and Spaniards in New Galicia, 1524–1550* (Albuquerque: University of New Mexico Press, 2010); and Laura E. Matthew, *Memories of Conquest: Becoming Mexicano in Colonial Guatemala* (Chapel Hill: University of North Carolina Press, 2012). Gonzalo Lamana applies a similarly novel approach to the history of the Andean conquest(s) in *Domination without Dominance: Inca-Spanish Encounters in Early Colonial Peru* (Durham, N.C.: Duke University Press, 2008).

6. In the introduction to the *Indian Conquistadors*, 14–15, Susan Schroeder identifies four categories of indios conquistadores (at least for the sixteenth century): forced auxilliaries, temporary volunteers, warrior-colonists, and settlers. The indios fronterizos discussed in this chapter might best be described as a mixture of the third and fourth categories: their ancestors having settled in the region as colonists, they took on the role of frontier militia.

7. Restall designates the conventional interpretation—that the conquest of Mesoamerica was undertaken and completed in a few decades—as the "Myth of Completion" in Chapter 4 of *Seven Myths of the Spanish Conquest*. New studies continue to disprove this myth. Yanna Yannakakis has tracked the role of indigenous conquistadors in Oaxaca through the sixteenth, seventeenth, and much of the eighteenth centuries in *The Art of Being In-between*.

8. The use of the term Colotlán Frontier in this study is a direct translation of "La Frontera de Colotlán," the official designation used by Spanish colonial authorities to describe the large gobierno constituting most of the communities included in this book. Outsiders and inhabitants alike sometimes referred to the region in the plural, "Las Fronteras de Colotlán."

9. My use of the term "Frontier Indians" to describe the indigenous inhabitants of the Colotlán region is a direct translation of the Spanish indios fronterizos. As noted, it was used by these communities as a self-identifier to mark the special status earned through their participation in the colonial project. The term indios flecheros or "Indian archers" was also also used and was reflective of their service as militiamen.

10. Examples of other revolts commonly considered "precursors" include the comuneros in New Granada, a 1765 tax revolt in Quito, and numerous other rebellions throughout the Americas. Brazil was not exempt from late colonial conspiracies and revolts, either, as in the case of the 1789 Inconfidenca Mineira, considered by many Brazilians as an important precursor of their own eventual independence. Sinclair Thomson's *We Alone Will Rule: Native Andean Politics in the Age of Insurgency* (Madison: University of Wisconsin Press, 2003) provides an in-depth look at the sociocultural factors contributing to the Catarista portion of the Andean rebellions. Sergio Serulnikov, *Subverting Colonial Authority: Challenges to Spanish Rule in Eighteenth-Century Southern Andes* (Durham, N.C.: Duke University Press, 2003), analyzes the nature of indigenous leadership during those same events. See the last chapter of Ward Stavig's *The World of Túpac Amaru: Conflict, Community, and Identity in Colonial Peru* (Lincoln: University of Nebraska Press, 1999) for a discussion of the social relations underpinning the revolt. Other works include Alberto Flores Galindo's *Túpac Amaru II, 1780: sociedad colonial y sublevaciones populares* (Lima: Retablo de Papel Ediciones, 1976) and Ulises Casas's *Los comuneros en el contexto de la lucha de clases* (Bogotá: Galas de Colombia, 1983).

11. For New Spain, the social and political implications of the Bourbon reforms have been studied by a number of influential scholars, including Nancy Farriss, Hugh M. Hamill, Brian Hamnett, and John Tutino. Tutino's *From Insurrection to Revolution in Mexico: Social Bases of Agrarian Violence, 1750–1940* (Princeton, N.J.: Princeton University Press, 1986) provided a systemic analysis of rural violence and protest. Tutino explained the independence revolts as a function of economic stresses placed on agrarian production, an analysis that he extended to explain episodic rural violence throughout most of the modern era. François-Xavier Guerra, in *Modernidad e Independencias: Ensayos sobre las revoluciones hispánicas* (Madrid: MAPFRE, 1992) and elsewhere laid the groundwork for reinterpreting Spanish-American independence as a syncretic response to modern political thought that incorporated significant elements of the colonial past. In *The Independence of Spanish America* (Cambridge, U.K.: Cambridge University Press, 1998), Jaime E. Rodríguez O. emphasized the important role of events in Spain that set the stage for Spanish-American independence.

12. Examples abound. R. Douglas Cope's analysis of the Mexico City *tumulto* of 1692 in *The Limits of Racial Domination: Plebian Society in Colonial Mexico City, 1660–1720* (Madison: University of Wisconsin Press, 1994) provides a detailed look at the racial undercurrents of that incident. Jane Landers traces the evolution of an early-sixteenth-century maroon community into a recognized free black town in

"Cimarron and Citizen: African Ethnicity, Corporate Identity, and the Evolution of Free Black Towns in the Spanish circum-Caribbean," in *Slaves, Subjects, and Subversives: Blacks in Colonial Latin America*, eds. Jane G. Landers and Barry M. Robinson (Albuquerque: University of New Mexico Press, 2006), 111–45.

13. The field of postcolonial studies brought a new emphasis on cultural identity to the study of the Latin American colonial experience. Partha Chatterjee's *The Nation and Its Fragments: Colonial and Postcolonial Histories* (Princeton, N.J.: Princeton University Press, 1993) portrayed colonialism as fundamentally connected to racial exclusivity. For applications of this methodology to Latin America, see Susan Deans-Smith, "Culture, Power, and Society in Colonial Mexico," *Latin American Research Review* 33, no. 1 (1998): 257–77; Patricia Seed, "Poststructuralism in Postcolonial History," *The Maryland Historian* 24, no. 1 (1993): 9–28; Robin Fiddian, ed., *Postcolonial Perspectives on the Cultures of Latin America and Lusophone Africa* (Liverpool, England: Liverpool University Press, 2000); and Mabel Moraña, Enrique Dussel, and Carlos A. Jáuregui, eds., *Coloniality at Large: Latin America and the Postcolonial Debate* (Durham, N.C., and London: Duke University Press, 2008).

14. In *We Alone Will Rule*, Thomson analyzes the role of remembered indigenous pasts in the Great Rebellion in Upper Peru, as does Nicholas A. Robins in *Genocide and Millennialism in Upper Peru: The Great Rebellion of 1780–1782* (Westport, Conn.: Praeger, 2002). Robins presents the actions of the rebels against the Spaniards as an atypical case of genocide.

15. José María Miquel i Vergés, *Diccionario de Insurgentes* (Mexico City: Editorial Porrua, 1969). A Catalán nationalist, Miquel i Vergés was one of a number of prominent Spanish historians who moved to Mexico in 1939 as a result of the Spanish Civil War. Javier Malagón Barcelló, *El historiador español exiliado en México* (Mexico City: El Colegio de México, 2012), 106. Miquel i Vergés remained in Mexico until his death in 1964, and his *Diccionario de Insurgentes*, compiled over the course of his career and published posthumously, contains some 4,000 individual sketches of Mexican insurgents, with associated references.

16. "Calvillo condujó a Guadalajara 7,000 indios, grupo que fue adiestrado en el uso de la flecha y que al fin dieron pésimo resultado en la famosa batalla de Puente de Calderón." Miquel i Vergés, *Diccionario de Insurgentes*, 108. Calvillo's first name is mistakenly given as "José Pablo" in the entry.

17. The early historians of the conspiracies, protests, and insurrections leading up to the independence of New Spain constructed their studies as biographies of the most prominent insurgents. The lives of Miguel Hidalgo y Costilla and José María Morelos y Pavón were glorified for at least the century and a half following their revolt in biographies and national histories, beginning with classic works such as Carlos María de Bustamante's *Cuadro histórico de la Revolución Mexicana, iniciada el 15 de septiembre de 1810 por el c. Miguel Hidalgo y Costilla, cura del pueblo de Dolores en el obispado de Michoacán*. (Mexico City: Ediciones de la Comisión Nacional para la Celebración del Sesquicentenario de la Proclamación de la Independencia Nacional y del Cincuentenario de la Revolución Mexicana, 1961), and Lucas Alamán's *Historia de Méjico desde los primeros moviminetos que prepararon su independencia en el año 1808 hasta la época presente* (Mexico City: Impr. de J. M. Lara, 1849–52).

18. The lack of historical memory of the colonial region known as the Colotlán Frontier is similar to the fate of San José de Gracia, famously "remembered" in Luis Gonzalez's *San José de Gracia: Mexican Village in Transition*, trans. John Upton (Austin: University of Texas Press, 1974).

19. Technically, the Frontera de Colotlán was sometimes included in the Provincias Internas, but the distinction still holds.

20. The Fronteras de Colotlán officially ceased to exist after independence, as did many of the colonial identities that had evolved in conjunction with the region itself. The historiography of the central-western Sierra Madre during the colonial and independence periods primarily includes municipal studies, but most have lost a sense of the regional identity that played such an important role in the lives of its inhabitants throughout the colonial period. Of this group, *Historia de Colotlán* (Colotlán, Jalisco: R. H. Ortega, 1991), eds. Renato Haro Ortega et al., is the most useful, as it begins with the Spaniards' first entrance into the region and traces (albeit sporadically) the development of the area throughout the colonial period. María del Carmen Velazquez Chávez's *Colotlán: Doble frontera contra los bárbaros* (Mexico City: Universidad Nacional Autónoma de México, 1961) also provides brief commentary on the Colotlán region's status in the late colonial period, but her work is much more valuable for the primary documents it contains, including the reproduction of a series of 1783 reports on the gobierno of Colotlán initiated by Viceroy Matías de Gálvez that includes several padrones from the district's cabeceras.

Bernardo Carlos Casas's detailed study of the city of Tlaltenango and the immediate surrounding area also provides brief but helpful information regarding the development of that particular district, including sporadic demographic data from several of Tlaltenango's *padrones* (colonial census sheets). Bernardo Carlos Casas, *Tlaltenango: una ciudad amurallada* (Guadalajara, México: Impre-Jal, 1986). In his *Monografia del municipio de Calvillo* (Aguascalientes, Mexico: Gobierno del Estado de Aguascalientes, 1991), Toribio Hernández-López furnishes similar information concerning the pueblo of Valle de Huejúcar, in the eastern portion of the greater Colotlán region, now renamed Calvillo and part of the state of Aguascalientes. The *Monografía* provides relatively little information about the larger indigenous population outside of the close vicinity of the pueblo itself. Gordon Darkenwald produced a study of the municipality of Calvillo in the early twentieth century, *Calvillo: An Isolated Mexican Community* (master's thesis, Clark University, 1933), that includes excellent topographical information, illustrating the remote setting of the region.

21. Several works with a slightly broader focus discuss the histories of the modern Mexican states of Jalisco, Zacatecas, Aguascalientes, and Nayarit from a conventional perspective, providing some information relevant to the late colonial status of the indigenous population of the greater Colotlán region, but only to the degree that it fits into the standard national narratives. See, for instance, Elías Amador, *Bosquejo histórico de Zacatecas* (Zacatecas, Mexico: Tall. Tip. Pedroza, 1943); Richard L. Garner, "Zacatecas, 1750–1821: The Study of a Late Colonial Mexican City" (PhD diss., University of Michigan, 1970); José María Muriá et al., *Jalisco, una historia compartida* (Guadalajara, México: Gobierno del Estado de Jalisco, 1987); Agustín R. González, *Historia del Estado de Aguascalientes* (Aguascalientes, Mexico: Tip. de F. Antúnez, 1974); and Jesús Gómez Serrano, *Aguascalientes en la historia, 1786–*

1920 (Aguascalientes, Mexico: Gobierno del Estado de Aguascalientes, 1988). José Antonio Gutiérrez Gutiérrez's takes a more inclusive regional approach in *Aguascalientes y su región de influencia hasta 1810: sociedad y política* (Guadalajara, Mexico: Sistema de Educación Media Superior de la Universidad de Guadalajara: Amigos de la Historia de los Altos de Jalisco, 1998). Usually defined in contrast to the term gente de razón (literally "rational people," or non-indios), gente de pueblo refers to the primarily indigenous popular classes. These studies draw from and intersect with many of the more prominent early studies of the independence period, such as Alamán, *Historia de Méjico*; Ernesto Higuera, *Hidalgo; reseña biográfica con una iconografía del iniciador de nuestra independencia* (Mexico City: Colección Medallones Mexicanos, 1955); José Mancisidor, *Hidalgo, Morelos, Guerrero* (Mexico City: Editorial Grijalbo, 1956); Hugh M. Hamill Jr., *The Hidalgo Revolt: Prelude to Mexican Independence* (Gainesville: University of Florida Press, 1966).

By far the most useful reference work for this region during the colonial period is Peter Gerhard, *The North Frontier of New Spain* (Princeton, N.J.: Princeton University Press, 1982), a historical geography that details the development of the northwestern portion of the viceroyalty on a district-by-district basis. Gerhard's excellent and comprehensive study of the political structure of northern New Spain provides extensive information on every district in the region during the colonial period, and it proved singularly valuable as I initially worked through the demographic and jurisdictional history of the region.

22. The problematic results of the often arbitrary, geometric borders imposed by European colonial regimes without much regard for African cultural variance are well known. See, for instance, Ruth Roach Pierson et al., eds., *Nation, Empire, Colony: Historicizing Gender and Race* (Bloomington: Indiana University Press, 1998); Alfred Abioseh Jarrett, *The Under-Development of Africa: Colonialism, Neo-Colonialism, and Socialism* (Lanham, Md.: University Press of America, 1996); and Mahmood Mamdani, *Citizen and Subject: Contemporary Africa and the Legacy of Late Colonialism* (Princeton, N.J.: Princeton University Press, 1996).

23. The database includes entries for 802 insurgents and a smaller number of royalist officials. It was compiled from the following sources: AGN, Indiferente de Guerra, vol. 109b, exp. 1, folios 1–194, 1791; AHEA Judicial-Penal, caja 33, exp. 30; caja 34, exp. 6; caja 47, exp. 18; caja 284, exp. 18, caja 288, exp. 24; AHEZ Fondo Poder Judicial Colonial, caja 22, exp. 20; Fondo Poder Judicial Civil, caja 55, exp. 28; caja 57, exps. 9, 21–34; Fondo Ayuntamiento de Zacatecas, Serie Cabildo, Subserie Acuerdos y Despachos, Cronología 1629–1824, caja 1; Archivo Parroquial de Huejúcar, Jal.; Archivo de la Real Audiencia de Guadalajara, held at the Biblioteca Pública del Estado de Jalisco (BPEJ) Ramo Bienes de Difuntos, caja 197, exp. 8; prog.1943; caja 202, exp. 4, prog. 1994; caja 202, exp. 12, prog. 2002; caja 202, exp. 13, prog. 2003; caja 202, exp. 14, prog. 2004; caja 204, exp. 2, prog. 2012; caja 204, exp. 6, prog. 2016; caja 210, exp. 2, prog. 2081; caja 210, exp. 5, prog. 2084; caja 242, exp. 11, prog. 2647; caja 242, exp. 3, prog. 2639; caja 251, exp. 21, prog. 2775; Ramo Civil, caja 1, exp. 174–75, prog. 1944; caja 1, exp. 194, Ramo Criminal, caja 2, exp. 16; caja 7, exps. 2, 6, and 12; caja 9, exp. 14; caja 10, exp. 6; caja 15, exp. 1; caja 17, exp. 15; caja 22, exps. 2 and 8; caja 23, exps. 4, 7, and 9; caja 24, exps. 7–8; caja 31, exp. 19; caja 33, exps. 1–523; caja 41, exps. 4, 9,

and 24; caja 42, exp. 23; caja 44, exp. 1; caja 58, exp. 4; caja 64, exps. 8 and 18; caja 66, exp. 7; caja 68, exp. 1; caja 109, exp. 5; caja 110, exp. 3; caja 114, exp. 2; caja 118, exp. 13; caja 167, exp. 4; and Ramo Manuscritos, V10E4, V10E4, V37E70, V41E38. When statements are made in the chapter based on analysis of these data, the source will be identified as Insurgent Database. Additional information for the database was also drawn from David Carbajal López, *La Minería en Bolaños*, 1748–1810 (Colotlán, Jalisco: Universidad de Guadalajara-Campus Universitario del Norte, 2002), 146–48, 216–17; Van Young, *The Other Rebellion*, 98; and Figueroa and Yguiniz, *Biblioteca Histórica Jalisciense*, 203–14.

24. The growth of Borderlands scholarship helped to fuel this transition, and recent works on particular areas of northern New Spain have infused studies of frontier settings with a heavy dose of ethnohistorical emphasis. This work attempts to examine cultural interchange from more than just the European or Euro-American viewpoint, or even to place indigenous perspectives in the forefront of historical analysis. Donna J. Guy and Thomas E. Sheridan, eds., *Contested Ground: Comparative Frontiers on the Northern and Southern Edges of the Spanish Empire* (Tucson: University of Arizona Press, 1998); Cynthia Radding, *Wandering Peoples: Colonialism, Ethnic Spaces, and Ecological Frontiers in Northwestern Mexico, 1700–1850* (Durham, N.C.: Duke University Press, 1997); David J. Weber, *The Spanish Frontier in North America* (New Haven, Conn.: Yale University Press, 1992); and Daniel Usner, *Indians, Settlers, and Slaves in a Frontier Exchange Economy: The Lower Mississippi Valley before 1783* (Chapel Hill: University of North Carolina Press, 1992).

25. Also occasionally referred to in the plural, "Las Fronteras de Colotlán."

26. Radding, *Wandering Peoples*, 310. Like this study of Colotlán, Radding's approach to the history of Sonora's indigenous communities privileges ethnic relations and cultural transformation as primary factors in shaping broader social and economic structures. However, Radding also positions herself in the sphere of subaltern studies by focusing on the particular experience of peasant communities and writing "history from below" in an effort to present previously overlooked perspectives.

27. For further reading on mining in this region during the colonial era, see Peter Bakewell, *Silver Mining and Society in Colonial Mexico: Zacatecas, 1546–1700* (Cambridge, U.K.: Cambridge University Press, 1971), and David Brading, *Miners and Merchants in Bourbon Mexico*, 1763–1810 (Cambridge, U.K.: Cambridge University Press, 1971).

28. The development of this identity is discussed in detail in subsequent chapters. The term indios fronterizos (frontier Indians) signified the special status of the inhabitants of many of the indigenous pueblos in the area; they served as militia against the more "barbarous" groups to the north (and to the west in the sierra of Nayarit up until the 1720s), and enjoyed exemptions from tribute and other privileges. AGN, Indios, vol. 44, exp. 100, 126–27, 1720.

29. The term vecino referred to property-owning citizens of a pueblo, villa, or city. My use of the term in this book follows that of the frontier indigenous communities, who employed it in more specific reference to Spanish, creole, or Hispanicized residents of neighboring settlements.

Chapter 1

1. Again, see Restall, *Maya Conquistador*; Sousa and Terraciano, "The 'Original Conquest' of Oaxaca"; Wood, *Transcending Conquest*; Chuchiak, "The Sins of the Fathers"; Yannakakis, *The Art of Being In-between*; Castañeda de la Paz, "Central Mexican Indigenous Coats of Arms and the Conquest of Mesoamerica," Altman, *The War for Mexico's West*; and Matthew, *Memories of Conquest* for examples of this new emphasis on the role of indigenous allies in the conquest of Mesoamerica.

2. Guy and Sheridan, *Contested Ground*; Radding, *Wandering Peoples*; Weber, *The Spanish Frontier in North America*; and Usner, *Indians, Settlers, and Slaves in a Frontier Exchange Economy*.

3. Gerhard, *The North Frontier of New Spain*, 39–51, 70–78, 97–104, 148–51.

4. These included the expeditions of Francisco Cortés (1524) and Nuño de Guzmán (1530–31), both accompanied by indigenous allies. Viceroy Antonio de Mendoza mounted an expedition to the region in response to the Mixtón war in 1541. These events are covered in excellent detail in Altman's groundbreaking study, *The War for Mexico's West*, 6–56. According to Altman, Guzman's indigenous allies suffered heavy casualties and received little reward for their service.

5. Gerhard, *The North Frontier of New Spain*, 148.

6. Altman's *The War for Mexico's West* places the Mixtón war in the context of the Spanish colonization of Nueva Galicia.

7. Haro Ortega et al., *Historia de Colotlán*, 36–37. This and all subsequent translations are the author's unless otherwise noted. These events from the Mixtón war bear a striking resemblance to the later Pueblo Revolt in New Mexico. The Pueblos utilized a similar rallying cry, promising that "who shall kill a Spaniard will get an Indian woman for a wife, and he who kills four will get four women, and he who kills ten or more will have a like number of women." Cited in Ramón A. Gutiérrez, *When Jesus Came, the Corn Mothers Went Away: Marriage, Sexuality, and Power in New Mexico, 1500–1846* (Stanford, Calif.: Stanford University Press, 1991), 132. Gutiérrez uses marriage as a basis for analyzing cultural interaction among indigenous communities, Franciscan friars, and Spanish settlers in colonial New Mexico.

8. The "Indio Mariano" uprising is discussed below.

9. See Altman, *The War for Mexico's West*, for a detailed account of Mendoza's expedition. Luis González Obregón also provided a narrative of the Mixtón war in his book *Rebeliones indígenas y precursores de la independencia mexicana en los siglos XVI, XVII, y XVIII*, 2nd ed. (Mexico City: Ediciones Fuente Cultural, 1952).

10. Alfredo Chavero, *Lienzo de Tlaxcalla* (Mexico City: Litográfica del Timbre, 1892), figures 58, 61, and 70. The name Colotlán meant "place of scorpions" in Náhuatl.

11. AGN, Provincias Internas, vol. 129, folios 151–317, 1709. Encomiendas were royal grants of the right to the labor and tribute of a designated group of indios. The fact that they were not successfully established in the Colotlán region meant that the indio pueblos of the Frontera de Colotlán would enjoy more freedom from tribute and obligations to local landowners than in many other areas of New Spain.

12. "Certificación de la Real Provisión, librada a favor de los Yndios Tlaxcaltecas de San Luis de Colotlán, por el Exmo. Señor Don Luis de Velasco, who was the Vice-

roy of this New Spain, on the 14th of March of 1591, in which are listed the Privileges what were conceded to them at the time in which they came to Populate this land." AGN, Indiferente de guerra, vol. 109b, exp. 1, folios 178–185. Also see AGN, Correspondencia de Virreyes, vol. 178, 145–54, 30 de Noviembre 1794. Here and throughout the book, original capitalization and spelling have been kept, with occasional modernization for purposes of clarification.

13. AGN, Correspondencia de Virreyes, vol. 178, 145–54, 30 de Noviembre 1794. For more on the Tlaxcalan colonies, see Eugenio Sego, *Aliados y Adversarios: Los colonos Tlaxcaltecas en la frontera septentrional en Nueva España* (San Luis Potosí, Mexico: El Colegio de San Luis, 1998).

14. Literally a "Republic of Indians," serving as the political body of an indigenous pueblo, officially recognized by the Spanish government. The "Señores de Republicas" were the officeholders, with the "empleos de la Republica" being the offices themselves. The use of this political concept would persist in Colotlán far later in the colonial period than in many other areas of the Spanish Empire.

15. "Certificación de la Real Provisión, librada a favor de los Yndios Tlaxcaltecas de San Luis de Colotlán." AGN, Indiferente de guerra, vol. 109b, exp. 1, folios 178–185. Also see AGN, Correspondencia de Virreyes, vol. 178, 145–54, 30 de Noviembre 1794.

16. Bret Blosser discusses the somewhat symbiotic relationship of these militias and their Spanish colonial counterparts in Nueva Galicia in "'By the Force of Their Lives and the Spilling of Blood': Flechero Service and Political Leverage on a Nueva Galicia Frontier," in eds. Laura E. Matthew and Michel R. Oudijk, *Indian Conquistadors: Indigenous Allies in the Conquest of Mesoamerica* (Norman: University of Oklahoma Press, 2007). For the standard text on militia rights and privileges in the late colonial period, see Lyle N. McAlister, *The "Fuero Militar"' in New Spain, 1764–1800* (Gainesville: University Press of Florida, 1957).

17. Laura Matthew found that the indigenous allies of the Spanish during the conquest and settlement of Guatemala also maintained a sense of their special status as "Indian Conquistadors" throughout the colonial period. In fact, Matthew calls the 1524 conquest of Guatemala a "Nahua-Spanish invasion," noting that the Spanish and their indigenous allies followed patterns of Aztec imperial expansion that predated the arrival of the Spanish. Nahuatl-speaking descendants of these indigenous conquistadors formed a distinct "Mexicano" identity separate from the local indigenous population. Exemption from tribute formed an important part of this identity. Matthew, *Memories of Conquest*, 39–50, 230.

18. AGN, Correspondencia de Virreyes, vol. 178, folios 145–154, 30 de Noviembre 1794; AGN, Reales Cédulas Originales, vol. 34, exp. 46, 94–95, 1709; Gerhard, *The North Frontier of New Spain*, 73–77; Alberto Santoscoy, ed., *Nayarit: Colección de documentos inéditos, históricos y etnográficos, acerca de la sierra de ese nombre* (Guadalajara: Ignacio Díaz y Macedo, 1899), xx.

19. AGN, Indios, vol. 33, exp. 105, 61–62, 1696; Gerhard, *The North Frontier of New Spain*, 77, 130–32.

20. Missions had been founded in Juchipila and Tlaltenango as early as the 1530s. The Franciscans continued to establish several other missions in the area throughout the seventeenth and early eighteenth centuries. Gerhard, *The North Frontier*

of New Spain, 21–22, 75, 102, 150. For more on the Jesuit evangelization efforts in Nayarit, see Phil C. Weigand, *Ensayos sobre el Gran Nayar: entre coras, huicholes y tepehuanos*, trans. Adela Iglesias Morineau (Zamora, Mich.: El Colegio de Michoacán, 1992), 155–59. For a more general discussion of the role of the church in colonial society, see John F. Schwaller, ed., *The Church in Colonial Latin America* (Wilmington, Dela.: SR Books, 2000).

21. William B. Taylor's extensive analysis of the professional and social aspects of priestly life in *Magistrates of the Sacred: Priests and Parishioners in Eighteenth-Century Mexico* (Stanford, Calif.: Stanford University Press, 1996) provides the most thorough analysis of any single social relationship in late colonial New Spain. Taylor's book contains detailed parish-level data that are crucial for understanding northern Nueva Galicia in the late colonial period, despite the fact that he only covers the Colotlán region as a small part of a study with a much broader scope. His book also does not address the distinctive indigenous history of the region. Nonetheless, his data and descriptions of church institutions and structures, lay culture, and pueblo-level politics and social relations invaluable as a reference tool, and his technique of concentrating on a particular social sphere throughout New Spain (the relationship of priest to parishioner) and then narrowing his analysis to a smaller region (the Diocese of Guadalajara) serves as an instructive model for my analysis of indultados.

22. Although there was certainly intermarriage among the three barrios over the colonial period, pueblo governance maintained the official distinction all the way up until independence. Even as late as 1826, a visiting British naval officer noted that the local indigenous population preserved the notion of the three ethnic barrios. George Francis Lyon, *Journal of a Residence and Tour in the Republic of Mexico, in 1826, with some account of the Mines* (London: John Murray, Albemarle Street, 1828), 1:280.

23. "Informes sobre las fronteras de San Luis Colotlán, 1783," AGN, Indiferente de Guerra, vol. 83, exp. 2, folio 61. Also cited and discussed in Velazquez Chávez, *Colotlán: Doble frontera contra los bárbaros*, 23–115. The writer's identification of what he termed a "corrupt Nahuatl" could signify the development of a hyrbid vernacular in the more multicultural or Hispanicized pueblos, where Nahuatl-speaking Tlaxcalans lived and intermarried with local groups. All of the indigenous languages in the area with the exception of Tepecano-Tepehuan related to Nahuatl; Gerhard, *The North Frontier of New Spain*, 42, 76–77.

24. Since the introduction of the Tlaxcalan colonies in the late sixteenth century, the Colotlán militias had been composed primarily of local indios who served in return for a fuero, exempting them from tribute. This customary practice came under attack in the last decade of the eighteenth century, as reform-oriented viceroys attempted to restructure New Spain's military forces to counter both foreign and domestic threats. As more Spanish vecinos moved into the region in the late colonial period, the practice of employing these indios flecheros increasingly drew suspicion and complaints. Many of the Spanish residents claimed that the Indians "should only be tributaries" and that "it was not appropriate to put the arms of the King in their hands." Amador, *Bosquejo histórico de Zacatecas*, 2:110.

25. For a detailed account of the role of the repartimiento system in such abuses,

see Robert W. Patch, *Indians and the Political Economy of Colonial Central America, 1670–1810* (Norman: University of Oklahoma Press, 2013).

26. The 1783 report on San Luis de Colotlán proper notes that mulatos advenedizos joined indigenous communities "in order to enjoy [their] freedom and [tax] exemptions." Advenedizos could signify "upstart" or "immigrant" and probably refers to free blacks or mulattoes. Velazquez Chávez, *Colotlán: Doble frontera contra los bárbaros*, 17. Even the Coras and Tepehuanes intermarried with each other and with black and mulatto laborers. Cynthia Radding observed a similar integration of castas into indigenous pueblos in her study of Sonora, *Wandering Peoples*, 162–65. Also see Matthew Restall, ed., *Beyond Black and Red: African-native Relations in Colonial Latin America* (University of New Mexico Press, 2005).

27. Cheryl English Martin has traced this phenomenon in Chihuahua, perceiving a powerful, albeit incomplete process of cultural transformation. Martin, *Governance and Society in Colonial Mexico: Chihuahua in the Eighteenth Century* (Stanford, Calif.: Stanford University Press, 1996). Also see Martin, "Indigenous Peoples," in *The Countryside in Colonial Latin America*, eds. Louisa Schell Hoberman and Susan Migden Socolow (Albuquerque: University of New Mexico Press, 1996), 187–212.

28. Ann Twinam has contributedly greatly to our understanding of the fluidity of ethnic categories in the colonial period. See Twinam, "The Etiology of Racial Passing: Constructions of Informal and Official 'Whiteness' in Colonial Spanish America," in *New World Orders, Violence, Sanction, and Authority in the Early Modern Americas*, eds. John Smolenski and Thomas J. Humphrey (Philadelphia: University of Pennsylvania Press, 2005), 249–72; and Twinam, *Public Lives, Private Secrets: Gender, Honor, Sexuality, and Illegitimacy in Colonial Spanish America* (Stanford, Calif.: Stanford University Press, 1999).

29. In fact, even as late as the 1860s and early 1870s, the Coras, Huicholes, and Tepehuanes retained a loosely cohesive identity separate from the Hispanicized mestizo majority of Mexico's population, as was evident in a joint uprising of several thousand members of the three groups under Manuel Lozada against the republican government. Thomas B. Hinton, ed., *Coras, huicholes y tepehuanes* (Mexico City: Instituto Nacional Indigenista, 1972), 157–60.

Twentieth-century anthropological studies of the Coras, Tepehuanes, and Huicholes also confirm that traditional rituals and languages survived Spanish attempts to forcibly assimilate the region's indigenous inhabitants. This rich anthropological literature includes Gilardo González Ramos, *Los coras* (Mexico City: Instituto Nacional Indigenista, 1972); Hinton, *Coras, huicholes y tepehuanes*; Carl Lumholtz, *Unknown Mexico; A Record of Five Years' Exploration Among the Tribes of the Western Sierra Madre; in the Tierra Caliente of Tepic and Jalisco; and Among the Tarascos of Michoacan, by Carl Lumholtz* (Glorieta, N.M.: Rio Grande Press, 1973); Weigand, *Ensayos sobre el Gran Nayar*; Barbro Dahlgren de Jordán, *Los coras de la sierra del Nayarit* (Mexico City: Universidad Nacional Autónoma de México, Instituto de Investigaciones Antropológicas, 1994); and José Luis Iturrioz Leza et al., eds., *Reflexiones sobre la identidad étnica* (Guadalajara, México: Universidad de Guadalajara, 1995). Gerhard's *The North Frontier of New Spain* also contains useful ethnohistorical data.

30. This cultural transformation was a broad trend, but it did not fully integrate

all of the previous indigenous groups. The term indios fronterizos signifies the special status of the inhabitants of many of the indigenous pueblos in the area; they served as militia against the more "barbarous" groups to the north (and to the west in the sierra of Nayarit up until the 1720s), and enjoyed exemptions from tribute and other privileges. AGN, Indios, vol. 44, exp. 100, 126–27, 1720. Ben Vinson III and Matthew Restall translate the term "indio fronterizo" as "frontiersman" and have argued that it conveyed a greater prestige than "indio flechero" or "indio amigo." Vinson and Restall, "Meanings of Military Service in the Spanish American Colonies," in Restall, *Beyond Black and Red*, 29–40.

31. In *Colotlán: Doble frontera contra los bárbaros*, Velazquez Chávez termed the district capital of San Luis Colotlán a doble frontera, signifying the dual function of Spanish control of the pueblo of San Luis de Colotlán in order to provide protection for the route from the mines of Zacatecas to Guadalajara and to promote the pacification of the neighboring indigenous population. Philip Wayne Powell described the important role of the mestizo captain Miguel Caldera in this process in *Mexico's Miguel Caldera: The Taming of America's First Frontier, 1548–1597* (Tucson: University of Arizona Press, 1977).

32. "Informes sobre las fronteras de San Luis Colotlán, 1783," in Velazquez Chávez, *Colotlán: Doble frontera contra los bárbaros*, 23–115. All of the indigenous languages in the area with the exception of Tepecano-Tepehuan were versions of Nahuatl; Gerhard, *The North Frontier of New Spain*, 42, 76–77.

33. In Huejúcar, for instance, the original document granting the privileges to the Tlaxcalan settlers was kept in the pueblo archive. AGN, Indiferente de guerra, vol. 109b, exp. 1, folios 178–85. This is discussed further in chapter 2. See Yannakakis, *The Art of Being In-between*, 191–219, for a similar interpretation of the role of the indios conquistdores in the Sierra Norte in Oaxaca.

34. This seems to have been the case in the Tepehuan Revolt of 1616–17, for instance. Peter Gerhard suggested the likely hypothesis that many Tepehuanes migrated southward to the Colotlán region after the rebellion. Gerhard, *The North Frontier of New Spain*, 74. Charlotte M. Gradie discusses the origins of the revolt and the Tepehuanes relationship with Jesuit missionaries in *The Tepehuan Revolt of 1616: Militarism, Evangelism, and Colonialism in Seventeenth-Century Nueva Vizcaya* (Salt Lake City: University of Utah Press, 2000).

35. In 1644, the Audiencia in Guadalajara considered Colotlán a "presidio," or bulwark against indigenous groups not yet incorporated into the empire. AGN, Reales Cédulas, vol. 2, exp. 36, folio 59, March 18, 1644. "Pidiendo informes sobre [. . .] los gastos que ocasionan el sostenimiento de los presidios de Acaponeta, Colotlán, Venado, y otros."

36. Gerhard *The North Frontier of New Spain*, 73–76, 111–13.

37. AGN, Indiferente de guerra, vol. 109b, exp. 1, folios 9–10. "Sublevaciones de indios [. . .] de la sierra de Colotlán." AGN, Reales Cédulas, vol. 34, exp. 46, folios 94–95, July 12, 1709; "Aprueba lo que hizo con motivo del descubrimiento de unas minas de plata en la sierra de Colotlán," AGN, Reales Cédulas, vol. 34, exp. 59, folios 133–35, July 29, 1709. The "crucifixion" of Silva and its subsequent commemoration is described in more detail in Barry M. Robinson, "The Limits of Loyalty in Colotlán: Subversion, Pardon, and Society in Late Colonial New Spain, 1780–1821"

(PhD diss., Vanderbilt University, 2005), 35–36. The practice of ritual rememberance of Silva's death lasted until at least the 1780s. Antonio de Vivanco to Viceroy Martín de Mayorga. AGN, Indiferente de guerra, vol. 109b, exp. 1, folios 9–10. Blosser also references this event in "'By the Force of Their Lives and the Spilling of Blood,'" in Matthew and Oudijk, *Indian Conquistadors: Indigenous Allies in the Conquest of Mesoamerica*, 307–8. He points out that the colonial authorities' decision to issue a general pardon, however atypical, was justified by the strategic imperative of maintaining a tenuous peace on the frontier.

38. Beatriz Rojas, comp., *Los Huicholes: documentos históricos* (Colonia Tlacopac, INI; Tlalpan, D.F.: CIESAS, 1992), 44–45; "Jalisco, Mezquitic," in *Colección Enciclopedia de los municipios de México* (Mexico City: Secretaría de Gobernación, 1987–88), 13:439.

39. AGN, Reales Cédulas Originales, vol. 32, exp. 81, folios 1–2; exp. 160, folio 1, December 1704 and July 1705; José María Muriá, director, *Historia de Jalisco* (Guadalajara, México: Gobierno de Jalisco, Secretaría General, Unidad Editorial, 1980–82), 36.

40. "Sublevaciones de indios [. . .] de la sierra de Colotlán." AGN, Reales Cédulas, vol. 34, exp. 46, folios 94–95, July 12, 1709; "Aprueba lo que hizo con motivo del descubrimiento de unas minas de plata en la sierra de Colotlán," AGN, Reales Cédulas, vol. 34, exp. 59, folios 133–35, July 29, 1709.

41. Antonio de Vivanco to Viceroy Martín de Mayorga. AGN, Indiferente de guerra, vol. 109b, exp. 1, folios 9–10.

42. Patricia Seed, *Ceremonies of Possession in Europe's Conquest of the New World, 1492–1640* (Cambridge, U.K. Cambridge University Press, 1995), 69–99.

43. See Rebecca Earle, *The Return of the Native: Indians and Mythmaking in Spanish America, 1810–1930* (Durham, N.C.: Duke University Press, 2008), for different examples of such claims.

44. Carbajal López, *La Minería en Bolaños*, 45–46.

45. Phil C. Weigand, *Evolución de una civilización prehispánica: arqueología de Jalisco, Nayarit y Zacatecas* (Zamora, Michoacán: El Colegio de Michoacán, 1993), 378.

46. The name "Tonati" is a variation of the Nahuatl word for the sun god, Tonaituh, and here refers to the native ruler of Nayarit. Hubert Howe Bancroft includes a detailed account of the conquest of Nayarit in Hubert Howe Bancroft, *History of Mexico: Vol. III, 1600–1803* (San Francisco: A. L. Bancroft & Company, 1883), 310–32.

47. Jean A. Meyer, *Breve historia de Nayarit* (Mexico City: Colegio de México, Fideicomiso Historia de las Américas: Fondo de Cultura Económica, 1997); Muriá, *Historia de Jalisco*, 37–40.

48. Gerhard, *The North Frontier of New Spain*, 70–73; Carbajal López, *La Minería en Bolaños*, 71–76. Corregidores were the equivalent of alcaldes mayores, thus, the corregidor of Bolaños was the royal district governor of that district.

49. AGN, Reales Cédulas, vol. 119, exp. 120, folio 1; vol. 159, exp. 150, folio, 1; vol. 160, exp. 242, folio, 1; vol. 173, exp., 227 and 292, folio 1. Gerhard, *The North Frontier of New Spain*, 70–73. A number of examples illustrate the chaotic nature of their governance. In the case of Juan Pascual, an Indian resident of Colotlán accused of rape, the audiencia of Guadalajara disputed the jurisdiction of the gobierno of Colotlán for four years between 1773 and 1777. AGN, Provincias Internas, vol. 130, exp.

1, folios. 1–83, 1773–77. In 1803, the districts of Aguascalientes and Juchipila were joined to the intendancy of Zacatecas. In late 1806, the military gobierno of Colotlán and Nayarit was broken up into nine sections, each to be governed by a subdelegate. AGN, Provincias Internas, vol. 130, exp. 4, folios 268–426, 1782; AGN, Reales Cédulas Originales, vol. 176, exp. 140, folios 1, 1800; AGN, Reales Cédulas Originales, vol. 187, exp. 274, folios 1, 1803; AGN, Reales Cédulas Originales, vol. 197, exp. 269, folios 5, 1806.

50. Gerhard, *The North Frontier of New Spain*, 76, 102, 150.

51. Report of Miguel Antonio Gómez, Cura of Jerez, 1783. AGN, Indiferente de Guerra, vol. 83, exp. 2, pp. 36–37, 50–53.

52. *Informe del Cura de Xerez*, no. 7, 1783, cited in Velazquez Chávez, *Colotlán: Doble frontera contra los bárbaros*, 18, 50–51.

53. AGN, Provincias Internas, vol. 130, exp. 4, folios 268–426, 1782. Barbara and Stanley Stein have found that Spanish residents of Mexico City formed a *Junta de Ciudadanos* in 1785 for the similar purpose of advocating the rights of Spanish merchants and landowners over indigenous laborers. Both the Mexico City and Colotlán juntas used the rhetoric of Indians with *poca subordinación* (little subordination) in their efforts to garner viceregal support to put pressure on indigenous communities to provide labor. Stanley J. Stein and Barbara H. Stein, *Apogee of Empire: Spain and New Spain in the Age of Charles III, 1759–1789* (Baltimore: Johns Hopkins University Press, 2003).

54. Carbajal López, *La Minería en Bolaños*, 121–70; Brading, *Miners and Merchants in Bourbon Mexico*, 190–91.

55. AGN, Minería, vol. 97, 1791.

56. AGN, Provincias Internas, vol. 210, exp. 4, folios 97–125, 1792–93.

57. AGN, Correspondencia de virreyes Marques de Branciforte, vol. 181, folios 99–100, 30 de Marzo 1795. In 1798 violence erupted at a tobacco production center between a security guard and unos indios de Colotlán. AGN, Intendencias, vol. 78, exp. 6, 1798. For another incident, in Tlaltenango, see Taylor, *Magistrates of the Sacred*, 387–88.

58. Enrique Florescano, writing more generally about the entirety of New Spain, describes the indigenous reaction to this process in *Memory, Myth, and Time in Mexico: From the Aztecs to Independence* (Austin: University of Texas Press, 1994), 181–83.

59. The Bolaños mines remained active until the outbreak of the independence struggle, but production had dropped substantially by 1798. Carbajal López, *La Minería en Bolaños*, 11–21; Gerhard, *The North Frontier of New Spain*, 72–73.

60. According to Lyle N. McAlister, "The militia of New Spain was drawn from all classes of population except Indians." McAlister, *The "fuero militar" in New Spain*, 2.

61. Amador, *Bosquejo histórico de Zacatecas*, 2:110.

62. My emphasis. Pedro Gorostiza, *Reglamento provisional para el regimen, gobierno y subsistencia de las milicias de la frontera de San Luis Colotlan* (Mexico City: Signed by Revilla Gigedo, 1792. Microfilm, Providence, R.I.: Brown University), 1–21. McAlister relates that these new units were granted their own *fuero*, "and, in addition, the pardos enlisted in them were granted exemption from tribute for the duration of their service." McAlister, *The "fuero militar" in New Spain*, 67–69.

63. BPEJ Ramo Civil, caja 174, exp. 5, prog. 1944, México 28 de Noviembre de 1792, "Sobre que los oficiales Felix Calleja y Simón de Herrera ejecuten e informen sobre lo que se les previno por el Excmo. Virrey para que vaya consiguiendo el mejor Gobierno y felicidad de los *indios Colotlenses*."

64. AGN, Correspondencia de virreyes Marqués de Branciforte, vol. 178, folios 145–54, 1794.

65. Ibid.

66. AGN, Indios, vol. 100, exp. 45, folio 137, 1807. The term gente de razón (literally, "rational people") referred to nonindigenous vecinos.

67. "Oficio de Señor Presidente al Gobernador de Colotlán," "Carta del Gobernador de Colotlán al Señor Presidente," in Juan Lopez, *La rebelion del indio Mariano: un movimiento insurgente en la Nueva Galicia, en 1801* (Guadalajara, Mexico: Ayuntamiento, 1985), 3:223, 267–68; Van Young, *The Other Rebellion,* 454–56.

Chapter 2

1. According to a 1783 report, Juanico's father had held the position of capitán protector general de la Frontera de Colotlán. AGN Indiferente de Guerra, vol. 83, exp. 2.

2. AGN, Indiferente de guerra, vol. 109b, exp. 1, folios 1–194.

3. Here Juanico is referring to the principales, leaders of the fronterizo pueblos.

4. "Carta escrita al mismo por aquel, y los demas cavecillas que se remitieron á Mexico, desde la Villa de Aguascalientes." AGN, Indiferente de guerra, vol. 109b, exp. 1, folio 177.

5. Brazil was not exempt from late colonial conspiracies and revolts, either, as in the case of the 1789 Inconfidenca Mineira, considered by most Brazilians as the most important precursor of their own eventual independence.

6. R. Douglas Cope's analysis of the Mexico City tumulto of 1692 in his book, *The Limits of Racial Domination: Plebian Society in Colonial Mexico City, 1660–1720*, provides a detailed look at the racial undercurrents of that incident (Madison: University of Wisconsin Press, 1994).

7. Nicholas A. Robins does a good job of portraying these new themes in the context of the Great Rebellion in Upper Peru, examining the diverse actions of the rebels in the context of an atypical case of genocide. Robins, *Genocide and Millennialism in Upper Peru: The Great Rebellion of 1780–1782* (Westport, Conn.: Praeger, 2002). See Ward Stavig, *The World of Túpac Amaru: Conflict, Community, and Identity in Colonial Peru* (Lincoln: University of Nebraska Press, 1999), for a useful discussion of the social context of the revolt. For more conventional interpretations, see Alberto Flores Galindo, *Túpac Amaru II, 1780: sociedad colonial y sublevaciones populares* (Lima: Retablo de Papel Ediciones, 1976), and Ulises Casas, *Los comuneros en el contexto de la lucha de clases.*

8. Juanico's story was first published in Robinson, "*The Limits of Loyalty in Colotlán*," and was later presented at the 2006 meeting of the American Historical Society.

9. See Carlos Rubén Ruiz Medrano, *Las sombrías aventuras del rey tlaxcalteco Juan Vicencio de Córdova y los rebeldes de Colotlán, Jalisco, 1777–1783* (San Luis Po-

tosí: Colegio de San Luis, 2011), for another perspective on Juan Vicencio de Córdova and the Señores Colotecos.

10. "Declaración de Dn José Lorenzo Aguaio," AGN, Indiferente de guerra, vol. 109b, exp. 1, folio 110.

11. AGN, Californias, vol. 40, exp. 1&5, folios 1–153, 300–473; AGN, Indios, vol. 66, exp. 82, folios 120v–125v.

12. AGN, Indios, vol. 66, exp. 82, folios 120v–125v.

13. AGN, Californias, vol. 40, exp. 2 and 5, folios 154–229, 300–473.

14. AGN, General de Parte, vol. 58, exp. 68, folios 91v–92.

15. AGN, Judicial, vol. 61, exp. 10, 107–25v, 1796–97. Villar did not return to the region for a number of years; he then chose to reside in the pueblo of Nochistlán, outside of the official bounds of the Colotlán Frontier, in the southeastern corner of the region. He would later be suggested as an "impartial and disinterested subject" to provide testimony in a land dispute between the pueblo of Huejúcar and the Countess of San Mateo Valparaiso.

16. " . . . como que por vivir entre ellos cerca de quarenta años, le acomoda mas seguir sus costumbres en mucha parte, que obserbar, las que son proprias de su sangre." AGN, Indiferente de guerra, vol. 109b, exp. 1, folio 16.

17. AGN, Indiferente de guerra, vol. 109b, exp. 1, folio 3. It is also possible that the men had some Spanish ancestry but still identified themselves as indios.

18. Although this pattern seems to have increased over the second half of the eighteenth century, Altman notes in *The War for Mexico's West* that the integration of free blacks and mulattoes into the indigenous pueblos of the region began in the earliest years of the conquest, 207.

19. Tanck de Estrada's *Atlas Ilustrado* provides the following population figures for these pueblos for the year 1790: San Luis de Colotlán (1,060 indios, 197 gente de razón), Mezquitic (456/60), Nostic (223/102), Totatiche (232/7), Asqueltán (317/0), Temastián (218/21), and Apozolco (189/50). The data for Apozolco are from 1793.

20. An indio flechero from Huejúcar reported that there was a "Gremio of the Pocos in the barrio of San Pedro," including "Nuñistas" and the Gonzales and Hernandez families. "Escrito presentado por un Soldado Flechero del Pueblo de Huajucar; . . . y su Declaración," AGN, Indiferente de guerra, vol. 109b, exp. 1, folios 108–109v.

21. The term literally meant "guild," and in New Spain gremios often served as occupational organizations for specific ethnic communities.

22. AGN, Indiferente de guerra, vol. 109b, exp. 1, folios 94–95; 106–9v; 114.

23. See, for instance, Radding, *Wandering Peoples*, 175–80, 236–38, 252–60.

24. BPEJ CIVIL caja 90, exp. 19, prog. 1010. Blosser, "By the Force of Their Lives and the Spilling of Blood," notes that Huejúcar deployed "certification documents in support of petitions regarding the pueblo's territorial integrity [throughout] the colonial period."

25. Don Lazaro de la Cruz and Don Manuel de Fernández. AGN, Indiferente de guerra, vol. 109b, exp. 1, folio 91.

26. " . . . lobos, Coyotes, y otras malas razas, ladrones, Abigeos, y quatreros agregados de otras partes en que apenas hai uno, u otro indio Natural de Guaxucar." "Petition of Don Lazaro de la Cruz and Don Manuel de Fernández, submitted by the

Protector de Indios Juan Fernández de Luera," AGN, Indiferente de guerra, vol. 109b, exp. 1, folios 85–88v.

27. "Andado con Villar." AGN, Indiferente de guerra, vol. 109b, exp. 1, folios 106–9v.

28. Gerhard, *The North Frontier of New Spain*, 75–78.

29. "Testimonios de varias certificaciones pertenecientes a los naturales de este pueblo sobre su participación en la conquista del Nayarith." BPEJ CIVIL caja 90, exp. 19, prog. 1010.

30. "Declaración de Domingo Santiago del Rio, Español," AGN, Indiferente de guerra, vol. 109b, exp. 1, folios 99v–100v.

31. Declaración de Don José Lorenzo de Aguaio," AGN, Indiferente de guerra, vol. 109b, exp. 1, folios 110–113v.

32. "Pues somos los contenidos en el poder." AGN, Indiferente de guerra, vol. 109b, exp. 1, folios 176–76v.

33. "Escrito presentado por el Teniente Gral que fue de la Frontera . . . Don Juose Manuel de Aguallo . . . en alegación contra el Pueblo de Colotlán, quien levantó discordia con unos y otros Pueblos," AGN, Indiferente de guerra, vol. 109b, exp. 1, folios 117–21.

34. Archivo General de Simancas (AGS) "Milicias de Colotlan. Tumultos y revueltas," 1785, Reference Number: ES.47161.AGS/19.8/SGU, 7015, 6. "Testimonios de las sumarias contra los cabecillas de tumultos y revueltas habidos en Colotlán," 7–11.

35. AGN, Indiferente de guerra, vol. 109b, exp. 1, folios 23–64, 94–109.

36. AGN, Indiferente de guerra, vol. 109b, exp. 1, folios 35v–36v.

37. Susan Kellogg discusses indigenous use of litigation in the early colonial period in *Law and the Transformation of Aztec Society, 1500–1700* (Norman: University of Oklahoma Press, 1995). In *Black Society in Spanish Florida* (Chicago: University of Illinois Press, 1999), 138, 183–84, Jane Landers has shown how Africans and their descendants in Florida and the broader circum-Caribbean used the Spanish legal system for their own purposes and often to great effect; Eric Van Young argued that indigenous pueblos utilized litigation against outsiders as a way of redirecting internal conflict. Van Young, "Conflict and Solidarity in Indian Village Life: The Guadalajara Region in the Late Colonial Period," *Hispanic American Historical Review* 64, no. 1 (February 1984): 55–80. Also see Taylor, *Magistrates of the Sacred*, 203–5, 370–95, and Malcolm Ebright, "Sharing the Shortages: Water Litigation and Regulation in Hispanic New Mexico, 1600–1850," *New Mexico Historical Review* 76, no. 1 (January 2001): 3–45.

38. AGN, Indiferente de guerra, vol. 109b, exp. 1, folios 105–7v, 142–48.

39. "Declaración of Dn. Gergorio Man.l de Fernández, indio Cacique and soldado del Barrio de Tochopa," AGN, Indiferente de guerra, vol. 109b, exp. 1, folios 132–32v.

40. In his two-volume history of the Mexican Revolution, *The Mexican Revolution* (Cambridge, U.K.: Cambridge University Press, 1986), 1:125, Alan Knight distinguished between "agrarian" and serrano rebels. The characteristics he put forth for serrano rebels have some relevance to the Colotlan region. According to Knight, regionalism and local relationships were "paramount" for the serranos. As the name suggests, the serranos often operated in the highland regions, where the "authority of state and landlord was tenuous." For Knight's serranos, the social divisions that eventually broke down into the opposing sides of the Revolution were vertical rather

than horizontal. In other words, serrano communities split along insider/outsider divisions rather than along class lines. Mineworkers, cowboys, and even local gentry often joined (or led) the serranos. This pattern clearly fits the Colotecos' faction during the battle for the allegiance of the Frontier Indians of Colotlán.

41. "Escrito presentado por el soldado Juan Antonio Ramírez," AGN, Indiferente de guerra, vol. 109b, exp. 1, folios 65–67v.

42. "Declaración de Don José Lorenzo Aguaio," AGN, Indiferente de guerra, vol. 109b, exp. 1, folios 110–13v. The observer then reports that Juanico Córdova and "those of his persuasion" later "formed a considerable intoxication" in the vicinity of the departed priest's home.

43. William B. Taylor has suggested that complaints from priests over lack of respect from parishioners could be used as a possible response to indigenous litigation against them. Taylor, *Magistrates of the Sacred*, 202–3.

44. AGN, Provincias Internas, vol. 129, exp. 12, folios 421–27, 1780.

45. AGN, Indiferente de guerra, vol. 109b, exp. 1, folios 172–73v.

46. "la provincia de Nayarit y . . . todos los Yndios de tierra adentro hasta mas allá de la Palma." AGN, Indiferente de guerra, vol. 109b, exp. 1, folio 105.

47. AGN, Indiferente de guerra, vol. 109b, exp. 1, folios 174–75v.

48. Ibid., folios 149–50.

49. In *The Nahuas After the Conquest: A Social and Cultural History of the Indians of Central Mexico, Sixteenth Through Eighteenth Centuries* (Stanford, Calif.: Stanford University Press, 1994), 299–305, James Lockhart demonstrated how linguistic cognates, with similar pronunciations and meanings in both languages, are particularly useful in societies with multicultural origins. "Cognate" cultural values could serve a similarly effective purpose, as seen in this case with Juanico.

50. AGN, Indiferente de guerra, vol. 109b, exp. 1, folios 176–76v.

51. Steve J. Stern, *The Secret History of Gender: Women, Men, and Power in Late Colonial Mexico* (Chapel Hill: University of North Carolina Press, 1995).

52. See, for instance, the case of Juan Lorenzo, an indio from Asqueltan, who killed his wife in a drunken rage. Never one to forego the opportunity of financial gain, however, Córdova offered to free Lorenzo upon payment of a one hundred peso fine. Lorenzo's father had not quite finished paying the money when Córdova freed a number of prisoners, including Lorenzo, who agreed to go with him to attack the pueblo of Huejúcar (see below). AGN, Indiferente de guerra, vol. 109b, exp. 1, folios 151–52v. The testimony of Lorenzo's father immediately follows his own. Córdova also imprisoned Gavriel Francisco Flores Espinosa for injuring a woman and embargoed his goods as a penalty, and to pay the curandero, and to get him out of jail. Córdova also got him to name him (Córdova) as heir to his estate. AGN, Indiferente de guerra, vol. 109b, exp. 1, folios 145–48.

53. "Declaración de Dn. Gregorio Manuel de Fernández indio Casique," AGN, Indiferente de guerra, vol. 109b, exp. 1, folios 132–33, February 3, 1781.

54. In the introduction to their edited volume on honor in colonial Latin America, Lyman L. Johnson and Sonya Lipsett-Rivera suggest that honor could be interpreted to, among other things, signify social status or demonstrate virtue. Although both were apparent in the case of Juanico's actions against the men who had mistreated their wives, Juanico's treatment of Don Gregorio clearly reinforced their respective

status in the social hierarchy. Johnson and Lipsett-Rivera, eds., *The Faces of Honor: Sex, Shame, and Violence in Colonial Latin America* (Albuquerque, N.M.: Dialogos, 1998).

55. AGN, Indiferente de guerra, vol. 109b, exp. 1, folios 85–88v.

56. "Statement of Don Pedro Davalos Montiel," BPEJ civil, caja 90, exp. 19, progresivo 1010, folio 7.

57. Juanico signs the letter as "Apoderado de la Frontera," and Calixto as "Apoderado"; after writing "Las Republicas, y Comunes, y por todos." AGN, Indiferente de guerra, vol. 109b, exp. 1, folios 89–92.

58. AGN, Indiferente de guerra, vol. 109b, exp. 1, folios 94–95v.

59. Ibid., folios 91–92.

60. "Declaración de Bernabe Rentería, Vecino de Colotlán," AGN, Indiferente de guerra, vol. 109b, exp. 1, folios 131–32.

61. "Declaración de Don Jose Lorenzo de Aguaio," AGN, Indiferente de guerra, vol. 109b, exp. 1, folio 111v.

62. "Declaración de Bernabe Rentería, Vecino de Colotlán," AGN, Indiferente de guerra, vol. 109b, exp. 1, folios 131–32.

63. "Declaración de Dn. Gregorio Manuel de Fernández indio Casique," AGN, Indiferente de guerra, vol. 109b, exp. 1, folios 132–33, February 3, 1781.

64. "Declaración del Soldado Salvador Mendoza," AGN, Indiferente de guerra, vol. 109b, exp. 1, folios 101–101v.

65. AGN, Indiferente de guerra, vol. 109b, exp. 1, folios 81–81v.

66. "Declaración del Soldado Salvador Mendoza," AGN, Indiferente de guerra, vol. 109b, exp. 1, folios 101–101v.

67. Testimony now housed in the Archivo General de Simancas (AGS) "Milicias de Colotlan. Tumultos y revueltas," 1785, Reference Number: ES.47161.AGS/19.8/SGU, 7015, 6. "Testimonios de las sumarias contra los cabecillas de tumultos y revueltas habidos en Colotlán," describes the assault on Huejúcar in great detail.

68. Considering that the divisions between the "true Común" and the Pocos centered on control over pueblo resources and government, it is likely that papers from the pueblo archive had been used to exclude the Pocos from full enfranchisement.

69. Morillo's killers were Manuel from Huejúcar and Fermin Reyes Tranquilino from Santiago Tlatelolco, a smaller pueblo between San Luis de Colotlán and Huejúcar. Both are described as Pocos. AGN, Indiferente de guerra, vol. 109b, exp. 1, folios 77–84. Most of the Huejúcar prisoners were soon set free, but the principales remained in the San Luis de Colotlán jail throughout the duration of this narrative. The Colotecos' actions during this assault followed patterns that had been established during the sacking of rebellious, unassimilated pueblos in the west.

70. AGN, Indiferente de guerra, vol. 109b, exp. 1, folios 93–93v, 189–91.

71. Fermin Reyes Tranquilino is listed as a zapatero, and Manuel as a cargadero. AGN, Indiferente de guerra, vol. 109b, exp. 1, folios 114–15, 189–91.

72. "Sus autoridades eran solo en sus vocas." Quote from "Escrito presentado por la Viuda del difunto Laurio Morillo, y sus tres Hijos . . . ," AGN, Indiferente de guerra, vol. 109b, exp. 1, folios 114–16v. María's phrase contains a double meaning that she may or may not have intended; that is discussed in the conclusion of the chapter. It also reflects the ingrained nature of New Spain's bureaucratic culture, even in areas

relatively distant from major urban centers. AGN, Indiferente de guerra, vol. 109b, exp. 1, folio 114v.

73. Ibid., folios 189–90v.

74. Ibid., folio 1.

75. Ibid., folios 4–7.

76. Ibid., folios 124–130v. As mayor of the closest villa to the northeastern portion of the Frontera, a number of the Spanish residents of the Colotlán region were subject to Jauregui's jurisdiction. The principales/repúblicas of the various pueblos of Colotlán were only supposed to exercise jurisdiction over indio residents.

77. Ibid., folio 129.

78. Ibid., folios 124–30v.

79. For the circum-Caribbean, see David P. Geggus, ed., *The Impact of the Haitian Revolution in the Atlantic World* (Columbia: University of South Carolina Press, 2001). For the reaction to the Tupac Amaru II revolt, see David Cahill, *From Rebellion to Independence in the Andes: Soundings from Southern Peru, 1750–1830* (Amsterdam: Aksant, 2002).

80. AGN, Indiferente de guerra, vol. 109b, exp. 1, folios 102–2v.

81. My emphasis. Ibid., folio 102v.

82. John Tutino has calculated that the Vivanco family estates would reach an annual income of some 20,000 pesos a year by 1800. Tutino, *Making a New World: Founding Capitalism in the Bajío and Spanish North America*, (Durham, N.C.: Duke University Press, 2011), 295.

83. AGN, Indiferente de guerra, vol. 109b, exp. 1, folios 170–71v.

84. Ibid., folios 186–88.

85. Ibid., folios 1–194.

86. Vivanco to Viceroy Martín de Mayorga. AGN, Indiferente de guerra, vol. 109b, exp. 1, folios 5–10.

87. AGN, Indiferente de guerra, vol. 109b, exp. 1, folios 15–16.

88. Again, this public ritual of submission and reconciliation reinforced the restructuring of Frontera' social relations by demonstrating Don Antonio's allegiance to the new powers-that-be. Ibid., folios 17–19.

89. AGN, Correspondencia de diversas autoridades, vol. 35i, exp. 121, folios 275, 288, 5 de Septiembre 1781.

90. Using the similar case of the indios conquistadores of Oaxaca, Yannakakis has argued that the late colonial Spanish tendency to impose a dichotomy of civilized Spaniards versus barbarous Indians onto the much more fluid and complex ethnic composition of the colonial system of the Spanish Americas put pressure on the very native intermediaries who were crucial to its persistence. Yannakakis, *The Art of Being In-between*, 192–224.

91. Matthew Restall has identified a similar racial fluidity in the Yucatan, where castas with varying degrees of African ancestry also used marriage and military service as a means of social mobility. Restall, *The Black Middle: Africans, Mayas, and Spaniards in Colonial Yucatan* (Stanford, Calif.: Stanford University Press, 2009).

92. As mentioned in the next chapter, the Colotecos' case resembles Alan Knight's serrano typology in *The Mexican Revolution*, although Knight does not use the insider-outsider terminology.

Chapter 3

1. The pueblo is now known as "Jiménez del Teúl" and is a municipio in the state of Zacatecas.

2. A 1783 report on San Luis de Colotlán notes that mulatos advenedizos later mixed with the indios "in order to enjoy [their] freedom and [tax] exemptions," Velazquez Chávez, *Colotlán: Doble frontera contra los bárbaros*, 17. The reports show that the indios' exemption, or fuero, depended on their status as frontier militiamen.

3. Susan Kellogg, "Hegemony Out of Conquest: The First Two Centuries of Spanish Rule in Central Mexico," *Radical History Review* 53 (1992): 27–46.

4. The surrounding settlements referred to here would presumably have been Chalchihuites, Fresnillo, Jerez, San Luís de Colotlán, and Sombrerete. Note that this command coincided with the 1704 uprising discussed in chapter 1. AGN, Indios, vol. 36, exp. 208, 187–87v, 1704.

5. The size of the land was 600 square varas, or just under 64 acres. AGN, Indios, vol. 44, exp. 100, 126v–27, 1720. At times I use the term "Teulenses" to avoid repetition of its synonym, "indios of San San Andrés del Teúl."

6. This is indicated in a viceregal order in 1721 specifying that "the Reverend Father Comisario General of Saint Francis, and in his absence the Provincial Father, provide the requested report concerning the claim by the naturales of the pueblo and frontier of San Andrés del Teúl relating to the lack of [religious] instruction." AGN, Indios, vol. 44, exp. 101, 127v–28, 1721.

7. AGN, Indios, vol. 44, exp. 102, 128–28v, 1721. For an excellent description of the Campa Cos family and their enterprises in the region, see Frédérique Langue, *Los Señores de Zacatecas: Una Aristocracia Minera del Siglo XVIII Novohispano* (Mexico City: Fondo de Cultura Económica, trans. 1999). José de la Campa Cos is discussed on 137.

8. Other lieutenants were located in Huejúcar, Mexquitic, and Huejuquilla. See Gerhard, *The North Frontier of New Spain*, 75, for a good explanation of these various jurisdictions.

9. Commercial agricultural production in the Colotlán region mostly included corn, with Zacatecas's wheat coming primarily from the Bajío. See Peter Bakewell, *Silver Mining and Society in Colonial Mexico: Zacatecas, 1546–1700* (Cambridge, U.K.: Cambridge University Press, 1971) 60–74, 237–65.

10. They submitted at least two different petitions, in 1723 and again in 1724. The 1723 petition mentioned the Hacienda of San Sebastián (in the present-day municipio of Etzatlán). The 1724 petition mentioned one José Borrego, of whom I have found no other mention. AGN, Indios, vol. 47, exp. 70, 118–88v, 1723; AGN, Indios, vol. 50i, exp. 30, 42–43, 1724. So far I have been unable to pinpoint the exact location of the land claimed by the pueblo in the Valley of Ameca. The Ameca River begins about 23km west of Guadalajara and flows westward and northwestward along the Jalisco/Nayarit border into Banderas Bay.

11. Fernando de la Campa Cos came to New Spain in 1705 to participate in the pacification of Nayarit as a colonel in the Spanish infantry alongside his brother Antonio, a general. He purchased haciendas and invested in numerous mines in the Zacatecas region with some 50,000 pesos from his own money and that of his first

wife. On July 14, 1727, he received the title of Count of San Mateo Valparaiso. At his death in 1742 he left his heirs a total of 1,283,278 pesos, 4 reales, and 9 granos. His fortune included more than a dozen haciendas in Sombrerete, Nieves, Fresnillo, and elsewhere. For a more detailed account, see Langue, *Los Señores de Zacatecas*, 192–93, passim.

12. AGN, Indios, vol. 44, exp. 133, 164v–65, 1721; AGN, Indios, vol. 46, exp. 26, 33–40, 1722.

13. Statement from a January 1797 report from the governor of Colotlán to the viceroy. AGN, Judicial, vol. 61, exp. 10, 107–25v, 1796–97.

14. Robert Shadow has estimated a decline of some 50 percent in the population of the Colotlan region from 1726 to 1742, a demographic drop that would certainly reduce the pueblo's need for land. By the early 1770s, the region's population had rebounded to pre-1726 levels. Robert Shadow, "La frontera norteña de la Nueva Galicia: las parroquias de Colotlán 1725–1820," in *Lecturas Históricas del Norte de Jalisco*, ed. Miguel Caldera. (Guadalajara, Mexico: Colegio de Jalisco, 1991), 91.

15. According to Langue, the Count built two chapels in the Ameca area. He notes that "la evangelización, para el conde de San Mateo, iba de la mano con la pacificación de esta zona 'fronteriza.'" Langue, *Los Señores de Zacatecas*, 274.

16. Literally, the cura of a doctrina, or pastor of a "proto-parish administered by the regular clergy for people [usually indigenous] who were in principle still neophytes but beyond the initial stage of conversion." Taylor, *Magistrates of the Sacred*, 530.

17. According to Taylor, obvenciones were "periodic fees and collections to which parish priests were entitled." Taylor, *Magistrates of the Sacred*, 532.

18. Circumstances surrounding the establishment of the benefice as described by the principales of the pueblo of San Andrés del Teúl, AGN, Judicial, vol. 61, exp. 10, 107–25v, 1796–97, p. 2 (108). San Luís de Colotlán was secularized in 1754–55, Juchipila in 1769, and Tlaltenango after 1772. As a part of Bourbon measures to counter the power and influence of the church, most of the Colotlán region was secularized in the second half of the eighteenth century, becoming part of the Diocese of Guadalajara. A small portion of the region, however, including San Andrés del Teúl and Nueva Tlaxcala, fell under the jurisdiction of the Diocese of Durango. Gerhard, *The North Frontier of New Spain*, 76, 102, 150.

19. In the local historical memory of the Zacatecas region in present-day Mexico, Doña Ana María de la Campa y Cos, third child and heir of the Count of San Mateo de Valparaíso, is remembered as a benefactress who funded a number of public works in the city of Zacatecas and in Sombrerete. For a discussion of the immense fortune of the house of San Mateo de Valparaiso and Jaral (the estate of the Countess's deceased husband), see Langue, *Los Señores de Zacatecas*, 273–78, passim.

20. Ibid., 194. During the war for independence, insurgent forces sacked the huge hacienda of their grandson, Juan Nepomuceno de Moncada y Berrio, Count of San Mateo, Marquis of Jaral, and Third Marquis of Moncada, who had raised a troop to support the royalist commander Félix María Calleja.

21. Oliverio Sarmiento Pacheco has written a history of this hacienda. Pacheco, *San Mateo, Valparaíso: Valle, Estancia, y Hacienda* (Valparaíso, Zacatecas: self-published, 2005).

22. AGN, General de Parte, vol. 76, exp. 79, 62–63, 1796.

23. Ibid.

24. AGN, General de Parte, vol. 75, exp. 345, 304v–5v, 1796.

25. The subdelegado of Fresnillo was technically subject to the intendant of Zacatecas, not the governor of Colotlán, but the governor could claim jurisdiction because of the involvement of one of his pueblos. See Gerhard, *The North Frontier of New Spain*, for a more detailed description of the introduction of the intendancy system.

26. Marripa, "the servant," was most likely the hacienda manager. As the lieutenant in charge of Nueva Tlaxcala, Servín de la Mora held authority over the pueblo of San Andrés and was subject to the oversight of the governor of Colotlán. *Corralitos* means "little corrals."

27. This was done without the authorization of the governor of Colotlán. AGN, General De Parte, vol. 75, exp. 345, 304v–5v, 1796.

28. A more specific description of the principales' identity can be found below. AGN, Judicial, vol. 61, exp. 10, 107–25v, 1796–97.

29. Teulenses' Account of the Encounter at Corralitos in December 1795. AGN, Judicial, vol. 61, exp. 10, 107–25v, 1796–97.

30. AGN, General De Parte, vol. 75, exp. 345, 304v–5v, 1796.

31. Ibid.

32. Ibid.

33. AGN, Judicial, vol. 61, exp. 10, 107–25v, 1796–97.

34. Ibid.

35. As Taylor discusses in *Magistrates of the Sacred*, the forests around the Zacatecas mining region had largely been depleted in the seventeeth century, and the sierra near San Andrés and down to Bolaños was rapidly disappearing in the eighteenth. Consequently, the increased value of timber as a commodity fueled some of the conflict between the indios of Teúl and Lieutenant Servín de la Mora. Taylor, *Magistrates of the Sacred*, 36–38.

36. AGN, Judicial, vol. 61, exp. 10, 107–25v, 1796–97.

37. Ibid.

38. Ibid. It is important to remember that, as described in the previous chapter, Don Felipe had been a key figure in the power struggle of 1780–85, when he was most certainly *not* viewed as an "impartial disinterested subject of integrity" by the Colotecos and their allies.

39. Ibid.

40. Ibid.

41. AGN, Judicial, vol. 61, exp. 10, 107–25v, 1796–97.

42. Ibid.

43. Ibid.

44. Ibid.

45. Ibid.

46. In using such language, the Countess (or more properly, Molina), was characterizing the indios of San Andrés as indios bárbaros in need of "pacification," rather than as indios fronterizos, militiamen, and loyal subjects of the king.

47. "Statement of José Rafael de Molina, agent of the Countess of San Mateo de Valparaiso, requesting that the Justicia of the Valle de Valparaiso be permitted to restore possession of the Ameca Valley to the Countess." AGN, General de Parte, vol. 76, exp. 79, 62–63, 1797.

48. The Teulenses' readiness to "command" the Countess' vaqueros and Molina's

remarks about the indios' "insolence" demonstrate the gap between the Teulenses' conception of their fronterizo status and the hacienda's characterization of them as Indian bandits, acting above their station.

49. Excerpt from the statement of José Rafael de Molina, agent of the Countess of San Mateo de Valparaiso, requesting that the Justicia of the Valle de Valparaiso be permitted to restore possession of the Ameca Valley to the Countess. AGN, General de Parte, vol. 76, exp. 79, 62–63, 1797.

50. "Statement of Molina," AGN, General de Parte, vol. 76, exp. 79, 62–63, 1797.

51. AGN, General de Parte, vol. 76, exp. 79, 62–63, Nov. 7, 13, 1797.

52. AGN, General de Parte, vol. 76, exp. 80, 63, Nov. 20, 1797.

53. AGN, General de Parte, vol. 76i, exp. 224, 168v–70, 1799.

54. Ibid.

55. Ibid.

56. Ibid. Alan Knight's serrano model also works in the case of the Teulenses. While less ethnically diverse than San Luis de Colotlán or Huejúcar, the pueblo of San Andrés did not hesitate to make cross-ethnic social alliances when it was expedient. Knight also argued that a significant element of banditry accompanied rebellion in serrano frontier regions, where rebels exhibited "relative freedom of mobility, a familiarity with violence, [and] resistance to urban political control and culture." These descriptions could just as easily be applied to Teulenses like José María Calzada as it was to the Pocos in the previous chapter. Knight, *The Mexican Revolution*, 1:115–127.

57. "Tomarles confesión y demás." AGN, General de Parte, vol. 76i, exp. 224, 168v–70, 1799.

58. Unfortunately, Cisneros's status and origin are unnoted. AGN, General de Parte, vol. 76i, exp. 224, 168v–70, 1799.

59. The Countess may have died by this point, as some undocumented sources give 1799 as the year of her death. Regardless of the actual date, the *mayorazgos* into which she had divided her estate were disputed among her heirs for several years, at least until 1812. Langue, *Los Señores de Zacatecas*, 272–75.

60. Trelles Villa de Moros notes that the lands of the two pueblos are "scanty" and "very rocky," and "for this reason, stimulated by necessity, they dispute [the ownership of these lands] with the Hacienda del Cuidado." Archivo de la Real Audiencia de Guadalajara (ARAG), held at the Biblioteca Pública del Estado de Jalisco (BPEJ), Ramo Civil, caja 259, exp. 12, prog. 3513; and caja 218, exp. 26, prog. 2798.

61. John Tutino's landmark study, *From Insurrection to Revolution in Mexico: Social Bases of Agrarian Violence, 1750–1940* (Princeton, N.J.: Princeton University Press, 1986), is a primary example. Tutino's connection of regional patterns of insurgency to land and labor pressures in the Central Highlands, Bajío, San Luis Potosí, and Jalisco provides a solid basis for understanding and comparing the variety of economic pressures put on New Spain's rural population in the late colonial period. His distinction between the experience of estate residents and villagers as a primary factor in fostering loyalty or rebellion represents a very real and marked difference in rural life, but, as he acknowledges, this goes only so far in explaining why particular people, communities, or regions chose to take up arms. Like most scholars, Tutino does not differentiate between the Jalisco rebels from the more immediate Guadalajara hinterland, who formed the basis for his discussion of Jalisco, and the several

thousand insurgents from Colotlán, who more closely resembled the inhabitants of the Central Highlands—as described by Tutino—than the "central Jalisco" insurgents he discusses. In fact, most accounts of the insurrection describe these rebels from Colotlán as indios despite their multiethnic fronterizo background.

62. In fact, David Brading lists the Countess's husband, the Marquis of Jaral, as "one of the greatest landowners in New Spain" in *Miners and Merchants in Bourbon Mexico*, 69. As Frédérique Langue notes in *Los Señores de Zacatecas*, the "Señores of Zacatecas"—like the Campa Cos family, peninsulars or not far removed—managed their huge *latifundios* as massive dowries and birthrights for the next generation of New World nobility.

63. Whereas Lieutenant Servín de la Mora and his allied vecinos from Nueva Tlaxcala are clearly seen as outsiders, the willingness of the Teulenses to oversee their own nonindigenous tenants in the Ameca Valley—individuals like Rafael Cisneros, whose legitimacy Molina contested in his appeals to the viceroy and Governor Trelles—further challenges descriptions of late colonial indigenous communities as "closed." Eric Van Young, for instance, attributes widespread "popular" participation in the independence-era insurgencies to "forms of localist autodefense and cultural resistance within a context of ethnic conflict between indigenous and nonindigenous social sectors." Yet Van Young's depiction of indigenous pueblos as communities significantly closed to outsiders does not precisely fit the Colotlán case. The context of indigenous versus nonindigenous ethnic conflict that he describes is clearly evident there, but the concept of indio, and more specifically of indio fronterizo, is malleable enough to include allied newcomers or "outsiders" from outside the pueblo, such as the mulatos advenedizos who married into these communities. Van Young, *The Other Rebellion*, 520–22.

64. Of the broader large-scale social conditions proposed as explanations for revolt—or at least setting the necessary conditions—evidence from the Colotlán region suggests that the introduction of the position of subdelegado throughout many indigenous pueblos—a creation of the intendancy system—had one of the most powerful effects on pre-independence social relations. So far, this has been analyzed most successfully, but not completely, by Taylor in *Magistrates of the Sacred*.

65. I do not mean to imply that such relationships were equally advantageous, or symmetrical. Fernando Campa Cos, in particular, exploited his relationship with the inhabitants of the Colotlán pueblos. During his lifetime, he acquired some fifty-six "sitios de ganado mayor" situated near Huejuquilla in the north of the region, "beyond the Sierra Madre." Langue, *Los Señores de Zacatecas*, 274.

66. ARAG, BPEJ, Ramo Criminal, caja 41, exp. 24, progresivo 658. "Ante el Presidente y vocales de la Junta de Seguridad Pública, contra Ramón Alegría, nombrado por los insurgentes Gobernador de Colotlán." Alegría later asked for, and received, a royal pardon.

67. The role of religion in the construction of identity is a relatively understudied aspect of the late colonial and independence period. Matthew O'Hara's *A Flock Divided: Race, Religion, and Politics in Mexico, 1749–1857* (Durham, N.C.: Duke University Press, 2009) is one recent effort to address this. He focuses primarily on Mexico City and the surrounding region and pays particular attention to the intersection of ethnic identity and religious institutions.

68. Chapter 5 of this book examines the role of the clergy in the Colotlán region

in greater detail. For an excellent, detailed analysis of the role of parish priests in late colonial New Spain, see Taylor, *Magistrates of the Sacred*.

69. Northern Jalisco and the area known as Los Altos served as a hotbed of the Cristero Revolt in the late 1920s. Jean Meyer, *The Cristero Rebellion: The Mexican People Between Church and State, 1926–1929* (Cambridge, U.K.: Cambridge University Press, 1976).

Chapter 4

1. Literally, "las revoluciones de este Cañón." My emphasis. BPEJ Criminal, caja 33, exp. 1, prog. 523, folio 42.

2. Ibid., 37.

3. Document is cited in Carlos Ramírez Esparza, *El Padre Calvillo: Caudillo de la Guerra de Independencia*, (Guadalajara, Mexico: Gobierno de Jalisco, Secretaria General, Unidad Editorial, 1987), 14.

4. For previous accounts of Hidalgo's rebellion in the context of the other Spanish-American independence struggles, see Jay Kinsbruner, *Independence in Spanish America: Civil Wars, Revolutions, and Underdevelopment* (Albuquerque: University of New Mexico Press, 2000) for a succinct account; Christon Archer, ed., *The Wars of Independence in Spanish America* (Wilmington, Dela., 2000) for a thematic approach; and Lester D. Langley, *The Americas in the Age of Revolution, 1750–1850* (New Haven, Conn.: Yale University Press, 1996) for a comparative focus that includes the American Revolution. Additionally, John Lynch's *Latin American Revolutions, 1808–1826: Old and New World Origins* (Norman: University of Oklahoma Press, 1994) provides an updated version of his 1973 classic on the revolutionary period in Latin America. Robert Harvey's *Liberators: Latin America's Struggle for Independence, 1810–1830* (London: John Murray, 2000) is a detailed and very readable story of the most famous military leaders of the period.

5. Many early historians of the conspiracies, protests, and insurrections leading up to the independence of New Spain constructed their studies as biographies of the most prominent figures of the insurgencies, a practice that tended to inhibit the study of rebellious regions not directly under the control of these heroes. This uneven treatment was particularly apparent in the cases of regional leaders who fail to fit the ideal model of a rebel hero-priest, as in the case of Padre Calvillo, whose participation has since been downplayed, ignored, or even altered, presumably to avoid the problematic issue of his eventual abandonment of the insurgent cause. Historians have also tended to avoid serious analysis of the pardon process, itself. See, for example, Alamán, *Historia de Méjico*; Ernesto Higuera, *Hidalgo: reseña biográfica con una iconografía del iniciador de nuestra independencia* (Mexico City: Colección Medallones mexicanos, 1955); José Mancisidor, *Hidalgo, Morelos, Guerrero* (Mexico City: Editorial Grijalbo, 1956); Hamill, *The Hidalgo Revolt*; Virginia Guedea, *José María Morelos y Pavón, cronología* (Mexico City: Universidad Nacional Autónoma de México, Instituto de Investigaciones Históricas, 1981).

6. The regional nature of the Colotlán insurrection is especially important in light of the "spacio-semiotic fragmentation" of New Spanish society during the period, which Van Young has discussed. Also significant is his contention that there

was no "unified discursive field in which a broadly consensual antiregime politics might flourish." Van Young, *The Other Rebellion*, 253. The nature of the rebellion in Colotlán strongly supports this notion of regional specificity.

7. See, for instance, John Tutino's *From Insurrection to Revolution in Mexico: Social Bases of Agrarian Violence, 1750–1940* (Princeton, N.J.: Princeton University Press, 1986). See also Juan Ortiz Escamilla, "El bajo clero mexicano durante la guerra civil de 1810" in *El nacimiento de México,* ed. Patricia Galeana (Mexico City: Archivo General de la Nación: Fondo de Cultura Económica, 1999), 11–19; Ernesto de la Torre Villar, *Los "Guadalupes" y la Independencia, con una selección de documentos inéditos* (Mexico City: Editorial Jus, 1966); Karl M. Schmitt, "The Clergy and the Independence of New Spain," *Hispanic American Historical Review* 34, no. 3 (August 1954): 289–312.

8. Eric Van Young's findings in *The Other Rebellion* served as a fulcrum for this shift, presenting a fundamental challenge to long-standing, conventional interpretations of Mexican independence. He wrote, "Popular insurgency in New Spain in the years 1810–1821, to the degree it can be treated as a single entity, sought primarily to effect some sort of standoff in a prolonged process of cultural resistance by rural communities against forces of change both internal and external, rather than to achieve the observed outcome of the political-military struggle, the consolidation of independence from Spain." Van Young, *The Other Rebellion*, 496. Archer suggested a similar process in *Wars of Independence in Spanish America*, 95. This project has employed a similar method of analysis of overlooked local circumstances supported by well-documented *Namierization* (or empirical evidence of "who the guys were,") as Van Young put it in *The Other Rebellion*, 42. While Van Young bases much of his analysis on an empirical sample of 1,284 insurgents from all over New Spain, although mostly central Mexico, the following analysis incorporates a more geographically dense sample of 802 insurgents from the Colotlán region.

9. Scholarship on the Atlantic World has moved beyond studies of one particular imperial sphere. Some of the notable transimperial examples include David Gaspar and David Geggus, *A Turbulent Time: The French Revolution and the Greater Caribbean* (Bloomington: Indiana University Press, 1997); Adam Zamoyski, *Holy Madness: Romantics, Patriots, and Revolutionaries, 1776–1871* (London: Weidenfeld & Nicolson, 1999); Hilary Beckles and Verene Shepherd, eds., *Caribbean Slavery in the Atlantic World* (Princeton, N.J.: Markus Wiener, 1999); Jane Landers, *Atlantic Creoles in the Age of Revolutions* (Cambridge, Mass.: Harvard University Press, 2010); Landers, *Black Society in Spanish Florida* (Urbana: University of Illinois Press, 1999); and Jorge Cañizares, *How to Write the History of the New World: Histories, Epistemologies, and Identities in the New World* (Stanford, Calif.: Stanford University Press, 2001). Camilla Townsend put together a direct comparison of North and South America in the early republican period in her recent book, *Tales of Two Cities: Race and Economic Culture in Early Republican North and South America* (Austin: University of Texas Press, 2000).

10. In his concise study of the Spanish-American independence movements, Jay Kinsbruner has argued that the conflicts were both civil wars and revolutions. Kinsbruner, *Independence in Spanish America: Civil Wars, Revolutions, and Underdevelopment* (Albuquerque: University of New Mexico Press, 2000).

11. On the North American historiography, see Colin Gordon, "Crafting a Usable Past: Consensus, Ideology, and Historians of the American Revolution," *William and Mary Quarterly* 46, no. 4 (1989): 675. A number of increasingly influential "neo-Whig" historians, including Bernard Bailyn, brought (elite) ideology back into prominence as the principal causal factor in the American Revolution. Bailyn, *The Ideological Origins of the American Revolution* (Cambridge, Mass.: Belknap Press of Harvard University Press, 1967). The consensus version of the Revolution has also been promoted by Gordon Wood, who maintained Bailyn's assumptions concerning the primacy of ideas in directing the course of the Revolution, first in his earlier writings and then in an eloquent but controversial argument for the *Radicalism of the American Revolution*. Wood, *The Creation of the American Republic, 1776–1787* (Chapel Hill, N.C.: Institute of Early American History and Culture and the University of North Carolina Press, 1969), and Wood, *The Radicalism of the American Revolution* (New York: Alfred A. Knopf, 1992). Interestingly, at the beginning of the twentieth century, Carl Becker anticipated (or perhaps encouraged) the semantic shift that brought the "revolutionary" designation into question, by considering whether the central issue of the American Revolution concerned "home rule" or "who should rule at home." Becker, *The History of Political Parties in the Province of New York, 1760–1776* (Madison: University of Wisconsin Press, 1909), 22.

12. For a review of these precursor revolts across the empire, see Anthony McFarlane, "Rebellions in Late Colonial Spanish America: A Comparative Perspective," *Bulletin of Latin American Research* 14, no. 3 (1995): 313–38.

13. For more on the Quito tax riots, see Kenneth Andrien, "Economic Crisis, Taxes and the Quito Insurrection of 1765," *Past and Present* 129 (1990): 104–31. For rebellion in New Granada, see John L. Phelan, *The People and the King: The Comunero Revolution in Colombia, 1781* (Madison: University of Wisconsin Press, 1978), and Rebecca Earle Mond, "Indian Rebellion and Bourbon Reform in New Granada: Riots in Pasto, 1780–1800," *Hispanic American Historical Review* 73 (1993): 99–124. Scarlett O'Phelan Godoy has written extensively on Tupac Amaru II and insurrection in the Andes; see Godoy, *Rebellions and Revolts in Eighteenth Century Peru and Upper Peru* (Köln: Böhlau, 1985), and Godoy, *La gran rebelión en los Andes: de Túpac Amaru a Túpac Catari* (Cuzco, Perú: Centro de Estudios Regionales Andinos Bartolomé de las Casas," 1995). Sinclair Thomson's *We Alone Will Rule: Native Andean Politics in the Age of Insurgency* (Madison: University of Wisconsin Press, 2003) is another excellent example.

14. Author's translation. "Representación del Intendente Abalos dirigida a Carlos III, en la que pronostica la independencia de America y sugiere la creación de varias monarquías en el Nuevo Mundo e isles Filipinas," document in Mario Rodríguez, *La revolución americana de 1776 y el mundo hispánico: ensayos y documentos* (Madrid: Editorial Tecnos, 1976), 57–58.

15. For a small selection of the numerous examples, see Isabel González Sánchez, *Haciendas, tumultos y trabajadores: Puebla-Tlaxcala, 1778–1798* (Mexico City: Instituto Nacional de Antropología e Historia, 1997); Ward Stavig, "Ethnic Conflict, Moral Economy, and Population in Rural Cuzco on the Eve of the Thupa Amaro II Rebellion," *Hispanic American Historical Review* 68, no. 4, (1988): 737–70; and William B. Taylor, *Drinking, Homicide, and Rebellion in Colonial Mexican Villages* (Stanford, Calif.: Stanford University Press, 1979).

16. Examples of this scholarship include Colin Calloway, *The American Revolution in Indian Country* (New York: Cambridge University Press, 1994); Calloway, *The World Turned Upside Down: Indian Voices from Early America* (Boston: Palgrave Macmillan, 1994); and Tom Hatley, *The Dividing Paths: Cherokees and South Carolinians through the Era of Revolution* (New York: Oxford University Press, 1995).

17. The term gente de pueblo refers to the nonelite popular classes of all races, as opposed to the *gente decente* (elites of Spanish descent).

18. See Rebecca Earle, *The Return of the Native: Indians and Mythmaking in Spanish America, 1810–1930* (Durham, N.C.: Duke University Press, 2008), for a fascinating discussion of indigenous symbolism in the late colonial and independence period.

19. "Apuntes relativos á los acontecimientos ocurridos en Colotlán en los memorables años de 1810 y siguientes hasta el 18., y servicios prestados p.r sus hijos, á la Causa de la Independencia proclamada p.r el Inmortal Hidalgo en el pueblo de Dolores en 15 de Septiembre del citado año 1810." Document published as a part of "Memoria histórica de Colotlán," from the manuscript collection of Sr. Lic. D. Mauro Villaseñor, in Ing. José Tomás Figueroa and Juan B. Yguiniz, eds., *Biblioteca Histórica Jalisciense* (Guadalajara, Mexico: Imprenta, Litografía, y Enc. de J. M. Yguíniz, 1909) section 1, no. 8–9, 167–216.

20. "Apuntes relativos á los acontecimientos ocurridos en Colotlán," Figueroa and Yguiniz, *Biblioteca Histórica Jalisciense*, section 1, no. 8, 188.

21. Ibid., 187–88.

22. Calvillo's willingness to host such a spiritually suspect event—remembering the conflicts between clergy and pious community members, and the Colotecos and many like-minded indigenous inhabitants in the 1780s—reflects his sympathetic and flexible approach toward popular customs and culture. Ibid., 188; Alejandro Villaseñor y Villaseñor, *Biografías de los héroes y caudillos de la Independencia*, (Mexico City: Imp. de "El Tiempo," de V. Agüeros, 1910), 165–66, 169.

23. "Apuntes relativos á los acontecimientos ocurridos en Colotlán," Figueroa and Yguiniz, eds., *Biblioteca Histórica Jalisciense*, section 1, no. 8, 188.

24. Villaseñor, *Biografías de los héroes*, 165–66, 169; Gutiérrez, *Aguascalientes y su región de influencia hasta 1810*, 55–57. Villaseñor states incorrectly that these events occurred in May 1811.

25. These were Teniente Vicente Nales, from Tlaltenango, and Teniente Manuel Campos and Miguel Guizas, from Coculiten. BPEJ Criminal, caja 33, exp. 1, prog. 523, 5, 10–11, 17, 23, 24, 26.

26. BPEJ Criminal, caja 41, exp. 2, prog. 658, 2.

27. AHEZ Judicial, caja 23, exp. 10.

28. "Todos los ranchos y pueblos cortos hasta el Valle [de Tlatenango] y Huejuquilla están insurgentados." Cited in Bernardo Carlos Casas, *Tlaltenango: una ciudad amurallada* (Guadalajara, México: Impre-Jal, 1986), 139.

29. BPEJ Ramo Criminal, caja 33, exps. 1–523. As mentioned in the introduction, these records form part of a biographical database that tracks 802 insurgents and a smaller number of royalist officials.

30. The *Memoria histórica de Colotlán* notes on 189 that "various companies of Indians numbering around four hundred from here [San Luis de Colotlán] and from the pueblos of Santiago, Santa María, Tlalcosahua y Huejúcar" joined the insurgency.

The captains included Victoriano Córdova and Marcos Escobedo. The indigenous of Tlaltenango, Zicacalco, Ocotlán, Coculiten, Teocaltiche, Tocatique also sent men.

31. BPEJ Criminal, caja 33, exp. 1, prog. 523, folio 42.

32. Ibid., 31; *Memoria histórica de Colotlán*, 189–90.

33. BPEJ Criminal, caja 33, exp. 1, prog. 523, folio 18.

34. Ibid. 34. "Aparicio Cervantes natural fue de Capitn. por nombramiento de los Justiciales de este Pueblo [de Tlaltenango] hasta Guadalajara."

35. Tlemole is apparently a pre-Hispanic sauce similar to what is now called *mole rojo*.

36. Insurgent Database.

37. "Contestación de Cruz," March 8, 1811, "Documento Número 199," and "Parte del Presb. D. José Francisco Alvarez, de la expedición de Huejúcar á Jerez," in Juan López, comp., *La Insurgencia de la Nueva Galicia en algunos documentos* (Guadalajara, México: Honorable Ayuntamiento de Guadalajara, 1984), 1:230, and 2:1–2.

38. According to Van Young, the widely held view that the Mexican struggle for independence was a predominantly mestizo movement is a "distortion" that does not fit the documentary evidence. He argues, instead, that indigenous rebels formed a significant majority of the insurgent population, roughly equal to their proportion of the population as a whole. Among other factors, he maintains that the traditionally narrow focus on relatively less indigenous areas like the Bajío, the area around Guadalajara, and the Pacific lowlands in the south have skewed observers' characterizations of insurgent ethnicity away from indigenous participation. He also identifies a misconceived tendency in the historiography to portray the independence struggle in the context of the predestined mestizaje that often accompanies nationalistic visions of Mexico's past, thereby driving out the very real presence of indigenous communities and individuals in the insurgency. Van Young, *The Other Rebellion*, 44–48.

39. My emphasis. Ibid., 45–46 and 141–64. Van Young argues that indigenous "village notables," on the whole, tended not to directly participate in the insurgency, especially not in numbers proportionate to their percentage of the population. This suggests that their ties to the Spanish regime limited the impetus they might otherwise have had to take on leadership roles in the insurgency.

40. Insurgent Database.

41. Van Young, *The Other Rebellion*, 128, maintains that indios were "more consistently prone than other people to self-exculpatory claims when caught up in the colonial regime's legal machinery."

42. Insurgent Database. According to Van Young, *The Other Rebellion*, 109, seven indigenous men purportedly forced into service by Camarena were still imprisoned in Guadalajara as late as March 1813.

43. BPEJ Criminal, caja 33, exp. 1, prog. 523, 43.

44. Alamán, *Historia de Méjico*, 2:16; Carlos María de Bustamante, *Cuadro histórico de la Revolución Mexicana, iniciada el 15 de septiembre de 1810 por el c. Miguel Hidalgo y Costilla, cura del pueblo de Dolores en el obispado de Michoacán* (Mexico City: Ediciones de la Comisión Nacional para la Celebración del Sesquicentenario de la Proclamación de la Independencia Nacional y del Cincuentenario de la Revolución Mexicana, 1961), 1:171–97.

45. BPEJ Criminal, caja 33, exp. 1, prog. 523, "Lista de individuos que se presentaron al indulto publicado con fecha del 6 de abril"; "Apuntes relativos á los acontecimientos ocurridos en Colotlán," Figueroa and Yguiniz, *Biblioteca Histórica Jalisciense*, section 1, no. 8, 188; Gutiérrez, *Aguascalientes y su región de influencia hasta 1810*, 57.

46. Miquel i Vergés, *Diccionario de Insurgentes*, 569–70.

47. Document cited in Carlos Ramírez Esparza, *El Padre Calvillo: Caudillo de la Guerra de Independencia* (Guadalajara, Mexico: Gobierno de Jalisco, Secretaria General, Unidad Editorial, 1987), 14.

48. Hamill, *The Hidalgo Revolt*, 194–201.

49. Purportedly, Ignacio Allende even planned to poison Hidalgo in conjunction with another estranged creole supporter; Hamill, *The Hidalgo Revolt*, 194–201. Later events marked Calvillo as a supporter of Hidalgo in this factious split, and evidence suggests that Hidalgo spared some of the Spaniards from execution at the urging of some of his associates. Calvillo may have acted on behalf of some of the gachupines (peninsular Spaniards) in this manner, particularly the Baron de Santa Cruz, who later served as an advocate for the granting of Calvillo's pardon. The baron's name was Guillermo García Caserta. He was a Spaniard from Cádiz and a nephew of the regidor of Guadalajara. Ramírez Esparza, *El Padre Calvillo*, 33–37.

50. Van Young, *The Other Rebellion*, 493–94.

51. BPEJ Criminal, caja 41, exp. 2, prog. 658, 1–4.

52. Ibid., 2.

53. Ibid., 1–4.

54. Ramírez Esparza, *El Padre Calvillo*, 13–15; Hamill, *The Hidalgo Revolt*, 201–2. For more on Calleja, see Hugh M. Hamill Jr.'s "Hidalgo and Calleja: The Colonial Bases of Caudillismo," in *Caudillos: Dictators in Spanish America*, ed. Hugh M. Hamill Jr. (Norman: University of Oklahoma Press, 1992), 99–106. For a general summary of the battle, see "Calderon Bridge," in *Encyclopedia of Battles in North America, 1517 to 1916*, eds. L. Edward Purcell and Sarah J. Purcell (New York: Facts On File, 2000), 42.

55. Insurgent Database.

56. Ibid.

57. Ibid.

58. Porlier's regiment was operating in the La Barca region near Lake Chapala, following a strategy soon to be applied in the Colotlán region of executing captured insurgents while offering royal pardon to those who would surrender voluntarily. "Contestación de Cruz," March 7, 1811, in Juan López, *La Insurgencia de la Nueva Galicia en algunos documentos*, 1:228–29; AGN, Infidencias, vol. 134, folio 252, exp. 106, 1810–12. "Que barra a las gavillas de Xalpa, Zacatecas, Juchipila, Tlaltenango y otras para que a un mismo tiempo se de el golpe a las gavillas gruesas."

59. General Cruz's exact words were: *El bribón del P. Calvillo está reuniendo bastante Indiada.* "Contestación de Cruz," March 8, 1811, Doc. 199 and Doc. 200, March 9, 1811, in Juan López, *La Insurgencia de la Nueva Galicia en algunos documentos*, 1:230–32.

60. "Alborotandolos, y juntando frente." AGN, Infidencias, vol. 131, folio 300, exp. 31, 1811, 173.

61. Alberto Santoscoy, "El Padre Pablo José Calvillo (Un Héroe de la Independencia)," *Diario de Jalisco*, Guadalajara, September 16, 1900, in *Alberto Santoscoy, Obras Completas* (Guadalajara, Mexico: Gobierno de Jalisco, Secretaría General, Unidad Editorial, 1986), 2:47.

62. "Álvarez to Cruz," March 31, 1811, Xerez, Doc. 219 in Juan López, *La Insurgencia de la Nueva Galicia en algunos documentos*, 2:1–2.

63. "Apuntes relativos á los acontecimientos ocurridos en Colotlán," Figueroa and Yguiniz, *Biblioteca Histórica Jalisciense*, section 1, no. 8, 190.

64. "Álvarez to Cruz," March 31, 1811, Xerez, Doc. 219 in Juan López, *La Insurgencia de la Nueva Galicia en algunos documentos*, 2:1–2.

65. BPEJ Criminal, caja 33, exp. 1, prog. 523, 1–73.

66. Doc. 224, April 7, 1811, in Juan López, *La Insurgencia de la Nueva Galicia en algunos documentos*, 2:10–11 and 2:8–9; Santoscoy, *Obras Completas*, 2:48; and Ramírez Esparza, *El Padre Calvillo*, 17.

67. Doc. 224, April 7, 1811, in Juan López, *La Insurgencia de la Nueva Galicia en algunos documentos*, 2:10–11.

68. Figueroa and Yguiniz, *Biblioteca histórica jalisciense*, 1:203.

Chapter 5

1. According to the officer recording the event, "only those designated by chance were shot." "Fueron diezmados solamente y fusilados solo los designados por la suerte." AGN, Infidencias, vol. 5, exp. 12, folios 1, register 38, 1810.

2. Consideration of the ritualistic aspect of pardon and confession in other cultural settings offers a useful comparative framework for textual analysis. In *Fiction in the Archives: Pardon Tales and Their Tellers in Sixteenth-Century France* (Stanford, Calif.: Stanford University Press, 1990), Natalie Zemon Davis reminds us of the importance of recognizing the fictional aspects often present in the construction of a pardon application, from formulaic methods of official record keeping to the influence of self-interested narrative license. Her work serves as a warning to not accept the wording of such documents at face value; it also is a reminder that the "tale behind the tale" can tell us much about the mentalities of our historical subjects. Such recognition of the value of pardon records has been relatively absent among scholars of late colonial Mexico, and other than several pages dedicated to the topic of pardon and ritual confession in Eric Van Young's *The Other Rebellion*, no other study has employed this approach in the context of Latin American independence.

3. "Proposición de Don José de la Cruz al Sr. Hidalgo para que se indulte, y contestación de éste y Allende," Document 207, in Juan E. Hernández y Dávalos, comp. *Coleccion de documentos para la historia de la guerra de independencia de Mexico de 1808 a 1821*, (Liechtenstein: Nendeln, Kraus Reprint, 1968), 2:403–4.

4. As Eric Van Young pointed out in *The Other Rebellion*, 118, the number of people pardoned during this period included "thousands upon thousands," and royalist field commanders did not always document every pardon they granted. Still, it is possible to detect a number of representative patterns in the nature and practice of the indulto process from extant records. In the instances where generalizations concerning the pardon process proved useful, they have been based on some 491

indulto records covering 1810 to 1820, in addition to and separate from the several hundred pardoned insurgents contained in the Insurgent Database. These records are not intended to contain exhaustive documentation representing the entire pardon process in independence-era New Spain, but they do represent all available records from the AGN and from other archival collections relevant to the Colotlán region. In addition to records covering events on the ground in Colotlán, the sources reviewed for this chapter include seventeen edicts pronounced by the viceregal government and currently housed in the Archivo General de la Nación in Mexico City. Indulto records from Nueva Galicia pertaining specifically to the Colotlán region are taken from the Criminal section of the Archivo de la Real Audiencia de Guadalajara at the Biblioteca Pública del Estado de Jalisco. Other sources include documents from J. E. Hernández y Dávalos's six-volume document collection on the wars of independence, *Coleccion de documentos para la historia de la guerra de independencia de Mexico de 1808 a 1821*; Genaro García's seven-volume set of *Documentos históricos mexicanos; obra conmemorativa del primer centenario de la independencia de México, la publica el Museo nacional de arqueología, historia y etnología, bajo la dirección de Genaro García, por acuerdo de la Secretaría de instrucción pública y bellas artes* (Mexico City, Museo nacional de aqueología, historia y etnología, 1910–12); José María Miquel i Vergés, *Diccionario de Insurgentes*; and Juan López, *La Insurgencia de la Nueva Galicia en algunos documentos*, 1–2.

5. Van Young, *The Other Rebellion*, 118.

6. AGN, Indios, vol. 6, exp. 1044, folio 283, 1595.

7. The chronological sequence of the 993 indulto documents in AGN confirms this interpretation, as they begin to appear with greater frequency in the late 1700s, then erupt numerically during the decade of the independence stuggle.

8. "¡Muera el mal gobierno! ¡Viva el Rey!" Crespo Rodas, Alberto, Mariano B. Gumucio y José de Mesa 1989. *La ciudad de La Paz* (La Paz, Bolivia: Alcaldía Municipal, 1989), 51, 100–101.

9. Note 11 contains a chronological list of the indulto decrees preserved in the AGN.

10. AGN, Bandos, vol. 31, exp. 25, folio 25, 1810.

11. The indulto decrees preserved in the AGN are: AGN, Bandos, vol. 31, exp. 25, folio 25, Oct. 15, 1810; AGN, Bandos, vol. 30, exp. 35, folios 35–36, Dec. 31, 1810; AGN, Bandos, vol. 31, exp. 35, folio 13, Feb. 11, 1811; AGN, Bandos, vol. 31, exp. 15, folio 15, April 5, 1811; AGN, Bandos, vol. 31, exp. 25, folio 25, July 30, 1811; AGN, Bandos, vol. 31, exp. 56, folio 56, April 1, 1812; AGN, Bandos, vol. 27, exp. 76, folio 90, Aug. 11, 1813; AGN, Bandos, vol. 27, exp. 29, folio. 65, June 22, 1814; AGN, Bandos, vol. 28, exp. 29, folio 65, March 13, 1815; AGN, Reales Cédulas, vol. 212, exp. 177, folio 12, May 30, 1815; AGN, Bandos, vol. 28, exp. 86, folio 167, Dec. 22, 1815; AGN, Bandos, vol. 28, exp. 123, folio 232, May 4, 1816; AGN, Bandos, vol. 28, exp. 125, folio 234, May 11, 1816; AGN, Casa de Moneda, vol. 75, exp. 19, folios 226–34, Jan. 25, 1817; AGN, Bandos, vol. 29, exp. 27, folio 78, June 28, 1817; AGN, Bandos, vol. 29, exp. 39, folios 90–91, Aug. 11, 1817; AGN, Reales Cédulas, vol. 224, exp. 87, folio 2, Oct. 20, 1820.

12. AGN, Infidencias, vol. 75, exp. 9, folio 13, 1815.

13. BPEJ Criminal, caja 33, exp. 1, prog. 523, "Lista de individuos que se presentaron al indulto publicado con fecha del 6 de abril."

14. Van Young, *The Other Rebellion*, 118–19.

15. AGN, Bandos, vol. 27, exp. 171, folio 212, 1814. A similar edict went out to the subdelegados of the Colotlán region in February 1816. BPEJ Civil, caja 284, exp. 3, prog. 3923: "Circular de 9 de febrero, sobre haber concedido el excelentísimo Sr. Virrey a los rebeldes el indulto con el saludable y piadoso fin de apartarlos del sistema de perdición y temporal que han adoptado."

16. A number of scholars have demonstrated the link between control over mobility and authority in the Spanish world. Steve Stern, for instance, has shown how control over a woman's mobility was central to male authority. As will be discussed later, the confinement of women associated with the insurgency in reformatory-style casas de recogidas highlights the paternal concerns of royal authorities troubled by social disorder during the insurgency. Stern, *The Secret History of Gender*, 75–77.

17. BPEJ Civil caja 284, exp. 3, prog. 3923; AGN, Infidencias, vol. 68, exp. 7, folio 75, 1816–17.

18. Such was the case of "elderly" insurgent Bernardo Fernandez, for example. AGN, Infidencias, vol. 136, exp. 5, folio 4, 1818.

19. AGN, Infidencias, vol. 42, exp. 5, folio 11, 1815.

20. AGN, Infidencias, vol. 167, exp. 4, folio 17, 1818.

21. This incident is cited in Van Young, *The Other Rebellion*, 120.

22. AGN, Infidencias, vol. 57, exp. 6, folio. 32, 1817–18.

23. In the case of Vicente Vargas, his family having been freed, in September 1819 he resumed his rebel activities. After royalist soldiers captured and shot him on October 14, a royalist colonel sentenced his *amasia* Rafaela Morales and four other women found in the company of his "gang" to four years labor and detainment, also in La Magdalena. Thus, while his wife's imprisonment served primarily as a tool to force Vargas's "repentance," the sentence of his mistress and her companions was clearly a punishment, as Vargas had already been killed. The cases of María Arias and Antonia Gonzales, two insurgent widows confined for a year and a half in the Casa de Recogidas in Irapuato, confirm the punitive nature of this practice. Miquel i Vergés, *Diccionario de Insurgentes,* 587; García, *Documentos históricos mexicanos,* 383–85.

24. In another example, María Estanislao Sánchez and her children, *muger é hijos del cavecilla Sebastian Gonzalez,* were exchanged for a royalist lieutenant captured by the rebel leader in March 1818. Miquel i Vergés, *Diccionario de Insurgentes,* 223; García, *Documentos históricos mexicanos,* 409–10, 428–29.

25. Out of the sixty-three cases I examined in which rebel family members were confined, only two women had been imprisoned before 1814. Desperation in the face of an enduring rebellion may have led royalist commanders to escalate their tactics. This point is discussed more fully in Barry M. Robinson, "La reclusión de mujeres rebeldes: el recogimiento en la guerra de independencia mexicana, 1810–1819," *Fronteras de la Historia* 15, no. 2 (2010): 225–44.

26. Space, time, and thematic coherence has not permitted an in-depth discussion here of the role of women in the pardon process and the insurgency as a whole. For just such a study, see Robinson, "La reclusión de mujeres rebeldes." One of the only other studies of the role of women in the insurgency is Janet R. Kentner, "The

Socio-Political Role of Women in the Mexican Wars of Independence, 1810–1821" (PhD diss., Loyola, University of Chicago, 1975).

27. AGN, Infidencias, vol. 150, exp. 7, folio 56, 1817.

28. AGN, Infidencias, vol. 44, exp. 4, folio 44, 1815.

29. Van Young notes that General José de la Cruz, the royal military commander of Nueva Galicia, was particularly disingenuous in this manner. Van Young, *The Other Rebellion,* 120.

30. AGN, Infidencias, vol. 151, exp. 31, folio 11, 1814–17; vol. 154, exp. 5, folio 11, 1819; vol. 154, exp. 9, folio 3, 1819.

31. AGN, Infidencias, vol. 57, exp. 4, folio 11, 1816.

32. AGN, Infidencias, vol. 116, exp. 16, folio 14, 1812.

33. AGN, Infidencias, vol. 58, exp. 8, folio 21, 1815.

34. AGN, Infidencias, vol. 101, exp. 4, folio 18, 1812; vol. 97, exp. 4, folio 12, 1814–16.

35. AGN, Infidencias, vol. 96, exp. 3, folio 12, 1817.

36. AGN, Infidencias, vol. 40, exp. 5, folio 56, 1815–17.

37. AGN, Infidencias, vol. 101, exp. 3, folio 33, 1812. Aside from priests and military officers, a number of other individuals recognized the value of serving as a "pardon broker." In 1811, for instance, a scribe from Sultepec asked royal authorities to grant him the right to administer pardons in his region, "flatteringly promising that he could bring over many rebels." AGN, Infidencias, vol. 175, exp. 53, folio 440, 1811.

38. AGN, Infidencias, vol. 48, exp. 9, folio 36, 1816.

39. The fiscal served as the legal council to an audiencia, or high court. AGN, Infidencias, vol. 110, exp. 1–4, folio 233, 1815–817.

40. AGN, Infidencias, vol. 57, exp. 2, folio 25, 1816–17.

41. AGN, Infidencias, vol. 99, exp. 5, fol. 58, 1811–16; AGN, Infidencias, vol. 40, exp. 6, folio 22, 1815–16.

42. Subsequently, José Batista, the royalist sergeant who had allowed Miranda to enter the church, was charged with failing to obey orders by allowing the prisoner to enter the church. Batista was eventually acquitted. AGN, Infidencias, vol. 59, exp. 4, folio 51, 1815–17.

43. AGN, Infidencias, vol. 102, exp. 1, folio 409, 1813–21.

44. AGN, Infidencias, vol. 157, exp. 80, folio 450, 1814.

45. AGN, Infidencias, vol. 120, exp. 8, folio 31, 1811–13.

46. AGN, Infidencias, vol. 157, exp. 62, folio 450, 1814.

47. AGN, Infidencias, vol. 18, exp. 5, folio 55, 1811–15.

48. AGN, Infidencias, vol. 108, exp. 3, folio 12, 1814.

49. AGN, Infidencias, vol. 11, exp. 8, folio 20, 1818.

50. AGN, Infidencias, vol. 71, exp. 3–4, folio 183, 31, 1814–20.

51. Miquel i Vergés, *Diccionario de Insurgentes,* 36, 68; García, *Documentos históricos mexicanos,* 452–53; AGN, Infidencias, vol. 84, exp. 3, folio 61, 1814–16.

52. "Unable to work." AGN, Carceles y Presidios, vol. 9, exp. 45, folios 158–60, 1813; Infidencias, vol. 151, exp. 88, folio 508, 1814–17.

53. AGN, Infidencias, vol. 137, exp. 1, folio 37, 1818–21.

54. AGN, Infidencias, vol. 112, exp. 3, folio 27, 1813–16.

55. "Bando declarando á los indios con iguales derechos que á los españoles, con-

cediéndoles ademas indulto," Documento 202, in Hernández y Dávalos, *Coleccion de documentos para la historia de la guerra de independencia de Mexico de 1808 a 1821*, 2:379–81. Thirty-nine of the 485 pardon cases studied specifically mentioned an indio applicant or applicants.

56. AGN, Infidencias, vol. 39, exp. 1, folio 248, 1814–18.

57. AGN, Infidencias, vol. 55, exp. 16, folio 10, 1811.

58. AGN, Infidencias, vol. 172, exp. 115, folio 492, 1812.

59. AGN, Infidencias, vol. 169, exp. 96, folio 357, 1816.

60. AGN, Infidencias, vol. 132, exp. 1, folio 104, 1818–21.

61. AGN, Infidencias, vol. 95, exp. 5, folio 80, 1815–17.

62. William Davis Robinson, *Memoirs of the Mexican Revolution; including a narrative of the expedition of General Xavier Mina. To which are annexed some observations on the practicability of opening a commerce between the Pacific and Atlantic oceans, through the Mexican isthmus, in the province of Oaxaca, and at the Lake of Nicaragua; and the vast importance of such commerce to the civilized world* (London: Lackington, Hughes, Harding, Mavor, & Lepard, 1821), 2:141.

63. Gutiérrez, *Aguascalientes y su región de influencia hasta 1810*, 10, 27. Pablo José was the son of Vicente Calvillo and María Jerónima Ximénez de Alvarado. The Church of Jesús Christ of Latter-day Saints, International Genealogical Index, Aguascalientes, Microfilm 1553589, sheet 41.

64. Toribio Hernández López, *Monografia del municipio de Calvillo* (Aguascalientes, Mexico: Gobierno del Estado de Aguascalientes, 1991), 31.

65. Baptismal records cited in Gutiérrez, *Aguascalientes y su región de influencia hasta 1810*, 28–29; LDS, International Genealogical Index: Aguascalientes, Microfilm 003, 1, 345; AGN, General de Parte, vol. 52, exp. 181, folios 201v–207, 1774.

66. Gutiérrez, *Aguascalientes y su región de influencia hasta 1810*, 30.

67. Taylor, *Magistrates of the Sacred*, 90–91; Gutiérrez, *Aguascalientes y su región de influencia hasta 1810*, 27.

68. "Seminario de Guadalajara: 305 años de formar sacerdotes." Accessed April 18, 2001, <http://www.informador.com.mx/lastest/2001/Marzo/17mar2001/17pro8a .htm>.

69. Taylor, *Magistrates of the Sacred*, 86–88.

70. It is possible that Calvillo spoke one of the indigenous languages of his home region, most likely Huichol. In his extensive study of Mexican clergy, Taylor, in Magistrates of the Sacred, discusses the practice of granting títulos de idioma to prospective clergymen without independent financial means in order to supply sufficient priests for remote indigenous parishes. Although Calvillo had access to at least moderate financial support through his family, he did end up ministering primarily to poorer indigenous parishes, and the fact that he grew up among a substantial Indian population lends credence to this possibility.

71. Gutiérrez, *Aguascalientes y su región de influencia hasta 1810*, 31–33.

72. Ibid., 48. After the fall of the city to Torres's rebels, Bishop Cabañas was forced to flee the city.

73. Santoscoy, *Nayarit: Colección de documentos inéditos*, 45.

74. Calvillo continued to maintain a home in Colotlán even after leaving the parish. Taylor, Magistrates of the Sacred, 81–97, 110; Bernardo Carlos Casas, *Tlaltenango:*

una ciudad amurallada, 134; Gutiérrez, *Aguascalientes y su región de influencia hasta 1810*, 34–36.

75. Santoscoy, *Nayarit: Colección de documentos inéditos*, 45.

76. Gutiérrez, *Aguascalientes y su región de influencia hasta 1810*, 34–38.

77. Gerhard, *The North Frontier of New Spain*, 64–65; Gutiérrez, *Aguascalientes y su región de influencia hasta 1810*, 38.

78. Archivo Histórico del Estado de Aguascalientes, (AHEA) Ramo Judicial-Penal caja 34, exp. 6, folios 1–4, "Sobre la sublevación de los indios de Jesús María debido al cateo de sus casas para averiguar quienes son los que han robado vacas de la región," February 6, 1810, Aguascalientes. Gómez Serrano, *Aguascalientes en la historia, 1786–1920*, 28–33.

79. AHEA Judicial-Penal caja 34, exp. 6, folios 1–4, February 6, 1810. Gómez Serrano, *Aguascalientes en la historia, 1786–1920*, 28–35. Roque Abarca would later be captured outside of Bolaños by Daniel Camarena, a confederate of Calvillo, who turned Abarca over to Hidalgo when the insurgents arrived in Guadalajara. Amador, *Bosquejo histórico de Zacatecas*, 2:21.

80. AHEA Judicial-Penal caja 34, exp. 6, folios 1–4, February 6, 1810; Gutiérrez, *Aguascalientes y su región de influencia hasta 1810*, 43; Gómez Serrano, *Aguascalientes en la historia, 1786–1920*, 28–35. Both Steve Stern and William B. Taylor have stressed the important roles of women in riots and resistance to Spanish authority. Stern argues, in particular, that "women responded fiercely in crises that threatened . . . the well-being of community families." An interpretation drawn from Stern might deem the escalation in Jesús María the result of "the status of women as gendered property," and the Indian men's "proprietary outrage." Stern, *The Secret History of Gende*, 206–9; Taylor, *Drinking, Homicide, and Rebellion in Colonial Mexican Villages*, 82–127, 153–56.

81. AHEA Judicial-Penal caja 34, exp. 6, folios 1–4, February 6, 1810; Gómez Serrano, *Aguascalientes en la historia, 1786–1920*, 30–32.

82. According to Van Young, many priests who were described by royalists as being able to "win the hearts of the people" (hence a "conscientious priest") were suspected of favoring the insurgent cause (a "disloyal citizen"). Van Young, *The Other Rebellion*, 248. Conflicts between subdelegates and parish priests were not uncommon during this period. Taylor argues that patterns of local politics in the late colonial period shifted from a model in which both royal authority (in the form of the subdelegates and district governors) and religious authority (in the form of the parish priests) exercised relatively similar influence on local pueblo officials and political events to a model in which royal authorities attempted to end parish priests' influence. Taylor also notes that "few alcaldes mayores and subdelegates were from the area or spoke the indigenous language, and few lived outside the cabecera. . . . Their contact was largely restricted to men; except as judges, they dealt mainly with their own dependents and lieutenants, village officials, trading partners, resident non-Indians, and the priests." Taylor, *Magistrates of the Sacred*, 345–69, 397–98, 422–23.

83. Farriss's *Crown and Clergy in Colonial Mexico* served as the standard study of clerical participation in the revolts for a long time. In this early and important study, Farriss makes a strong case for the important role played by clerical insurgents. She estimated that the 401 rebel clergymen listed in the Appendix of her book formed

only a small portion of the total number of rebellious clergy. Farriss, *Crown and Clergy in Colonial Mexico*, 198–99. Ortíz Escamilla estimates that of 4,000 parish priests in the various regions in which the insurgency caught on, some 400 actively joined the rebel forces. As Ortíz Escamilla notes, this number is particularly significant considering the fact that many clergy were too old to fight and many others remained neutral. Ortíz Escamilla, "El bajo clero mexicano durante la guerra civil de 1810," 11. See also D. A. Brading, *Church and State in Bourbon Mexico: The Diocese of Michoacán, 1749–1810* (Cambridge, U.K.: Cambridge University Press, 1994).

84. Van Young has recently challenged previously accepted estimates of the high number of clergymen involved in active rebellion. He argues that "perhaps 80 percent of New Spain's clergy remained at least passively loyal to the colonial regime during the decade of the insurgency," and he disputes the "conventional historical wisdom" that has described the Mexican clergy as generally "revolutionary." However, he concedes that a higher percentage of clergymen sided with the insurgency than did "other highly visible groups in the general population." In effect, rather than denying the significance of clerical participation, he argues that traditional, sweeping explanations for the motivation of clerical participation in the rebellions are suspect. Van Young, *The Other Rebellion*, 240–41, 585–86.

85. Farriss, *Crown and Clergy in Colonial Mexico*, 200.

86. The phrase "crisis of ecclesiastical privilege " is taken from Farriss's title. Ortíz Escamilla provides a good example of such arguments: "The war divided the members of the church and caused it to lose a good portion of its priests and parishes, perhaps the most active, enlightened and involved with the church and society. The priests that rebelled did not do so against the church, but against the government that tried to limit their privileges, rights, and goods." Ortíz Escamilla, "El bajo clero mexicano durante la guerra civil de 1810," 11. In "The Appropriation of Mexican Church Wealth by the Spanish Bourbon Government: The 'Consolidación de Vales Reales,' 1805–1809," *Journal of Latin American Studies 1 (1969): 85–113*, Hamnett argued that the Crown's efforts to "appropriate capital from the corporate reserves of the church and Indian pueblos" created widespread disaffection. On the other hand, Asunción Lavrin, "The Execution of the Law of Consolidation in New Spain: Economic Aims and Results," *Hispanic American Historical Review* 53, no. 1 (February 1973): 27–49, found no correlation between these efforts and indigenous insurgency. See Taylor, *Magistrates of the Sacred*, 22.

87. For a succinct discussion of the importance of the Virgen de Guadalupe, see Hamnett, *Roots of Insurgency*, 15–18. Some observers have argued that religion was not an important cause of rebellion. Hugh M. Hamill Jr. writes, for instance, that "[the Catholic religion] was never imperiled. Religion was not an issue during the Hidalgo revolt, although it was frequently—even blatantly—used as a weapon of propaganda." Hamill, *The Hidalgo Revolt*, 40–41.

88. Taylor, *Magistrates of the Sacred*; Schmitt, "The Clergy and the Independence of New Spain," 289, 299–305; Hamill, *The Hidalgo Revolt*, 132–37. Most higher-ranking clergymen opposed the rebellion. The fact that the lower ranks of the clergy split, rather than supporting the insurgency wholesale, also complicates an explanation of clerical participation based strictly on class and socioeconomic position. Van Young echoes this argument on 254–55 of *The Other Rebellion*.

89. AHEZ caja 57, exp. 11, folio 8, 26 de Febrero de 1811–4 de Marzo de 1811; BPEJ Manuscritos, caja 70, exp. 37, folios 163–64.

90. Van Young, *The Other Rebellion,* 202–23, 588n27.

91. Felipe Jiménez de la Rosa, *Ruta de Hidalgo, 1810–1811* (Mexico City: Impresora y Servicios Gráficos, 1960), 116–21.

92. AHEZ Judicial caja 22, exp. 16.

93. Villaseñor, *Biografías de los heroes,* 168–69. For more on the Count of Santiago de la Laguna and insurgent Zacatecas during this period, see Jaime E. Rodríguez O., "*We Are Now the True Spaniards": Sovereignty, Revolution, Independence, and the Emergence of the Federal Republic of Mexico, 1808–1824* (Stanford, Calif.: Stanford University Press, 2012), 142–45.

94. Padre Álvarez developed a reputation for brutality. Calvillo's men dubbed him the *cura chicharronero* (the "bungling priest"). According to Ortíz Escamilla, Álvarez was recognized for his ferocity during the pacification of the pueblos, and was known for burning the bodies of his enemies. General Cruz claimed that "Álvarez did not always comply with his obligations because he forced contributions, appropriated goods, and permitted the looting of the properties of insurgents simply to placate his troops; he sent those who should have been pardoned to the firing squad and pardoned those who he should have executed. Nevertheless, he could not be dispensed with because he was the only available force to maintain order in the canyon of Juchipila, Tlaltenango, and Teúl." Ortíz Escamilla, "El bajo clero mexicano durante la guerra civil de 1810," 16–17.

95. Santoscoy, *Nayarit: Colección de documentos inéditos,* 48.

96. BPEJ Criminal, caja 33, exp. 1, prog. 523, 50.

97. AGN, Infidencias, vol. 21, exp. 4, 1811. Although the Najeras's ethnicity is not specified, a number of indigenous and casta Najeras are listed in earlier padrones (1783) from the pueblo of Huejuquilla el Alto in the Colotlán Frontera. "Informes sobre las fronteras de San Luis Colotlán, 1783," AGN, Indiferente de Guerra, vol. 83, exp. 2.

98. AHEZ caja 22, exp. 16, folio 3. Villaseñor also reported that Terán did, in fact, know of Calvillo's presence in the town but incorrectly explained that "such was the fear that he had of Padre Calvillo" that Terán did not attempt to arrest him. Villaseñor, *Biografías de los heroes,* 168; Gutiérrez follows this account, *Aguascalientes y su región de influencia hasta 1810,* 65–69.

99. AHEZ Judicial caja 24, exp. 10, folio 16–17.

100. AHEZ Judicial caja 24, exp. 10, folio 21–23.

101. AHEZ Judicial caja 22, exp. 21, AHEZ Judicial caja 22, exp. 16; AHEZ Judicial caja 24, exp. 10.

102. AGN, Infidencias, vol. 21, folio 10, exp. 4, 1811; AGN, Infidencias, vol. 13, exp. 4, folio 8, 1811; AGN, Infidencias, vol. 134, folio 252, exp. 1–106, 1810–12; Alamán, *Historia de Méjico,* 2:312; Gutiérrez, *Aguascalientes y su región de influencia hasta 1810,* 78; Gómez Serrano, *Aguascalientes en la historia, 1786–1920,* 49; Miquel i Vergés, *Diccionario de Insurgentes,* 415.

103. Juan López, *La Insurgencia de la Nueva Galicia en algunos documentos,* 2:270–71. Lucas Alamán erroneously reports that, while Calvillo's wounds and illness may have kept him from active participation, he helped to direct the operation from Valle

de Huejúcar. Alamán, *Historia de Méjico*, 2:291–295; Miquel i Vergés, *Diccionario de Insurgentes*, 108–9; Gutiérrez, *Aguascalientes y su región de influencia hasta 1810*, 77–79; Villaseñor, *Biografías de los heroes*, 168.

104. Cited in Amador, *Bosquejo histórico de Zacatecas*, 2:117–21.

105. AGN, Infidencias, vol. 21, folio 10, exp. 4, 1811; AGN, Infidencias, vol. 13, folio 8, exp. 4, 1811; AGN, Infidencias, vol. 134, folio. 252, exp. 1–106, 1810–12; Alamán, *Historia de Méjico*, 2:312; Gutiérrez, *Aguascalientes y su región de influencia hasta 1810*, 78; Gómez Serrano, *Aguascalientes en la historia, 1786–1920*, 49; and Miquel i Vergés, *Diccionario de Insurgentes*, 415.

106. AGN, Infidencias, vol. 99, folio 21, exp. 8, 1811.

107. AGN, Infidencias, vol. 131, folio 300, exp. 1–64, 1811.

108. BPEJ, Manuscritos, vol. 77, exp. 37, prog. 177, March 9, 1811.

109. José Ignacio Paulino Dávila Garibi, *Biografía de un gran prelado, el exmo. e ilmo. Sr. Dr. D. Juan Cruz Ruiz de Cabañas y Crespo* (Mexico City: Editorial Jus, 1984), 250, 312.

110. BPEJ caja 31, exp. 10, prog. 523, 64–65.

111. Calvillo may have acted on behalf of some of the peninsular Spaniards during the period of Hidalgo's control over Guadalajara. The Baron de Santa Cruz later served as an advocate for the granting of Calvillo's pardon. Ramírez Esparza, *El Padre Calvillo*, 33–37.

112. The note reads: "As a true Spaniard and loyal vassal of our Catholic Monarch el Señor Don Fernando Séptimo (May God Save Him), desiring that men of honor finish cutting the thread of insurrection, I certify and in case of necessity swear that the causes of the tardiness of the parish priest Don Pablo José Calvillo in presenting himself to receive the grace of pardon have been a [kidney stone] that impedes him from mounting a horse and also a considerable injury that a horse gave him, and for surety of the applicant and the results that have been arranged I provide this in the Valley of Huajucar on the twenty-sixth day of the month of November of the year 1811." Ramírez Esparza, *El Padre Calvillo*, 45.

113. The fact that the ecclesiastical authorities initially showed less willingness than General Cruz to confirm Calvillo's pardon seems to contradict Schmitt's notion that church authorities generally demonstrated more lenience toward former insurgent priests than did civil authorities. Ramírez Esparza, *El Padre Calvillo*, 33–35; Gutiérrez, *Aguascalientes y su región de influencia hasta 1810*, 100–103; Schmitt, "The Clergy and the Independence of New Spain," 294–98.

114. Gutiérrez, *Aguascalientes y su región de influencia hasta 1810*, 119–26.

115. In addition to the three Najera brothers and José Felipe Gonzalez, Calvillo had also turned over Manuel de Luevano and an unidentified associate to the authorities at some point.

116. "Confesión del Presbítero Dn. Pablo José Calvillo," original image reproduced in Ramírez Esparza, *El Padre Calvillo*, 53–54.

117. AHEZ Judicial caja 23, exp. 10, folio 5; "Teul 25 de Noviembre de 1811," in Juan López, *La Insurgencia de la Nueva Galicia en algunos documentos*, 2:38.

118. "Memoria histórica de Colotlán," from the manuscript collection of Sr. Lic. D. Mauro Villaseñor, in Figueroa and Yguiniz, *Biblioteca Histórica Jalisciense*, section 1, no. 9, 203–4. "Upstanding man" is translated from hombre de bién in the origi-

nal, a term that was commonly used to designate a respectable gentleman. Michael P. Costeloe has identified the status of hombre de bien as the common denominator among the political leadership of the newly independent Mexico of the 1820s and 1830s, in "Hombres de Bien in the Age of Santa Anna," in *Mexico in the Age of Democratic Revolutions 1750–1850*, ed. Jaime E. Rodriguez (Boulder, Colo.: Lynne Rienner, 1994), 243–57.

119. "Memoria histórica de Colotlán," 203–4.

120. See Doc. 244, "Extractos de doce acciones de guerra, dadas por las fuerzas de Nueva Galicia"; Doc. 251, "Aviso de D. José de la Cruz sobre el Ataque a Teocaltiche defendido por Díaz Cosio los días 23 y 24 de Febrero"; Doc. 266, "Parte del Subdelegado de Hostotipaquillo contra los indios de Apozolco 5 de Julio y órdenes del Sr. Cruz al mismo y al gobernador de Colotlán"; Doc. 272, "Extracto de los partes de 50 acciones de guerra, publicadas por José de la Cruz, en el aniversario de 16 de Septiembre"; Doc. 335, "Extracto de cuarenta y ocho acciones de guerra del 22 de Febrero al 18 de Septiembre de 1813, según los partes de D. José de la Cruz"; and Doc. 341, "Partes de D. José de la Cruz sobre varias acciones de guerra en distintos puntos del 4 de Septiembre de 1813 al 3 de Febrero de 1814," in Juan López, *La Insurgencia de la Nueva Galicia en algunos documentos*, 2:38, 44, 110, 116–27, 180, 194–200.

121. "Aviso de D. José de la Cruz sobre el Ataque a Teocaltiche defendido por Díaz Cosio los días 23 y 24 de Febrero, 1812" Doc. 251 in Juan López, *La Insurgencia de la Nueva Galicia en algunos documentos*, 2:44.

122. Doc. 272:43a in Juan López, *La Insurgencia de la Nueva Galicia en algunos documentos*, 2:124–25.

123. AHMJ, Archivo Parroquial de Jerez, Area Sacramental, Sección Defunciones, Serie Partidas y Certificaciones, Subserie General, caja 148, lib. 5, exp. 1, May–June 1812.

124. "La Gavilla de Mamata." "Cruz to Venegas, Enero 1812," AGN Infidencias, vol. 134. After conquering Chimaltitan, Iturbe é Iraeta arrested the pueblo's priest and sent him to be judged by the Junta de Seguridad in Zacatecas.

125. Doc. 335:41, 43 in Juan López, *La Insurgencia de la Nueva Galicia en algunos documentos*, 2:186–87; Report of the Cura of Teul to Bishop Cabañas, July 25, 1813, in Rojas, *Los Huicholes: Documentos Históricos*, 112. Further details of this episode are reprinted in Laura Magriña Ocampo, "Coras y Tecualmes: De la Conquista de El Nayarit a la Guerra de Independencia," in *Participación indígena en los procesos de Independencia y Revolución Mexicana*, eds. Víctor Manuel Rojo Leyva et al. (Mexico City: Comisión Nacional para el Desarrollo de los Pueblos Indígenas, 2011), 133–47.

126. Report of the Cura of Teúl to Bishop Cabañas, July 25, 1813, in Rojas, *Los Huicholes: Documentos Históricos*, 112; BPEJ Criminal caja 33, exp. 1, prog. 523, 24.

127. Juan E. Hernández y Dávalos Manuscript Collection, Benson Latin American Collection, University of Texas at Austin, Item No. [HD 10-3.760], 942 Ortiz de Rosas, José Ignacio. "Oficio a Cruz sobre acción de Manuel Campos contra rebeldes," December 5, 1816.

128. Juan Bautista de Arizpe, "Nueva Galicia," *Gaceta del Gobierno de México*, April 1816, and "Zacetas," *Gaceta del Gobierno de México*, May 1816; Alamán, *Historia de Méjico*, 4:435, cited in Miquel I Vergés, *Diccionario de Insurgentes*, 266. Rebecca Earle discussed the nature of indigenous loyalty during the independence period in

"Creole Patriotism and the Myth of the 'Loyal Indian,'" Past and Present 172 (2001): 129–30. She points out that despite royalist and nationalist rhetoric about the steadfastness of indigenous loyalty, Indian communities sometimes sought advantage by switching sides, in pursuit of their own interests.

129. AGN, Operaciones de Guerra, Vol. 147, Exp. 23, Sept. 15, 1815–Dec. 17, 1815, 104–11.

130. "Memoria histórica de Colotlán," from the manuscript collection of Sr. Lic. D. Mauro Villaseñor, in Figueroa and Yguiniz, eds., *Biblioteca Histórica Jalisciense*, section 1, no. 9, 204–5.

131. Ibid., 206.

132. Ibid.

Epilogue

1. For an overview of how independence was achieved, see Virginia Guedea, "The Process of Mexican Independence," *American Historical Review* 105, no. 1 (February 2000): 116–130.

2. AGN, Infidencias, vol. 102, exp. 1, folio 409, 1813–21; AGN, Infidencias, vol. 137, exp. 1, folio 37, 1818–21.

3. By this point, a majority of New Spain's population, including previously fervent royalists, began to realize, as Virginia Guedea put it, that "they could no longer remain at the mercy of the political fluctuations of the Iberian Peninsula." Guedea, "The Process of Mexican Independence," 129.

4. Timothy Anna, Peter Guardino, and Torcuato Di Tella have all argued that Mexico's indigenous population played an important role in the electoral politics of the early postindependence period, but the political power of the indigenous population may have been overstated. Timothy Anna, *Forging Mexico, 1821–1835* (Lincoln: University of Nebraska Press, 2001), 123–27; Peter Guardino, *Peasants, Politics, and the Formation of Mexico's National State: Guerrero, 1800–1857* (Stanford, Calif.: Stanford University Press, 2002), 90–97; and Torcuato Di Tella, "Ciclos políticos en la primera mitad del siglo XIX," in *La fundación del estado mexicano, 1821–1855*, ed. Josefina Zoraida Vázquez (Mexico City: Nueva Imagen, 1994), 111–33. Juan Ortíz Escamilla and José Antonio Serrano Ortega's edited volume, *Ayuntamientos y liberalismo gaditano en México* (Zamora, Mexico: El Colegio de Michoacán-Universidad Veracruzana, 2007), also provides particular insight into the status of Indians after Mexican independence in certain locales, but the contributors find that political participation varied by locale.

5. For example, in a 1999 study of indigenous attitudes toward these 1820 and 1821 political developments, Michael T. Ducey recognized that the implementation of the ayuntamiento system of local political organization marked an important identity shift for the indios of New Spain. Ducey argued that indigenous insurgents in Papantla, Veracruz, embraced the Spanish repromulgation of the Constitution of Cádiz in 1820 and adopted new identities as "citizens." He interpreted these events as a positive development in the political status of indigenous villagers, claiming that "the transformation of repúblicas de indios into constitutionally based forms of local rule offered villagers opportunities to address the disputes over power that had

affected relations both between Crown officials and subjects and within the pueblos themselves." Ducey, "Village, Nation, and Constitution: Insurgent Politics in Papantla, Veracruz, 1810–1821," *Hispanic American Historical Review* 79, no. 3 (1999): 463–93. Ducey's study provides a very useful narrative of the insurgency in the Papantla region, and the divided loyalties he documents mesh well with the discussion provided in chapters 4 and 5 of this study. Interestingly, he also found evidence of interpueblo conflict between cabecera and subject pueblos, 466. However, it is not clear that it is in fact the indigenous inhabitants of Papantla, rather than particular insurgent commanders, who expressed the opinions he interprets as "nationalistic" or "protonationalistic."

6. "Correspondencia dirigida a la H. Ayuntamiento de Zacatecas sobre Juntas Electorales. Mes de Enero de 1821," AHEZ, Fondo Intendencia de Zacatecas (1785–1822) Gobierno, caja 3, exp. 37.

7. AHEZ, Fondo Intendencia de Zacatecas (1785–1822) Gobierno, caja 3, exp. 37, 4.

8. Hernández y Dávalos Manuscript Collection, Item No. HD 15-7.1956 Contrera, Gregorio. "Lista que denomina los Nombres y Clases de los oficiales empleados en las Milicias Locales de nueva criación en la comprehensión del Gobierno de Colotlán." Colotlán, LS. Jan. 13, 1822.

9. AHEZ, Fondo Intendencia de Zacatecas (1785–1822) Gobierno, caja 3, exp. 37, folio 10.

10. BPEJ Criminal, caja 33, exp. 1, prog. 523, folio 31.

11. BPEJ Civil caja 223, exp. 12, prog. 2910, folios 1–14.

12. "Correspondencia dirigida a la H. Ayuntamiento de Zacatecas sobre Juntas Electorales. Mes de Enero de 1821," AHEZ, Fondo Intendencia de Zacatecas (1785–1822) Gobierno, caja 3, exp. 37.

13. Juan Ortíz Escamilla, *Guerra y gobierno: los pueblos y la independencia de México* (Seville, Spain: Instituto Mora, 1997), 168–69. Macedonio Padilla had been a signatory to an 1815 declaration of loyalty to the king, written on behalf of the mining interests at Bolaños.

14. "Acta de lealtad al rey por parte de El Real y Minas de San Antonio de Bolaños. San Antonio de Bolaños, October 16–17, 1815. Doc. 807 in Hernández y Dávalos, *Coleccion de documentos para la historia de la guerra de independencia de Mexico de 1808 a 1821*, vol. 2, Item # HD-7-2.577.

15. AHEZ, Fondo Intendencia de Zacatecas (1785–1822) Gobierno, caja 3, exp. 37, folios 1–32.

16. "Pero creo que no lo quieren mucho por acá." "Carta de Pedro Celestino Negrete a Iturbide, Julio 6 de 1821," in *La correspondencia de Agustín de Iturbide después de la Proclamación del Plan de Iguala*, ed. Vito Alessio Robles (Mexico City: Archivo Histórico Militar Mexicano No. 1), 106–8.

17. Eric Hobsbawn launched the study of social banditry in *Primitive Rebels: Studies in Archaic Forms of Social Movement in the 19th and 20th Centuries* (New York: W. W. Norton, 1959). For a consideration of Mexican banditry in the long nineteenth century, see Chris Frazer, *Bandit Nation: A History of Outlaws and Cultural Struggle in Mexico, 1810–1920* (Lincoln: University of Nebraska Press, 2006).

18. Jesús y Laura Magriñá Jáuregui, "Estudio etnohistórico acerca del origen de los mexicaneros (hablantes del náhuatl) de la sierra Madre Occidental," *Dimensión*

Antropológica 26 (September-December, 2002): 27–81. Also see Jean Meyer, "El reino de Lozada en Tepic (1856–1873)," in *Esperando a Lozada* (Guadalajara, Mexico: El Colegio de Michoacán—Consejo Nacional de Ciencia y Tecnología, 1984), 235–56.

19. Stanley Linn Robe's *Azuela and the Mexican Underdogs* (Berkeley: University of California Press, 1979) traces Azuela's path through the region during the Mexican Revolution.

Bibliography

Archival Sources

Archivo General de la Nación, Mexico (AGN)

Sections:
Archivo de Guerra
Archivo Histórico de Hacienda
Ayuntamientos
Bandos
Capellanías
Carceles y Presidios
Clero Regular y Secular
Criminal
Documentos de Jalisco
Colección de Colección de Documentos para la Historia de la Guerra de Independencia de México: 1808–1821
Edictos de Inquisición
Expulsión de Españoles
General de Parte
Guerra y Marina
Indiferente de Guerra
Indios
Infidencias
Inquisición
Intendencias
Jesuitas
Justicia
Minería
Misiones
Operaciones de Guerra
Padrones
Provincias Internas

Real Audiencia
Reales Cédulas
Reales Ordenes
Subdelegados
Tierras
Títulos y Despachos de Guerra
Tributos

Archivo Histórico del Estado de Aguascalientes (AHEA)

Sections:
Protocolos Notariales (1592–1925), Indigenous pueblos and padrones
Ramo Judicial (1654–)
Cofradías (1790–1857)
Parish records

Archivo del Arzobispado de Guadalajara (AAG)

Sections:
Seminario (1696 to present)
Presbíteros (17th century to present)
Cofradías (1741–1850)
Visitas Pastorales de Obispos (1700–1800)
Padrones de Población (17th century to present)

Archivo Histórico Municipal de Jerez (AHMJ)

Archivo Histórico del Estado de Zacatecas (AHEZ)

Sections:
Ayuntamiento de la Ciudad (1557–1824)
Intendencia de Zacatecas (1785–1822)
Judicial (1557–1824)
Notarías (1614–1824)
Real Hacienda (1592–1824)
Tierras y Aguas (1586–1824)

Archivo Histórico del Estado de Jalisco (AHJ)

Archivo de la Real Audiencia de Guadalajara (ARAG), held at the Biblioteca Pública del Estado de Jalisco (BPEJ), Ramo Civil

Archivo Parroquial de Huejúcar, Jal (APH)

Archivo General de Simancas (AGS)

Archivo Histórico de la Provincia Franciscana (Zapopán-Jalisco)

Sections:
Colegio de Guadalupe, Zacatecas (18–19th centuries)
(Includes parish government records from 1800–1850)
Provincia de Santiago de Xalisco

Provincia de los Zacatecos
Papeles del Convento Dieguino de Aguascalientes

Church of Jesus Christ of Latter-day Saints, Microfilm collection

International Genealogical Index: Aguascalientes, Jalisco, Zacatecas; other microfilms

Individual Documents, Manuscripts, and Documentary Collections

Biblioteca histórica jalisciense. Guadalajara, Mexico: J. M. Yguíniz, 1909, vol. 1, no. 9., November 15– July 10, 1910.

Chavero, Alfredo, ed. *Lienzo de Tlaxcalla.* Mexico City: Litográfica del Timbre, 1892.

García, Genaro, ed. *Documentos históricos mexicanos; obra conmemorativa del primer centenario de la independencia de México, la publica el Museo nacional de arqueología, historia y etnología, bajo la dirección de Genaro García, por acuerdo de la Secretaría de instrucción pública y bellas artes.* Vol. 5. Mexico City: Museo nacional de aqueología, historia y etnología, 1910–12.

Gorostiza, Pedro. *Reglamento provisional para el regimen, gobierno y subsistencia de las milicias de la frontera de San Luis Colotlan establecidas con objecto a la defensa interior y exterior de esta provincia, y la del Nayarit.* Mexico City: Signed by Revilla Gigedo, 1792. Microfilm, Providence, RI, Brown University.

Gutiérrez Dávila, Julián. *Vida y virtudes de el siervo de Dios, el venerable padre D. Domingo Perez de Barcia, presbytero secular, fundador de la casa, y voluntario recogimiento de Mugeres, nombrado San Miguel de Bethlen, en la ciudad de Mexico,* 1720.

Hernández y Dávalos, Juan E., ed. *Coleccion de documentos para la historia de la guerra de independencia de Mexico de 1808 a 1821.* 6 vols. Liechtenstein: Nendeln, Kraus Reprint, 1968.

Humboldt, Alexander von. *Ensayo político sobre el reino de la Nueva España [por] Alejandro de Humboldt. Estudio preliminar, revisión del texto, cotejos, notas y anexos de Juan A. Ortega y Medina.* Mexico City: Editorial Porrua, 1966.

López, Juan, comp. *La Insurgencia de la Nueva Galicia en algunos documentos.* 2 vols. Guadalajara, México: Honorable Ayuntamiento de Guadalajara, 1984.

———. *La rebelion del indio Mariano: un movimiento insurgente en la Nueva Galicia, en 1801.* Vol. 3. Guadalajara, Mexico: Ayuntamiento de Guadalajara, 1985.

Orozco Farías, Rogelio, comp. *Fuentes históricas de la independencia de México, 1808–1821.* Docs. 20–24. Mexico City: Editorial Jus, 1967.

Ramírez Esparza, Carlos, ed. *El Padre Calvillo: Caudillo de la Guerra de Independencia.* Guadalajara, Mexico: Gobierno de Jalisco, Secretaria General, Unidad Editorial, 1987.

Robinson, William Davis. *Memoirs of the Mexican Revolution; including a narrative of the expedition of General Xavier Mina. To which are annexed some observations on the practicability of opening a commerce between the Pacific and Atlantic oceans, through the Mexican isthmus, in the province of Oaxaca, and at the Lake of Nicaragua; and the vast importance of such commerce to the civilized world.* 2 vols. London: Lackington, Hughes, Harding, Mavor, & Lepard, 1821.

Robles, Vito Alessio, ed. *La correspondencia de Agustín de Iturbide después de la Proclamación del Plan de Iguala*. City, State: Archivo Histórico Militar Mexicano No. 1.

Rojas, Beatriz, ed. *Los Huicholes: Documentos Históricos*. Mexico City: CIESAS, 1992.

Rueda, Laura, comp. *Descripciones franciscanas de la Provincia de Santiago de Xalisco, siglo XVIII*. Zapopan, Jalisco: Colegio de Jalisco, 1996.

Torre Villar, Ernesto de la, ed. *Los "Guadalupes" y la Independencia, con una selección de documentos inéditos*. Mexico City: Editorial Jus, 1966.

Secondary Literature

Alamán, Lucas. *Historia de Méjico desde los primeros moviminetos que prepararon su independencia en el año 1808 hasta la época presente*. Mexico City: Impr. de J. M. Lara, 1849–52.

Altman, Ida. *The War for Mexico's West: Indians and Spaniards in New Galicia, 1524–1550*. Albuquerque: University of New Mexico Press, 2010.

Amador, Elías. *Bosquejo histórico de Zacatecas*. Zacatecas, Mexico: Tall. Tip. Pedroza, 1943.

Andrien, Kenneth. "Economic Crisis, Taxes, and the Quito Insurrection of 1765." *Past and Present* 129 (1990): 104–31.

Archer, Christon, ed. *The Wars of Independence in Spanish America*. Wilmington, DE: Rowman and Littlefield, 2000.

Arendt, Hannah. *On Revolution*. Westport, CT: Greenwood Press, 1982.

Armitage, David. "The Declaration of Independence and International Law." *William and Mary Quarterly* 59, no. 1 (2002): 39–64.

Arrom, Silvia. *The Women of Mexico City, 1790–1857*. Stanford, CA: Stanford University Press, 1985.

Bailyn, Bernard. *The Ideological Origins of the American Revolution*. Cambridge, MA: Belknap Press of Harvard University Press, 1967.

Bakewell, Peter. *Silver Mining and Society in Colonial Mexico: Zacatecas, 1546–1700*. Cambridge, UK: Cambridge University Press, 1971.

Bancroft, Hubert Howe, *History of Mexico: Vol. III, 1600–1803*. San Francisco: A. L. Bancroft & Company, 1883.

Becker, Carl Lotus. *The History of Political Parties in the Province of New York, 1760–1776*. Madison: University of Wisconsin Press, 1909.

Beckles, Hilary, and Verene Shepherd, eds. *Caribbean Slavery in the Atlantic World*. Princeton, NJ: Markus Wiener, 1999.

Blosser, Bret. "'By the Force of Their Lives and the Spilling of Blood': Flechero Service and Political Leverage on a Nueva Galicia Frontier." In *Indian Conquistadors: Indigenous Allies in the Conquest of Mesoamerica*, edited by Laura E. Matthew and Michel R. Oudijk, 289–316. Norman: University of Oklahoma Press, 2007.

Brading, David A. *Church and State in Bourbon Mexico: The Diocese of Michoacán, 1749–1810*. Cambridge: Cambridge University Press, 1994.

———. *Los orígenes del nacionalismo mexicano*. Mexico City: Ediciones Era, 1980.

———. *Miners and Merchants in Bourbon Mexico, 1763–1810* (Cambridge, UK: Cambridge University Press, 1971).

Brinton, Crane. *The Anatomy of Revolution*. Revised ed. New York: Prentice Hall, 1952.

Burkholder, Mark. "From Creole to Peninsular: The Transformation of the Audiencia of Lima." *Hispanic American Historical Review* 52 (1972): 395–415.

Bustamante, Carlos María de. *Cuadro histórico de la Revolución Mexicana, iniciada el 15 de septiembre de 1810 por el c. Miguel Hidalgo y Costilla, cura del pueblo de Dolores en el obispado de Michoacán*. Mexico City: Ediciones de la Comisión Nacional para la Celebración del Sesquicentenario de la Proclamación de la Independencia Nacional y del Cincuentenario de la Revolución Mexicana, 1961.

Cahill, David. *From Rebellion to Independence in the Andes: Soundings from Southern Peru, 1750–1830*. Amsterdam: Aksant, 2002.

Calloway, Colin. *The American Revolution in Indian Country*. New York: Cambridge University Press, 1994.

———. *The World Turned Upside Down: Indian Voices from Early America*. Boston: Palgrave Macmillan, 1994.

Campbell, Leon. "A Colonial Establishment: Creole Domination in the Audencia of Lima during the late 18th century." *Hispanic American Historical Review* 52 (1972): 1–25.

Cañizares, Jorge. *How to Write the History of the New World: Histories, Epistemologies and Identities in the New World*. Stanford, CA: Stanford University Press, 2001.

Canny, Nicholas, and Anthony Pagden, eds. *Colonial Identity in the Atlantic World, 1500–1800*. Princeton, NJ: Princeton University Press, 1987.

Carbajal López, David. *La Minería en Bolaños, 1748–1810*. Colotlán, Jalisco: Universidad de Guadalajara-Campus Universitario del Norte, 2002.

Casas, Bernardo Carlos. *Tlaltenango: una ciudad amurallada*. Guadalajara, México: Impre-Jal, 1986.

Casas, Ulises. *Los comuneros en el contexto de la lucha de clases*. Bogotá: Galas de Colombia, 1983.

Castañeda de la Paz, María. "Central Mexican Indigenous Coats of Arms and the Conquest of Mesoamerica." *Ethnohistory* 56, no. 1 (Winter 2009): 125–61.

Chandler, D. S. "Creole Appointments and the Sale of Audencia Positions in the Spanish Empire Under the Early Bourbons 1701–1750." *Journal of Latin American Studies* 4 (1972): 187–206.

Chatterjee, Partha. *The Nation and Its Fragments: Colonial and Postcolonial Histories*. Princeton, NJ: Princeton University Press, 1993.

Chuchiak IV, John F. "The Sins of the Fathers: Franciscan Friars, Parish Priests, and the Sexual Conquest of the Yucatec Maya, 1545–1808." *Ethnohistory* 54, no. 1 (Winter 2007): 69–127.

Conway, Stephen. *The British Isles and the War of American Independence*. London: Oxford University Press, 2002.

———. "From Fellow-Nationals to Foreigners: British Perceptions of the Americas, circa 1739–1783." *William and Mary Quarterly* 59, no. 1 (2002): 65–100.

Cope, R. Douglas. *The Limits of Racial Domination: Plebian Society in Colonial Mexico City, 1660–1720*. Madison: University of Wisconsin Press, 1994.

Costeloe, Michael P. "Hombres de Bien in the Age of Santa Anna." In *Mexico in the Age of Democratic Revolutions 1750–1850*, edited by Jaime E. Rodriguez, 243–57. London: Lynne Rienner, 1994.

Crespo Rodas, Alberto, Mariano B. Gumucio, and José de Mesa. *La ciudad de La Paz*. La Paz, Mexico: Alcaldía Municipal, 1989.

Dahlgren de Jordán, Barbro. *Los coras de la sierra del Nayarit*. Mexico City: Universidad Nacional Autónoma de México, Instituto de Investigaciones Antropológicas, 1994.

Darkenwald, Gordon. "Calvillo: An Isolated Mexican Community." Master's thesis, Clark University, 1933.

Dávila Garibi, José Ignacio Paulino. *Biografía de un gran prelado, el exmo. e ilmo. Sr. Dr. D. Juan Cruz Ruiz de Cabañas y Crespo*. Mexico City: Editorial Jus, 1984.

Davis, David Brion. *Revolutions: Reflections on American Equality and Foreign Liberations*. Cambridge, MA: Harvard University Press, 1990.

Davis, Natalie Zemon. *Fiction in the Archives: Pardon Tales and Their Tellers in Sixteenth-Century France*. Stanford, CA: Stanford University Press, 1990.

Deans-Smith, Susan. "Culture, Power, and Society in Colonial Mexico." *Latin American Research Review* 33, no. 1 (1998): 257–77.

Ducey, Michael T. "Village, Nation, and Constitution: Insurgent Politics in Papantla, Veracruz, 1810–1821." *Hispanic American Historical Review* 79, no. 3 (1999): 463–93.

Dym, Jordana. *From Sovereign Villages to National States: City, State, and Federation in Central America, 1759–1839*. Albuquerque: University of New Mexico Press, 2006.

Earle, Rebecca. "Creole patriotism and the myth of the 'loyal Indian.'" *Past and Present* 172 (2001): 129–30.

———. "Indian Rebellion and Bourbon Reform in New Granada: Riots in Pasto, 1780–1800." Hispanic American Historical Review 73 (1993): 99–124.

———. *The Return of the Native: Indians and Mythmaking in Spanish America, 1810–1930*. Durham, NC: Duke University Press, 2008.

Ebright, Malcolm. "Sharing the Shortages: Water Litigation and Regulation in Hispanic New Mexico, 1600–1850," *New Mexico Historical Review* 76, no. 1 (January 2001): 3–45.

English Martin, Cheryl. *Governance and Society in Colonial Mexico: Chihuahua in the Eighteenth Century*. Stanford, CA: Stanford University Press, 1996.

———. "Indigenous Peoples." In *The Countryside in Colonial Latin America*, edited by Louisa Schell Hoberman and Susan Migden Socolow, 187–212. Albuquerque: University of New Mexico Press, 1996.

Farriss, Nancy. *Crown and Clergy in Colonial Mexico, 1759–1821: The Crisis of Ecclesiastical Privilege*. London: Athlone P., 1968.

Fiddian, Robin, ed. *Postcolonial Perspectives on the Cultures of Latin America and Lusophone Africa*. Liverpool, England: Liverpool University Press, 2000.

Figueroa, José Tomás, and Juan B. Yguiniz, eds. *Biblioteca Histórica Jalisciense*. Guadalajara, Mexico: Imprenta, Litografía, y Enc. de J. M. Yguíniz, 1909.

Flores Galindo, Alberto. *Túpac Amaru II, 1780: Sociedad colonial y sublevaciones populares*. Lima: Retablo de Papel Ediciones, 1976.

Florescano, Enrique. *Memory, Myth, and Time in Mexico: From the Aztecs to Independence*. Austin: University of Texas Press, 1994.

Frazer, Chris. *Bandit Nation: A History of Outlaws and Cultural Struggle in Mexico, 1810–1920*. Lincoln: University of Nebraska Press, 2006.

Garner, Richard L. "Zacatecas, 1750–1821: The Study of a Late Colonial Mexican City." PhD diss., University of Michigan, 1970.

Gaspar, David, and David Geggus. *A Turbulent Time: The French Revolution and the Greater Caribbean.* Bloomington: Indiana University Press, 1997.

Geggus, David P., ed. *The Impact of the Haitian Revolution in the Atlantic World.* Columbia: University of South Carolina, 2001.

Gerhard, Peter. *The North Frontier of New Spain.* Princeton, NJ: Princeton University Press, 1982.

Gómez Serrano, Jesús. *Aguascalientes en la historia, 1786–1920.* Aguascalientes, Mexico: Gobierno del Estado de Aguascalientes, 1988.

González, Agustín R. *Historia del Estado de Aguascalientes.* Aguascalientes, Mexico: Tip. de Francisco Antúnez, 1974.

González Obregón, Luis. *Rebeliones indígenas y precursores de la independencia mexicana en los siglos XVI, XVII, y XVIII.* 2nd ed. Mexico City: Ediciones Fuente Cultural, 1952.

González Ramos, Gilardo. *Los coras.* Mexico City: Instituto Nacional Indigenista, 1972.

González Sánchez, Isabel. *Haciendas, tumultos y trabajadores: Puebla-Tlaxcala, 1778–1798.* Mexico City: Instituto Nacional de Antropología e Historia, 1997.

Gordon, Colin. "Crafting a Usable Past: Consensus, Ideology, and Historians of the American Revolution." *William and Mary Quarterly* 46, no. 4 (1989): 671–695.

Gradie, Charlotte M. *The Tepehuan Revolt of 1616: Militarism, Evangelism, and Colonialism in Seventeenth-Century Nueva Vizcaya.* Salt Lake City: University of Utah Press, 2000.

Greene, Jack P. "The American Revolution." *American Historical Review* 105, no. 1 (February 2000): 93–102.

Guardino, Peter. *The Time of Liberty: Popular Culture in Oaxaca, 1750–1850.* Durham, NC: Duke University Press, 2005.

Guedea, Virginia. *José María Morelos y Pavón, cronología.* Mexico City: Universidad Nacional Autónoma de México, Instituto de Investigaciones Históricas, 1981.

———. "The Process of Mexican Independence." *American Historical Review* 105, no. 1 (February 2000) 116–30.

Guerra, François-Xavier. *Modernidad e Independencias: Ensayos sobre las revoluciones hispánicas.* Madrid: MAPFRE, 1992.

Gutiérrez Gutiérrez, José Antonio. *Aguascalientes y su región de influencia hasta 1810: sociedad y política.* Guadalajara, Mexico: Sistema de Educación Media Superior de la Universidad de Guadalajara: Amigos de la Historia de los Altos de Jalisco, 1998.

Gutiérrez, Ramón A. *When Jesus Came, the Corn Mothers Went Away: Marriage, Sexuality, and Power in New Mexico, 1500–1846.* Stanford, CA: Stanford University Press, 1991.

Guy, Donna J., and Thomas E. Sheridan, eds. *Contested Ground: Comparative Frontiers on the Northern and Southern Edges of the Spanish Empire.* Tucson: University of Arizona Press, 1998.

Hamill, Hugh M., Jr., ed. *Caudillos: Dictators in Spanish America.* Norman: University of Oklahoma Press, 1992.

———. *The Hidalgo Revolt: Prelude to Mexican Independence.* Gainesville: University of Florida Press, 1966.

Hamnett, Brian. "The Appropriation of Mexican Church Wealth by the Spanish

Bourbon Government: The 'Consolidación de Vales Reales,' 1805–1809." Journal of Latin American Studies 1 (1969): 85–113.

———. *Roots of Insurgency: Mexican Regions, 1750–1824*. Cambridge, UK: Cambridge University Press, 1986.

Haro Ortega, Renato, ed. *Historia de Colotlán*. Colotlán, Jalisco: R. H. Ortega, 1991.

Harvey, Robert. *Liberators: Latin America's Struggle for Independence, 1810–1830*. London: John Murray, 2000.

Hatley, Tom. *The Dividing Paths: Cherokees and South Carolinians through the Era of Revolution*. New York: Oxford University Press, 1995.

Hernández-López, Toribio. *Monografia del municipio de Calvillo*. Aguascalientes, Mexico: Gobierno del Estado de Aguascalientes, 1991.

Higuera, Ernesto. *Hidalgo; reseña biográfica con una iconografía del iniciador de nuestra independencia*. Mexico City: Colección Medallones mexicanos, 1955.

Hinton, Thomas B., ed. *Coras, huicholes y tepehuanes*. Mexico City: Instituto Nacional Indigenista, 1972.

Hobsbawm, Eric J. *Primitive Rebels: Studies in Archaic Forms of Social Movement in the 19th and 20th Centuries*. New York: W. W. Norton, 1959.

———. *Revolutionaries: Contemporary Essays*. New York: Pantheon Books, 1973. Iturrioz Leza, José Luis, Julio Carrillo de la Cruz, and Gabriel Pacheco Sandoval, eds. *Reflexiones sobre la identidad étnica*. Guadalajara, México: Universidad de Guadalajara, 1995.

Jarrett, Alfred Abioseh. *The Under-Development of Africa: Colonialism, Neo-Colonialism and Socialism*. Lanham, MD: University Press of America, 1996.

Jiménez de la Rosa, Felipe. *Ruta de Hidalgo, 1810–1811*. Mexico City: Impresora y Servicios Gráficos, 1960.

Johnson, Lyman L., and Sonya Lipsett-Rivera, eds. *The Faces of Honor: Sex, Shame, and Violence in Colonial Latin America*. Albuquerque: University of New Mexico Press, 1998.

Kellogg, Susan. "Hegemony Out of Conquest: The First Two Centuries of Spanish Rule in Central Mexico." *Radical History Review* 53 (1992): 27–46.

———. *Law and the Transformation of Aztec Society, 1500–1700*. Norman: University of Oklahoma Press, 1995.

Kentner, Janet. "The Socio-Political Role of Women in the Mexican Wars of Independence, 1810–1821." PhD diss.: Loyola University of Chicago, 1975.

Kerber, Linda K. *Women of the Republic: Intellect and Ideology in Revolutionary America*. Chapel Hill: University of North Carolina Press, 1980.

Kinsbruner, Jay. *Independence in Spanish America: Civil Wars, Revolutions, and Underdevelopment*. Albuquerque: University of New Mexico Press, 2000.

Knight, Alan. *The Mexican Revolution*. 2 vols. Cambridge, UK: Cambridge University Press, 1986.

Lamana, Gonzalo. *Domination without Dominance: Inca-Spanish Encounters in Early Colonial Peru*. Durham, NC: Duke University Press, 2008.

Landers, Jane. *Atlantic Creoles in the Age of Revolutions*. Cambridge, MA: Harvard University Press, 2010.

———. *Black Society in Spanish Florida*. Urbana: University of Illinois Press, 1999.

Landers, Jane, and Barry Robinson, eds. *Slaves, Subjects, and Subversives: Blacks in Colonial Latin America*. Albuquerque: University of New Mexico Press, 2006.

Langley, Lester D. *The Americas in the Age of Revolution, 1750–1850*. New Haven, CT: Yale University Press, 1996.

Langue, Frédérique. *Los Señores de Zacatecas: Una Aristocracia Minera del Siglo XVIII Novohispano*. Mexico City: Fondo de Cultura Económica, trans. 1999.

Lavrin, Asunción. "The Execution of the Law of Consolidation in New Spain: Economic Aims and Results." *Hispanic American Historical Review* 53, no. 1 (February 1973): 27–49.

Lopez, Juan. *La rebelion del indio Mariano: un movimiento insurgente en la Nueva Galicia, en 1801*. Vol. 3. Guadalajara, Mexico: Ayuntamiento, 1985.

Lumholtz, Carl. *Unknown Mexico: A Record of Five Years' Exploration among the Tribes of the Western Sierra Madre; in the Tierra Caliente of Tepic and Jalisco; and among the Tarascos of Michoacan*. Glorieta, NM: Rio Grande Press 1973.

Lynch, John. *Latin American Revolutions, 1808–1826: Old and New World Origins*. Norman: University of Oklahoma Press, 1994.

McAlister, Lyle N. *The "fuero militar" in New Spain, 1764–1800*. Gainesville: University of Florida Press, 1957.

McFarlane, Anthony. "Rebellions in Late Colonial Spanish America: A Comparative Perspective." *Bulletin of Latin American Research* 14, no. 3 (1995): 313–38.

Magriña Ocampo, Laura. "Coras y Tecualmes: De la Conquista de El Nayarit a la Guerra de Independencia." In *Participación indígena en los procesos de Independencia y Revolución Mexicana*, edited by Víctor Manuel Rojo Leyva, José Luis Reyes Utrera, and Adrián Fernando Rangel Aguilar, 133–47. Mexico City: Comisión Nacional para el Desarrollo de los Pueblos Indígenas, 2011.

Malagón Barcelló, Javier. *El historiador español exiliado en México*. Mexico City: El Colegio de México, 2012.

Mamdani, Mahmood. *Citizen and Subject: Contemporary Africa and the Legacy of Late Colonialism*. Princeton, NJ: Princeton University Press, 1996.

Mancisidor, José. *Hidalgo, Morelos, Guerrero*. Mexico City: Editorial Grijalbo, 1956.

Matthew, Laura E. *Memories of Conquest: Becoming Mexicano in Colonial Guatemala*. Chapel Hill: University of North Carolina Press, 2012.

Matthew, Laura E., and Michel R. Oudijk, eds. *Indian Conquistadors: Indigenous Allies in the Conquest of Mesoamerica*. Norman: University of Oklahoma Press, 2007.

Merritt, Jane. *At the Crossroads: Indians and Empires on a Mid-Atlantic Frontier, 1700–1763*. Chapel Hill: University of North Carolina Press, 2003.

Meyer, Jean A. *Breve historia de Nayarit*. Mexico City: Colegio de México, Fideicomiso Historia de las Américas: Fondo de Cultura Económica, 1997.

———. *The Cristero Rebellion: The Mexican People between Church and State, 1926–1929*. Cambridge, UK: Cambridge University Press, 1976.

Miquel i Vergés, José María. *Diccionario de Insurgentes*. Mexico City: Editorial Porrua, 1969.

Muriá, José María, director. *Historia de Jalisco*. Guadalajara, México: Gobierno de Jalisco, Secretaría General, Unidad Editorial, 1980–82.

Muriá, José María, Cándido Galván, and Angélica Peregrina. *Jalisco, una historia compartida*. Guadalajara, México: Gobierno del Estado de Jalisco, 1987.

Norton, Mary Beth. *Liberty's Daughters: The Revolutionary Experience of American Women, 1750–1800*. Ithaca, NY: Cornell University Press, 1996.

O'Hara, Matthew. *A Flock Divided: Race, Religion, and Politics in Mexico, 1749–1857*. Durham, NC: Duke University Press, 2009.

O'Phelan Godoy, Scarlett. *La gran rebelión en los Andes: de Túpac Amaru a Túpac Catari*. Cuzco, Perú: Centro de Estudios Regionales Andinos "Bartolomé de las Casas," 1995.

———. *Rebellions and Revolts in Eighteenth Century Peru and Upper Peru*. Köln: Böhlau, 1985.

Ortiz Escamilla, Juan. "El bajo clero mexicano durante la guerra civil de 1810." In *El nacimiento de México*, edited by Patricia Galeana, 11–19. Mexico City: Archivo General de la Nación, Fondo de Cultura Económica, 1999.

Ortiz Escamilla, Juan, and José Antonio Serrano Ortega, eds. *Ayuntamientos y liberalismo gaditano en México*. Zamora, Mexico: El Colegio de Michoacán-Universidad Veracruzana, 2007.

Patch, Robert W. *Indians and the Political Economy of Colonial Central America, 1670–1810*. Norman: University of Oklahoma Press, 2013.

Phelan, John L. *The People and the King: The Comunero Revolution in Colombia, 1781*. Madison: University of Wisconsin Press, 1978.

Powell, Philip Wayne. *Mexico's Miguel Caldera: The Taming of America's First Frontier, 1548–1597*. Tucson: University of Arizona Press, 1977.

Purcell, L. Edward, and Sarah J. Purcell, eds. *Encyclopedia of Battles in North America, 1517 to 1916*. New York: Facts on File, 2000.

Radding, Cynthia. *Wandering Peoples: Colonialism, Ethnic Spaces, and Ecological Frontiers in Northwestern Mexico, 1700–1850*. Durham, NC: Duke University Press, 1997.

Ramírez Esparza, Carlos. *El Padre Calvillo: Caudillo de la Guerra de Independencia*. Guadalajara, Mexico: Gobierno de Jalisco, Secretaria General, Unidad Editorial, 1987.

Restall, Matthew, ed. *Beyond Black and Red: African-Native Relations in Colonial Latin America*. Albuquerque: University of New Mexico Press, 2005.

———. *The Black Middle: Africans, Mayas, and Spaniards in Colonial Yucatan*. Stanford, CA: Stanford University Press, 2009.

———. *Maya Conquistador*. Boston: Beacon Press, 1998.

———. *Seven Myths of the Spanish Conquest*. New York: Oxford University Press, 2003.

Roach Pierson, Ruth, Nupur Chaudhuri, and Beth McAuley, eds. *Nation, Empire, Colony: Historicizing Gender and Race*. Bloomington: Indiana University Press, 1998.

Robins, Nicholas A. *Genocide and Millennialism in Upper Peru: The Great Rebellion of 1780–1782*. Westport, CT: Praeger, 2002.

Robinson, Barry M. "La reclusión de mujeres rebeldes: el recogimiento en la guerra de independencia mexicana, 1810–1819. *Fronteras de la Historia* 15, no. 2 (2010): 225–244.

Rodríguez, Mario. *La revolución americana de 1776 y el mundo hispánico: ensayos y documentos*. Madrid: Editorial Tecnos, 1976.

Rodríguez O., Jaime E. "The Emancipation of America." *American Historical Review* 105, no. 1 (February 2000): 131–52.

———. *The Independence of Spanish America*. Cambridge, UK: Cambridge University Press, 1998.

——, ed. *Mexico in the Age of Democratic Revolutions 1750–1850*. London: Lynne Rienner, 1994.

——. *"We Are Now the True Spaniards": Sovereignty, Revolution, Independence, and the Emergence of the Federal Republic of Mexico, 1808–1824*. Stanford, CA: Stanford University Press, 2012.

Rojas, Beatriz. *Los Huicholes: documentos históricos*. Colonia Tlacopac, INI; Tlalpan, DF: CIESAS, 1992.

Ruiz Medrano, Carlos Rubén. *Las sombrías aventuras del rey tlaxcalteco Juan Vicencio de Córdova y los rebeldes de Colotlán, Jalisco, 1777–1783*. San Luis Potosí, México: Colegio de San Luis, 2011.

Santoscoy, Alberto. *Obras Completas Tomo II*. Guadalajara, Mexico: Gobierno de Jalisco, Secretaría General, Unidad Editorial, 1986.

Schmitt, Karl M. "The Clergy and the Independence of New Spain." *Hispanic American Historical Review* 34, no. 3 (August 1954): 289–312.

Schwaller, John F., ed. *The Church in Colonial Latin America*. Wilmington, DE: SR Books, 2000.

Seed, Patricia. *Ceremonies of Possession in Europe's Conquest of the New World, 1492–1640*. Cambridge, UK: Cambridge University Press, 1995.

——. "Poststructuralism in Postcolonial History." *Maryland Historian* 24, no. 1 (1993): 9–28.

Sego, Eugenio. *Aliados y Adversarios: Los colonos Tlaxcaltecas en la frontera septentrional en Nueva España*. San Luis Potosí, Mexico: El Colegio de San Luis, 1998.

Serulnikov, Sergio. *Subverting Colonial Authority: Challenges to Spanish Rule in Eighteenth-Century Southern Andes*. Durham, NC: Duke University Press, 2003.

Shadow, Robert. "La frontera norteña de la Nueva Galicia: las parroquias de Colotlán 1725–1820." In *Lecturas Históricas del Norte de Jalisco*, edited by Manuel Caldera and José María Muría, 87–109. Guadalajara, Mexico: Colegio de Jalisco, 1991.

Sousa, Lisa, and Kevin Terraciano. "The 'Original Conquest' of Oaxaca: Nahua and Mixtec Accounts of the Spanish Conquest," *Ethnohistory* 50, no. 2 (Spring 2003): 349–400.

Stavig, Ward. "Ethnic Conflict, Moral Economy, and Population in Rural Cuzco on the Eve of the Thupa Amaro II Rebellion." *Hispanic American Historical Review* 68, no. 4 (1988): 737–70.

——. *The World of Túpac Amaru: Conflict, Community, and Identity in Colonial Peru*. Lincoln: University of Nebraska Press, 1999.

Stanley, J. Stein, and Barbara H. Stein. *Apogee of Empire: Spain and New Spain in the Age of Charles III, 1759–1789*. Baltimore: Johns Hopkins University Press, 2003.

Stern, Steve. *The Secret History of Gender: Women, Men, and Power in Late Colonial Mexico*. Chapel Hill: University of North Carolina Press, 1995.

Tanck de Estrada, Dorothy. *Atlas ilustrado de los pueblos de Indios, Nueva España, 1800*. Mexico City, El Colegio de México, El Colegio Mexiquense, Comisión Nacional para el Desarrollo de los Pueblos Indígenas, Fomento Cultural Banamex, 2005.

Taylor, William B. *Drinking, Homicide, and Rebellion in Colonial Mexican Villages*. Stanford, CA: Stanford University Press, 1979.

——. *Magistrates of the Sacred: Priests and Parishioners in Eighteenth-Century Mexico*. Stanford, CA: Stanford University Press, 1996.

Thomson, Sinclair. *We Alone Will Rule: Native Andean Politics in the Age of Insurgency*. Madison: University of Wisconsin Press, 2003.

Torre Villar, Ernesto de la. *Los "Guadalupes" y la Independencia, con una selección de documentos inéditos*. Mexico City: Editorial Jus, 1966.

Townsend, Camilla. *Tales of Two Cities: Race and Economic Culture in Early Republican North and South America*. Austin: University of Texas Press, 2000.

Tutino, John. *From Insurrection to Revolution in Mexico: Social Bases of Agrarian Violence, 1750–1940*. Princeton, NJ: Princeton University Press, 1986.

———. *Making a New World: Founding Capitalism in the Bajío and Spanish North America*. Durham, NC: Duke University Press, 2011.

Twinam, Ann. "The Etiology of Racial Passing: Constructions of Informal and Official 'Whiteness' in Colonial Spanish America." In *New World Orders, Violence, Sanction, and Authority in the Early Modern Americas*, edited by John Smolenski and Thomas J. Humphrey, 249–72. McNeil Center for Early American Studies. Philadelphia: University of Pennsylvania Press, 2005.

———. *Public Lives Private Secrets: Gender, Honor, Sexuality, and Illegitimacy in Colonial Spanish America*. Stanford, CA: Stanford University Press, 1999.

Van Young, Eric. "Conflict and Solidarity in Indian Village Life: The Guadalajara Region in the Late Colonial Period." *Hispanic American Historical Review* 64, no. 1 (February 1984): 55–80.

———. *The Other Rebellion: Popular Violence, Ideology, and the Mexican Struggle for Independence, 1810–1821*. Stanford, CA: Stanford University Press, 2001.

Velazquez Chávez, María del Carmen. *Colotlán: Doble frontera contra los bárbaros*. CITY, México: Universidad Nacional Autónoma de México, 1961.

Villaseñor y Villaseñor, Alejandro. *Biografías de los héroes y caudillos de la Independencia*. Mexico City: Imp. de "El Tiempo," de V. Agüeros, 1910.

Weber, David J. *The Spanish Frontier in North America*. New Haven, CT: Yale University Press, 1992.

Weigand, Phil C. *Ensayos sobre el Gran Nayar: entre coras, huicholes y tepehuanos*. Zamora, Michoacán: El Colegio de Michoacán, 1992.

———. *Evolución de una civilización prehispánica: arqueología de Jalisco, Nayarit y Zacatecas*, translated by Adela Iglesias Morineau. Zamora, Michoacán: El Colegio de Michoacán, 1993.

Wood, Gordon S. *The Creation of the American Republic, 1776–1787*. Chapel Hill: Institute of Early American History and Culture and University of North Carolina Press, 1969.

———. *The Radicalism of the American Revolution*. New York: Alfred A. Knopf, 1992.

Wood, Stephanie. *Transcending Conquest: Nahua Views of Spanish Colonial Mexico*, Norman: University of Oklahoma Press, 2003.

Yannakakis, Yanna. *The Art of Being In-between: Native Intermediaries, Indian Identity, and Local Rule in Colonial Oaxaca*. Durham, NC: Duke University Press, 2008.

Zamoyski, Adam. *Holy Madness: Romantics, Patriots and Revolutionaries, 1776–1871*. London: Weidenfeld & Nicolson, 1999.

Index

Page numbers in italics refer to figures and tables.